Bright Lights and Bacon Rolls

Malcolm D.Y. Treen

Published in 2020 by FeedARead.com Publishing

Third Edition

A CIP catalogue record for this title is available from the British Library.

Cover photo taken by Simon Smith

Dedications

To my dear mum, Blanche Treen, without whom none of the following events would have occurred. She insisted when I was young that I had piano lessons, saying, 'You can always get a job in a pub, if everything else fails, people may even buy you drinks.' Thankfully, because of her, this never came to pass.

Also, to my ever-patient wife, Mary, and my beautiful daughters Laura and Hannah; I love you all deeply, including our wonderful grandchildren, Zach and Safi, who have given us so much joy and fun.

And to all my work colleagues who even now, almost fifty years on, are still some of my best chums and especially to Paul Faraday who liked my early ramblings enough to allow me to have a special place on his LWT website.

Finally, to Paul Burton, whose enthusiasm and keen interest means these pages can now be read by the many not just the few.

Malcolm D.Y. Treen

4

List of Chapters

Foreword

Although I never had the pleasure of meeting her, I am very grateful to Malcolm Treen's Mum. If she had not spotted a job vacancy in her newspaper for trainees to join a new television station, and persuaded her son to apply, we would not have the pleasure of reading the pages that follow.

This book is an autobiographical tale of Malcolm's career journey from young wide-eyed trainee in the sound department, to battle hardened location manager and onwards later to production manager, as a freelancer. A voyage that roves from the brightly lit studio floors to the darkened perspiration perfumed control rooms of the television centre, to location filming on the mean streets of London, to bomb scarred Northern Ireland during the 'troubles', across the Atlas Mountains of Morocco, deep into the Red-Light district of Amsterdam and much more besides.

But let us be honest this book is really about a very special place to have worked – London Weekend Television, better known as LWT. It was one of over a dozen separate television companies that made-up ITV, Britain's then only commercial television network.

When ex-LWT staffers, those of us lucky enough to be still alive and kicking, bump into each other by chance all these years later, like anyone else, pleasantries are exchanged. How are you doing? The family? The kids? But at another level there is a deeper communication going on. A knowing smile. A glance, eye contact held for just a little longer than it would be in other circumstances. It is unspoken because we know that we all went through a unique shared experience in a special company at a more innocent, never to be recaptured, time. At LWT, we were all sprinkled with a magical invisible dust that left its warm sustaining glow on us for the rest of our lives. To capture the essence of it, and communicate it to others, none of us has managed to do anywhere near adequately. Until now, that is. In this book, Malcolm has picked it, bottled it, matured it, poured it into a glass for you to sit back and relish.

Do you need to have worked at LWT to enjoy this book? Not at all. If you did, it is a fond, delicious, and nostalgic wallow. If you did not work there, and just sat on your sofa and watched the programmes, and didn't we all, it is an eye-opening page-turning insight into what it was really like to work on the other side of the screen to make these programmes and bring them to your living rooms.

Not just at LWT, but within commercial television generally, it was a time of militant trade unions, with their crazy Machiavellian working practices and demarcation rules. We even went on strike. The management was, of course, aware of this but if the station sold the space and filled its advertising breaks, there was ample revenue to pay our salaries, make the programmes and some profit too. It was a system that worked. From the 'fun factory' that was LWT, emerged some of the best television programmes ever made and some of the finest practitioners of the art at all levels. The programme formats and the names of the people who made them, and appeared in them, still resonate through the industry today. You will recognise so many of them as you read this book.

Working at LWT was like swimming in a warm exotic lagoon protected by a sturdy reef. It would be many years before the reef was breached letting in the sharks circling ominously in the darker waters beyond. It was lovely while it lasted.

It was no holiday though. We worked hard, very hard. When Malcolm writes about ninety-hour weeks, he is not joking. Sleeping in a nearby B&B after a ridiculously long day of filming was no luxury for him, it was a necessity, as a car journey home in a state of near exhaustion with a crack of dawn start the next day would have been far too risky. There were many moments of great stress. Malcolm's story about being sent down a railway line in Morocco to flag down an express train hurtling toward the point on the line where we were filming is not just a story. I was there – and is all true! But the stress is always defused with overriding good humour throughout this book.

I had the privilege of working with Malcolm particularly during his filming on location stints. My job kept me mostly in the relative safety of whatever temporary production office we had established for the duration of filming. While I fretted over coloured cardboard strips that in those pre-computer days represented the scenes that had to be completed each day, and hoped that we had not gone over budget, Malcolm's role took him into the thick of it. The front line where the bullets flew all round. The crazy, eccentric sometime obstructive, more often lovely public, the police, the officials, the huge crews and casts, the numerous and massive technical vehicles, the complex equipment, lights, cables, all needing to be parked, accommodated, watered, fed, motivated, galvanised and made to work as a unit to produce the scheduled quota of daily filming and then at the end of the day got safely back to base.

So, thank you Malcolm for so many things. For being interested in the people around you during those great days at LWT and beyond (the 'beyond' is about how it does not measure up to the LWT times). For taking the trouble to observe and remember what they said and did, and always seeing the humour, the irony, sometimes the pathos in every situation you encountered. It takes an unselfish person interested more in others than himself to do that. Most of all thanks for transforming your working life into such a readable and enjoyable book.

The sound of Malcolm's reassuring voice from some windswept film location crackling over the loudspeaker of my Motorola walkie-talkie back in the production office (mobile phones were a rare luxury in those days!), telling me that filming was completed and everyone was returning to base, still echoes in my head as I read and reread this book. 'It's a wrap, David. Over.'

Thanks Malcolm. Over and out.

David FitzGerald
Production Manager LWT, 1975-1990
London, March 2017

Chapter One

A Rum Job

Just as some people want to climb Mount Everest or others want to break world records, in the autumn of 1968, Malcolm D.Y. Treen was walking into the main reception area of London Weekend Television's Wembley Studios. At the age of nineteen, he was about to realise his own relatively short but lifelong ambition. The excitement in him was obvious; because for as long as he could remember he had always wanted to work in television, preferably on 'something' to do with animals, and now here he was about to start his career in what was to turn out to be one of the most notable television stations in Britain. The excitement in the building was also obvious, even though there were still two months to go before LWT went on air. Everyone seemed at fever pitch and you felt you could almost touch that atmosphere. Yes, I had arrived from the family home in Newbury to start work as a trainee in the sound department and I was working on the theory the animals bit would come later; sadly, it never did.

The interview for the job had been extraordinary. Associated Rediffusion had lost their seven-day week franchise after thirteen years and the licence had been split between Thames Television, who would broadcast from Monday to Friday until seven o'clock, and LWT providing the weekend service. The staff of Rediffusion had been given the opportunity to either stay on and work for LWT or go off to work for Thames. The split was about fifty-fifty. They were all rather proud that most of them had been made redundant on the Friday and walked away with a lump sum in their back pockets, only to re-enter the same building on the

11

Monday but working for a different company. When I later found this piece of information out, it finally explained the number of new cars in the staff car park that autumn. One person was reported to have worked over his hours on the Sunday and started his new job on the Monday on double time. LWT had advertised for twelve sound and camera trainees to help re-build their staff levels. My mother, a plain-speaking Mancunian lass, had seen the job advertised in the Daily Telegraph and had said in her usual witch-like predictive manner, 'If you apply for that, you'll get it.'

Some four weeks later, I found myself in a comfortable chair being offered tea and biscuits by the then head of personnel, Roy van Gelder. Also present were Derek Cochrane, head of cameras, and Brian Penny, head of sound. The manner was relaxed and informal. We talked of sound recording and taking pictures – and even hedgehogs! I possessed both a camera and a tape recorder and we had about twenty hedgehogs or so that visited my parents' garden regularly every evening, so I used to photograph them and record their wonderful snuffling noises. We tried at one point to give them individual names but as one hedgehog looks pretty much like another, except to other hedgehogs, my father and I gave up on that idea. I was asked whether I fancied sound or cameras the most. For some unknown reason I chose sound. As I left, and almost as an aside, Brian Penny asked me if I had applied anywhere else for employment. I confessed that I did have an interview with the BBC that very afternoon as a trainee film sound recordist. 'Well, let's see if we can beat the BBC on this one, shall we?' he said with a wink and a nod. I knew I had got the job.

I think the BBC building I attended was somewhere in Great Portland Street. I know I was escorted into a room where three rather stuffy gentlemen sat behind a desk. I sat in a very low seat in front of them, the sun straight in my face as I struggled to see theirs, instead of just three silhouettes. I was called Mr Treen and not Malcolm, as I had been that morning at Station House just off the North Circular road, where LWT had their offices. I had achieved two 'A' levels, one in Economics and the other in English, which I admit had no technical content whatsoever. However, combined with seven 'O' levels, I presumed that anybody worth their salt would realise that, if nothing else, I was at least capable of learning. Once I had passed the interview, I knew I would be dispatched to Evesham for about nine months, which was where the BBC did most of their training. They handed me a piece of card and explained that it was a circuit diagram. Somewhere it was connected-up wrongly. They then asked if I could show them where the error was and how to connect it properly. I had lost interest in physics at school at a very early age, when given the demonstration of a bell ringing in a jar, the air being removed and the bell no longer being audible. 'My God, I shall be using that every working day of my life!' I remember thinking cynically to myself at the time. I then went off into a daydream, visualising a fire engine rushing along the street with a huge glass jar over it and a device fitted, so that the bell (yes, I am afraid to confess that they had them in those days!) could not be heard in residential areas at night! Someone pushed a switch and removed the air and hey presto, silence! And when it came to the demonstration of chucking a load of iron filings over a piece of paper with a magnet underneath and watching the magnetic pattern form, well good trick but what possible practical purpose could that ever have served? Was I really doomed to wander around for the whole of my adult life, armed with a load of iron filings in my pocket, so that I could throw them over a piece of paper at a moment's notice to show someone a magnetic field? I am afraid the subject had left me cold. I slowly rotated the card, so that the drawing was now upside down, gazed at it again and then looked up to see if my silent miming act had got a laugh. Needless-to-say, it hadn't. In fact, it caused the card to be removed sharply from my grasp and an alternative was produced.

'Try this one, it is much easier,' said a voice tinged with both despair and impatience. I didn't dare do the same gag twice.

'No, er, sorry I'm afraid I can't.'

It was just like appearing in front of a magistrate's court; the three heads quickly nestled together in a whispered consultation and then came the verdict.

'No, we're very sorry, Mr Treen, but you obviously do not seem to have the technical qualifications for the job.'

With that I stood up and left. I did think about protesting that this was a trainee position and that given the ability to learn, which I clearly possessed, I would be an ideal candidate. But if that was not the case, then why had they bothered asking me to an interview in the first place? After all, it was obvious from the form I filled in that all my qualifications had nothing remotely to do with the gibberish on the card I was holding. The very word trainee means that they train you, surely does it not? However, I had already decided that if everyone was like these three at the BBC, I really didn't want to be there and LWT were obviously going to be a much friendlier place to inhabit and work. They had managed in a very short space of time not only to frighten me but also to make me angry. Perhaps they were in a desperate hurry to get home, after having been interviewing all day, who knows? But after what must have been a record three-and-a-half-minute interview, I was back outside the room with a snarl on my face and was just about to leave when a lady handed me a form. 'If you fill this in now, I'll get you the money from the petty cash,' she said rather helpfully. It was for my travelling expenses, no mention of which, I feel obliged to point out, had been made at LWT. How ironic that it was the BBC who paid for my trip up to London, but Independent Television, in a letter that arrived some two days later, who gave me the job!

Back at that autumn morning in the LWT reception, I was escorted to Brian Penny's office. He was alarmed to see that I was obviously carrying a suitcase. I explained I was going to find somewhere to stay after work. He would hear none of it and I was ushered off the premises and told only to come back after I had found somewhere to rest my head that night. He said he would keep my suitcase in his office until at least a temporary home had been found for my body. I then went and found the bed and breakfast that had been recommended by the company.

The next morning, the lovely lady who ran my new lodgings brought me a cup of tea to my room.

'My word,' she remarked. 'You were tired last night.'

'How can you tell?' I asked sleepily.

'You haven't ruffled the bed at all. You slept all night in the exact spot where you landed.'

They were wonderful, exciting days, so much to learn, so much to take in and the 'dirty dozen', as we twelve sound trainees became known, clinging to one another for friendship and support. My first drama was a production called *Gareth* by Alan Owen from a *Company of Five* series that LWT were making, starring Ann Bell and Ray Smith, who later went on to play 'Spikings' the boss in the LWT crime drama, *Dempsey and Makepeace*.

Back then, LWT's schedules included comedy programmes like *It's Tommy Cooper*. Cooper's shows were a joy to work on, not only for me as an amateur magician, but also because of the director, Bill Turner, who was a charming man. He in turn had just as charming a producer, Bill Hitchcock, who was married to the very famous comedy actress, Liz Fraser. Bill Turner had a wonderful catchphrase, which was, 'Bless him, bless him. Thank him very much.'

The problem with the show for a would-be boom operator was that although all the sketches we did were scripted, Tommy's opening routine, with his usual casualty of tricks presented off his table, was not. Now this routine in rehearsal would simply mean Tommy standing by his table for five minutes or so while they got the camera angles and lighting right and Tommy saying, 'Patter, patter, patter,' for a sound level. On the night, it was often something like twenty minutes of carnage, mirth and merriment, that none of us had ever heard or seen before, with even Cooper himself corpsing on occasions. Now this was fine if you were anything but the cameraman or the boom operator, who I have seen laughing so much, that the cameraman would have to resort to 'locking the camera off' to avoid the wobbles, even though it was mounted on a sturdy pedestal. In turn, the boom operator (I personally have done this!) would lock the boom off, knowing the head height of the shot could not now vary because he had just seen the cameraman lock off the camera. You really had to be there but those opening routines were sometimes just side splittingly funny and I struggled many times to focus because of the tears in my eyes.

Bill Turner also had an interest in magic and when he found out that I too was an enthusiast he gave me an old book from his collection. A generous act from a truly generous and likeable fellow.

There were also situation comedies like *On the Buses*, starring Reg Varney, *Please Sir!*, starring John Alderton, and *Doctor in the House*, with the late Barry Evans, who made us all madly jealous by having Susan George as his girlfriend at one point. Susan would often come and watch the show being recorded. Believe me, if there is one thing that can put a young boom operator right off his stroke, it was the sight of Susan George, often in what appeared to be the smallest mini skirt ever invented by man, sitting in the front row of the audience.

As a quick aside, *Doctor in the House* also starred George Layton, who along with Jonathan Lynn, wrote some of the many episodes that were recorded. I am pleased to say that many years later I saw George in a play at the New End Theatre in Hampstead. He remembered me but more so my wife who looked after the fan mail for the cast. I explained I had swung a boom over his head while he was in the series, but never hit him. George looked at me and smiled, 'Well, no, you wouldn't would you,' he said, indicating his smallness of stature. A lovely man all those years ago and has not altered one jot.

Anyway, back to the early days at LWT. David Frost was soon to be on live on screen three-nights-a-week hosting *Frost on Friday*, *Frost on Saturday* and *Frost on Sunday*, where Ronnie Barker and Ronnie Corbett both developed and honed their talents and skills. On one memorable occasion, live on a Sunday evening, that emotional singer Vicki Carr completely missed her entry into a song said, 'Sorry Harry, I blew it,' to Harry

Rabinowitz the musical director. And with that they started the song again.

Also during this period, Dickie Davis, who had in his early days been known as Richard, was set to present *World of Sport* every Saturday live for five hours. Meanwhile, a northern journalist called Michael Parkinson was to present *Sports Arena* on a Sunday morning, occasionally with a bit of a hangover having been 'Bromleyed' the night before. John Bromley was the producer and quite often took Michael out on a Saturday night. Being the professional he was, Michael's condition, of course, never showed on the screen. *On the Ball,* broadcast on a Saturday, and *The Big Match*, shown on a Sunday, would become the best football shows in town under the guidance of that godfather of football, Brian Moore, and aided and abetted in the early years by Jimmy Hill. Meanwhile, Humphrey Burton was about to launch *Aquarius*, a leading arts programme for many years, and *Upstairs, Downstairs* was soon to begin, and become, what is now a television legend. This list was endless and they were fantastic times.

Now I don't know, and I am willing to be corrected, there may well have been a 'nasty side' to Jack Williams, the producer of many of London Weekend's programmes but I never saw it. All I ever saw on the studio floor was a gentle man who also shared a big bag of sweets on recording days to calm people's nerves. He would also dash onto the set to rearrange the flowers on productions such as *Lillie*, often much to the chagrin of the stage manager.

Another such man was John Hawkesworth, a fine LWT producer, who worked most notably on *Upstairs Downstairs*. The only time I ever saw him angry was the day that Christopher Beeny and his motorbike had a

18

serious accident on the way to work on the day of a recording. Not surprisingly, chaos ensued. However, with 'the show must go' on motto ringing in everyone's ears, his lines were distributed to other members of the cast and scenes were shortened or cut. It made things difficult for the cast and crew, but we struggled through and somehow it got made. John was furious at the occurrence, not that the accident had happened, indeed the whole thing mortified him and he was deeply concerned for Christopher's well-being, but he was furious with himself. It seemed that bulletins were issued almost on an hourly basis on his progress and stability after John had yet again phoned the hospital for an update. John knowing that Chris rode the wretched machine to work had at one point toyed with the idea of having a clause inserted in his contract that he was not allowed to ride it on recording days. One of those strange things where you ponder that if he had have done that, would not only all the upset have been avoided, but more importantly the accident itself? Why hadn't he done it? Why hadn't he gone with his first instinct? Only John himself could answer that and it disturbed him greatly for many weeks afterwards to think that it might well have been in his domain to prevent that accident. But who does know what the fates hold in store for us and is there really any way we can prevent or control them?

Suddenly, two weeks after I walked through the front door of LWT, all the workers were summoned to a meeting in the yard where the outside broadcast garages were. A fascinating place, where all the vehicles used to facilitate any televised sport or recorded dramas were stored. A man stood on a box, who I was later to find out was the shop steward, and he explained that they had tried but failed to get any conclusive answers from management to the problems we all knew about and so things had finally come to a head.

'What problems?' I asked one of the senior sound people stood next to me.

'Shush, I'll tell you later,' he replied.

So, it was with great regret, the man on the box continued that we would have to have a show of hands. The hands went up and two people hurriedly counted the votes on either side of a split crowd. A verdict was declared and that was it. For the first, but certainly not for the only time in my career, I was now officially on strike.

'What happens now?' I said to the sound section union representative.

'We all have to leave the studios and go home.'

'But I haven't finished tidying those cables in the sound store.' I declared.

He sighed and then pronounced each word separately and slowly so that it would be sure to sink in, 'We're on strike.'

'Oh, right,' I nodded heavily, so he would know that I fully understood.

'You just leave everything, where it is and go home. Don't worry you'll still be paid because you're only a trainee. See you when it's over, I'll keep in touch.'

There was a drama series that had been on television around this time called *Man of Our Times* made by Rediffusion and starring George Cole. The story followed the ups and downs of a factory owner and his industrial troubles with the workforce and this incident could have been a scene straight out of it. I pondered on the train journey home as to whether art reflects life or life reflects art? Whatever the answer, the look on my mother's face reflected total disbelief as she opened the front door to discover her little worker stood on the

20

doorstep, with his suitcase in his hand, returning only two weeks after leaving home.

'We're on strike,' I announced, trying to sound and look as Bolshevik as Tom Courtenay in *Doctor Zhivago*.

'For how long?' my mother asked.

'I don't know,' I said, shrugging my shoulders. 'They said they would let me know.'

'Bloody rum job, this is,' she declared.

The strike dragged on for almost three weeks. Then finally I got the call to return to the studios and life resumed almost as we had left it. I was earning the glorious sum of twelve pounds per week and, as we got paid every four weeks, at the end of that period forty-eight pounds was mine for the keeping. Well, apart from the National Health Insurance contribution and the tax, which were deducted at source. Later would come the Union subscription, which you had to pay in those days, and the pension deduction. This meant for many years, whether I liked it or not, I contributed to the Labour Party's funds. What was quite nice about that system was that there were years when you got thirteen payments instead of twelve, so it felt like you were getting a month for free. As I said, halcyon days that may have become more speckled with sunshine, as the years have drifted away, than they really were. It took many years for folk to stop going around saying, 'It wasn't like this with Rediffusion.' In fact, I think that only came to a stop after thirteen years when LWT had eventually been in existence for longer than Rediffusion had!

I finally found permanent digs and my room was my own. I had minimal cooking facilities and a shared bathroom but as I tried to spend as little time as possible within its confines, none of the above bothered me that much. I would boil an egg in the morning and use the water from the pan to make my cup of tea. I had seen this on a situation comedy, probably *Hancock's Half Hour*, and decided what a wonderful use of time and resources this was. It worked wonderfully well except on the odd occasion when the egg cracked and the tea making went out of the window! Mostly I ate in the canteen at work, along with the rest of the 'dirty dozen'.

About two weeks after we had returned to the fold, Brian Penny told us one lunchtime that the film section needed a sound trainee. He asked if any of us would like to go and join them. I nearly put my hand up, but I thought somehow he would hold it against me and so I shook my head in a negative fashion, strangely enough as did everybody else. I always wonder to this day, what path my career would have taken and to where it would have taken me, if I had said yes to his request.

I am afraid to say that when I joined LWT we were making programmes in black and white and the cameras had turret lenses, the zoom lens had yet to make its appearance. The sound desks were not fitted with faders, as they are now, so that you can fade the sound up or down, but pots, round control knobs, with which you decreased or increased the volume. Looking at pictures of them now, they looked like something John Logie Baird himself would have used. The first colour production nearly ground to a halt when once again the union asked for more money. The reason? They claimed working under the extra lighting that was required for colour pictures was hotter and more uncomfortable. We got it and as I recall it was simply called 'colour money'!

The advent of the zoom lens caused consternation for any self-respecting boom operator, which basically was what I was being trained to be. With fixed lenses, you knew because you could look down and see exactly what size lens the camera was on and therefore how tight the shot was, but with the advent of the zoom lens you had no idea. Many heated discussions were had and at first, out of the normal four cameras per studio, only one would have the zoom lens fitted. Should there be a little flag on top of the camera that went in and out with the zoom? This would at least give some clue as to the size of the shot. No, we had to content ourselves with looking at the monitors on the studio floor, from our elevated position of some five-feet or so above the ground, which someone, usually from the make-up department, would always stand in front of at the crucial moment and the cry would go up from the gallery, 'Boom in shot. Cut!' The other problem of being five-feet above the studio floor and wearing headphones and glasses, was that when a tea break was called and you whipped the headphones off; nine times out of ten your glasses went with them. I smashed so many pairs over a very few weeks that I resorted to contact lenses, in order to save me the huge expense of replacement glasses. So a simple financial consideration is why I went down that road and not anything to do with cosmetic looks!

There were six camera crews and six sound crews. You worked your way up from trainee to sound assistant B then to sound assistant A then to sound balancer and then finally sound supervisor. That should be a question on a quiz show to see if any of my old colleagues can remember the order! I joined sound crew three and slowly began to learn my craft.

Some of the members of the department had come in from the hit and miss freelance world of films to find a more secure life in the television studios. Many of their stories and tales were legend. Indeed, my boss, Pat Wheeler, who was called the number one in charge of the floor, had worked on films like *Where No Vultures Fly* and one of the other number one's, a lovely man called Percy Britain, had worked on *The African Queen* with Humphrey Bogart. He had a picture of which he was immensely proud of himself with Bogart burning leeches off their legs with cigarettes. Pat would frequently answer the phone in the sound control room with the line, 'Paramount Stage Ten', which often threw the person on the other end into such confusion they would hang up! I held them in awe, even though Percy's training technique of standing by the boom with an old chair leg in his hand and every time you dipped into shot he would crack you on the shines with it, was a bit hard to take sometimes. Imagine in this politically correct world trying to do that now?! But by God it trained you very quickly how to become an ace boom operator. Well, at least to make sure you kept the wretched thing out of shot. Pat just simply terrified me and the other trainee on the crew, Adrian Rodger, and both of us spent many sleepless nights wondering if we were in the right job! However, once I learnt to operate a boom, and operate it well, thanks to the patience of Pat, I had a skill that no one could take away and many had a deep respect for.

There was immense rivalry between not only each sound crew, but also between cameras and sound. We always considered ourselves the poorer relations and frequently felt hard done by. In those days, there always seemed time to laugh. The camera department didn't laugh very much when the sound department produced a document which listed a job description of each trade. The senior cameraman was listed as training people and then pointing his camera under direction from the director. Every other grade lower down just simply had the phrase operates his camera under direction from the director. The sound list, of course, was astronomical, knowledge of microphones, technical understanding of public address rigs, lines knowledge for outside broadcasts, how to edit tape, how to operate a sound desk and it went on and on. I seem to remember it was some sort of thrust by the department to get more money than cameras – I remember we failed. The problem was that after the camera department caught sight of it, tempers were a little edgy for quite some time.

Finally, we were back to square one and practical jokes abounded and reached a startling pitch, when I put crazy foam into the headset of a cameraman, who always left them on his viewfinder. On this occasion, he went up to the camera and whacked them straight onto his head. He froze and stared straight ahead as he became aware of the cold foam now in each ear. Young camera trainees rushed for cover in order not to be seen laughing at him as he very slowly lifted the headphones off, displaying two wonderful white blobs protruding from each ear, which was the cause for more laughter. Eventually, John Morgan, who went on to be a director, found out it was me and I was warned for weeks by camera crew six that something very physical was going to happen to me and to expect the worst. They got me very subtly one evening after a show. The crew had had a drink in the bar and I strolled over to my car in the car park, thinking that it had been unusual to see camera crew six hovering around for so long that evening. I got in, started the engine, put it in gear and it went nowhere. I just couldn't understand. What they had done was jack the damn thing up and put it onto bricks but only just half an inch or so off the ground. I, of course, hadn't noticed this when I climbed aboard. Four of them appeared in a car from out of the darkness and drove round and round me in the car park, laughing their heads off. A police car went past on the main road and they hurriedly got my car off the bricks and let me go, just in case the police came back, not wanting to have been seen to be behaving badly in the eyes of the law. Old fashioned? It seems so now, doesn't it?

Chapter Two

Farewell Wembley

On the 20 July 1969, we did the live broadcast of *Man On the Moon* with David Frost hosting an all singing all dancing spectacular, which finally ended up with those amazing pictures of the small craft Eagle landing on the lunar surface and the voice of mission control being transmitted into the small hours of the following day. Even though I was working all night, I did have time for a quick kiss and cuddle by the schedules board, a highly romantic location, with my wife-to-be, Mary, who worked in the ticket office or audience participation as they used to call it. Unfortunately, Vic Gardiner, who was the managing director of LWT at the time, rounded the corner and caught the two of us at it and my heart rate galloped a bit. Probably not as fast as Neil Armstrong's, whose rate apparently went up from seventy-seven to one hundred and fifty-six as he got close to the moon's surface. Being a gentleman, Vic never said a word about his close encounter with us, until Mary left the company many years later to have Laura our first daughter. He managed to cause her severe embarrassment at her leaving party by mentioning this early morning rendezvous in his speech. I left the studios at about nine thirty on a bright sunlit July morning making the reverse journey back to my digs, having stayed longer than I needed to, simply because I knew I was watching history in the making and almost a fifth of the world's population had been watching it live on television with me. It's quite unbelievable now to think that the craft that Armstrong piloted onto the moon's surface had an onboard computer with less memory than a mobile phone!

Two of the sound trainees had clubbed together and were sharing a flat and I spent more time at their place than mine. Well, they had a television and loneliness was a terrible thing that I never really got used to. I am sure they looked upon me as a darn nuisance but they never said so and for that I will always be grateful to young Derek Brandon and Ken O'Neill. Colour had only just arrived and in the very early days we would scuttle off to the *World of* Sport studio control room on a Friday night, where there was one of the few colour monitors in the building, to watch *Rowan and Martin's Laugh-In*. The show was hysterical and one of the other bonuses in watching it was the presence of a young lady called Goldie Hawn, who we were all madly in love with.

Slowly making my way up the sound ladder, I eventually arrived in the control room as a grams' operator (gram, can you believe it, being short for gramophone?). As a sound balancer, you were either on the studio floor in charge of a sound crew or in the control room as the grams' operator. He or she is the one who plays in the music and sound effects of wind or thunder, or he used to be. A lot of what we used to play in on the night is now added in a dubbing suite after the show has been recorded. I can remember one wonderful day when I was doing an early morning Saturday children's programme, which if I recall was cheated and recorded on a Friday. By now, we were at the new studios on the South Bank in London. Spiderman was knocking about having just brought out a new cartoon or some such and he accidentally staggered into the control room and asked for directions to the wardrobe department. I stepped forward to show him the way and trod on his foot. His costume was very thin and there was no evidence of any shoes at all. He hopped about like mad holding his foot with his hand and yelling in pain. I remember thinking it wasn't everybody who when asked what had they done at work today, could reply that they had trod on the foot of a superhero and brought him to his knees!

Being a grams operator had its moments especially on live productions. I can remember working on *World of Sport* one Saturday. I always used to say you waited eight hours to get the end music wrong, I will explain why in a minute. One Saturday, all had been going well until Dickie Davis came to lead into a commercial break. David Scott, the director of the programme, was a lovely man who had the most beautiful transatlantic accent, which made listening to him all day at least easy on the ear. However, to counter that he would often wear very loud Bermuda t-shirts that didn't make looking at him easy on the eye! It was my job to play the short burst of music into and out of a commercial break and at the same time the vision mixer cut up the end or beginning of part caption. Dickie was leading into one of those breaks and saying something like, 'So there we are. We will be right back after the break.' He took a breath; I hit the play button on the tape machine, because he sounded for all the world to me like he had finished and the music burst forth. To my horror he continued to talk, admittedly shouting a bit over the top of the music to make himself heard, 'With much more action to come on *World of Sport.*' There was a cry from the director's box like a wailing banshee and I thought, look out here comes the bollocking. The adjoining door to the director's control room opened and there stood David Scott, who could not by any means be described as a small figure. I tried to crouch down behind the technical equipment in front of me, in the vague hope I would be less visible. 'Oh, my lovely,

I'd have done the same,' he yelled. 'I really thought he had finished too.' The vision mixer looked very smug because, despite me playing the music, she had not cut away to the caption but stayed on Dickie. This really made it look like one of Denis Norden's cock-ups – which in truth it was!

The end music for *World of Sport* was what we called pre-faded. This meant if you had the two-minute version on the tape machine at two minutes before the off-air time of the programme you pushed the play button and all being well two minutes later the roller caption, with all the credits on came to an end at the same time as your music did and everyone went off for a well-earned drink. That was the theory. It was also the most hectic part of the show, with reports coming in from here there and everywhere and so much chat in the control room, with talkback from a million different football grounds. It was always hard to concentrate the mind. If the studio asked for an overrun, which sometimes they did, and presentation allowed them, re-working out the end time with bedlam going on around you could be a bit daunting! So, a little bit of thought had to go into hitting the button at the right time. The full version of the theme, if I remember rightly, ran two minutes and seventeen seconds, so that added a further complication to the mathematics. There was one memorable moment when I hit the button at the appointed second, watched the tape go around and then watched a whole section of leader tape (which is blank tape with nothing on it) go past very slowly and then the proper tape reappeared again. The gram operator the week before had needed to go straight into the theme for some reason or other and had spliced a load of leader tape in between. For those of you who remember the tune, the first opening dum, dum, dum single drum beats and the start of the music. He never put it back the way he had found it. His name was Fred Varley, a lovely man, who wouldn't do a thing like that deliberately. I watched with horror, it had seemed as though there had been miles and miles of leader tape but in fact it made only a couple of seconds' difference. But you can see it only needed the machine to stop or falter and like I said you had sat there for eight hours just waiting to get the end music wrong!

The producer of *World of Sport* was a larger than life man who went by the name of John Bromley, affectionately known as 'Brommers'. He worked hard and he played hard. He worked his team hard and he played them hard. I always admired the sports department at LWT, they were a real team. Yes, they fell out now and again, but they all pulled together for the sake of that programme and by God did it show. Their professionalism was second to none. Of course, after five hours of live television output one was in inclined to partake of maybe one or two drinks afterwards to unwind. Eventually John went on to be controller of sport at the ITV Network Centre. Sadly, he was a character taken from us much too early by whatever hand does control these events in our lives or more correctly our deaths. I always think that all of us would benefit from someone being polite and at least pre-warning us by calling out a gentle 'last orders', instead of just turning all the lights out and suddenly closing the establishment down.

People have often asked me over the many years that I have been in this business we call show what the funniest thing is that I have ever seen. I must admit the one still rated amongst my favourites was a video shoot many years ago for a programme called *Love for Lydia*, which starred a young man called Jeremy Irons. I met

Jeremy again when we were working on a *Comic Relief* sketch for the BBC. We had a smashing chat going back down memory lane and like me he blames just one person for the relatively recent demise of our industry, but more of her later. *Lydia* was made in the dark days of television, when the camera was still large, but small enough to go outside and do drama inserts. It was still attached by its umbilical cord to a back pack, the technical term for which was camera control unit, and then to the scanner, which is the vehicle that the director and vision mixer sit in so they can monitor and cut the pictures, if more than one camera is being used.

I watched with interest as the senior cameraman, Jeff Sheppard, and the director, a gentle man called Chris Hodson, were setting up a shot to be taken from inside a rather splendid vintage car. The actors would climb into the car with the camera already in there beside them and the shot would continue as the car pulled away, panning off onto the snow scene viewed out of the window, which was made up of an obscene number of white drapes laid over the distant hillsides. John Ruffey, one of Jeff's crew was squashed into the car and for speed and quickness the C.C.U., which really should have been attached to the car, allowing the cable to unwind as it pulled away, but as I recall the boot was too small, was very ably going to be carried by Jeff. A quantity of cable was looped so it would just unwind as the car pulled away, and all that Jeff had to do was simply keep up with the moving vehicle and after all everybody knew that the car could only travel a relatively short distance before it ran out of cable. Now this is where I became privileged to two pieces of information that, I realised afterwards, I should have perhaps passed on. But you know how it is, you always assume that the grown-ups know what they're doing.

Wrong. To keep up with the car, Jeff would have to run a bit. The director had said to him, 'The car will pull away slowly and we will cut very quickly'. Meanwhile the floor manager had said to the car driver, 'As soon as they (meaning the actors) are in the back just pull away as normal.' Well, to give him his due, there was enough cable but that wasn't about to be the problem. If I have an excuse for not putting these two privileged pieces of information together, it is that only afterwards did I realise the floor manager had never actually had a conversation with the director. You're probably way ahead of me here! As the car pulled away, Jeff, bless him had no alternative but to try and keep up with the car. You could see it coming a mile off. I have never witnessed a cameraman running so fast in all my life, as Jeff did to the limits of his ability trying to stay abreast of the car that was accelerating away from him. In the end, he had no alternative but to let go of the C.C.U. and I must say the number of pieces that it shattered into amazed even me. The engineer looked at the mangled heap of waste metal on the floor, which only seconds before had been a living thing, turned around, sighed deeply, and threw his screwdriver over his shoulder into the pile of twisted and crushed debris. Everyone around looked very solemn faced; however I am sorry to say I spent nearly ten minutes laughing in some nearby bushes. Every time the mental image of those little legs going so fast by the side of the car appeared in my mind, the tears welled up in my eyes and I was off again into uncontrollable mirth. As Jeff has said himself since, his legs were a blur, putting even Road Runner to shame. The shot, as it turned out, was quite successful until the screen went blank and I believe was actually used in the final edited version of the episode.

I remember vividly swinging my boom between Christopher Blake and Jeremy Irons, in the studio in a pub set that was supposed to be early morning and Jeremy Irons holding a small whisky shot glass had the classic line as he raised it to his mouth, 'You see, that's the trouble with the first drink of the day, you're never quite sure whether it's going to stay down or come back up.'

Mel Martin, Christopher Blake, Peter Davison and Jeremy Northern were some of the other actors in the series. There was also one lovely lady, Sherrie Hewson, an inveterate giggler. I remember one day on location when I had to record a track of her crying, which we could later then lay over a scene. She confessed that she was useless at crying and she and I had to go off into the bushes, not an unpleasant task, armed with a tape recorder, so that well away from everyone else, she could compose herself and cry. She got the giggles and it took ages before I finally got the required length of crying material. The rest of the crew were deeply suspicious at the length of time I had been absent. I simply put this down to jealousy and Sherrie and I did nothing to dispel their suspicions, occasionally secretly winking at one another while making sure we could be seen!

I later worked on a production called *The Last Detective*, which starred Peter Davison, for Meridian Broadcasting, and again a charming man and great to meet him again after all these years. The first assistant was a man called Jon Older who was a pleasure to work with and the three weeks filming went like three days. Of course, we had the usual problems, artiste availability, Peter Davison getting a nasty ear infection for two days, which had a domino effect on everything. But despite these problems, it was fun. Now there's a word you don't often hear these days! The crew were all to a man and a woman charming and, dare I say, even the sparks.

Television is a strange industry and you need to work in it to really understand that some things may look crazy, but are usually necessary. The classic case for me of that was on *Love for Lydia*. During my lunch hour on location, I was wandering around a stunning house, which we were using the exterior of, and admiring the grounds. I walked away from the house to get a distant view of the entire establishment and way down the field, under a tree, a painter was hard at work.

'Hi Joe, how's tricks?'

'Oh, okay, thanks.'

I stared at his activity and my eyes just couldn't seem to take in what he was doing, so I asked, more for confirmation than out of curiosity, 'What are you doing?'

'I'm painting the grass green.'

'Pardon?'

'I'm painting the grass green. I have been for the last two days. They all came over and looked at the place for the picnic scene on Tuesday and they all decided the grass was just too brown, so I'm having to paint it green.'

'How big an area are you covering?'

'Well, as big as I can until the paint runs out or they tell me to stop.'

Such attention to detail was commonplace back then, but you try explaining that to your mother the next time you go home. 'Painting the grass green, I've never heard such rubbish! Your tea is on the table.'

'Thanks, Mum.'

'Go on, get eating, it'll be cold. Painting the grass green, whatever next?'

One thing you do learn as a boom operator is never to work with babies. Next time you find yourself watching a programme with a baby or toddler up to the age of about two in shot, please do pay attention to the eyeline if they are being held in someone's arms. There is a ninety per cent chance, I think you will find that it is looking up, while all around are talking and looking at one another. You will find that he or she is looking at the boom. You would probably have to employ the services of someone like David Attenborough to tell you why this phenomenon occurs. There must be some sort of built in survival instinct about being attacked at an early age by a bird that is still with us; I am sure he would know the answer. All I know is that whenever I put a boom above a baby or toddler, they would instinctively look up and not take their eyes off the thing or point at it and try to grab it. It had to be there to capture the sound but the baby would see it as some sort of wonderful toddler entertainment device put there purely for their edification and want to play with the thing during the whole of the scene.

As a temporary move to get me out of bedsit-land, and don't ask me how, Ken O'Neill and I found ourselves sharing a flat in Harrow and Wealdstone with a young man called Ian Southern. Ian was one of those chaps you meet in life that was already mature when you met him at the age of nineteen. You could see by his attitude he was a born survivor but that did not mean he was not a very hard worker. He had a very keen brain, loved Malt Whisky (before I had ever heard of it!), could spot a money-making opportunity three-miles away and had a Jaguar XJ6 by the time he was twenty-one, which I know Ken at one point called 'his vulgar tax loss.' On top of which he had a hell of a sense of humour and was an all-round good egg and I was very jealous of him. We have since met up again and he is in fact driving a Lexus and owns a boat! He came, some four years ago, to a function at Mary's place of work, which is the Transport Research Laboratory in Crowthorne. Mary gazed at his face looked at his name badge and suddenly yelled, 'Ian! It's me, Mary, Malcolm's wife!' He is still with the lovely Vena, an ex-sound section secretary, and we meet every three months or so for lunch and a good old natter. He hasn't changed one jot and is still a great guy and is now also a member of the XL's, a group for ex-LWT employees.

Ken and I were billeted in the same bedroom and by God it was a cold winter that year. You could tell how cold the room was because when you woke up in the morning the condensation was usually on the outside of the window!

We finally got a flat on our own and relieved Ian of the strain of sharing his flat with so many people but again my thanks to him for, without him, Ken and I would have been homeless for quite a while. It was a hard learning curve for us all and trying to show that you were not homesick was difficult but again we did have some laughs by way of compensation. I think we stayed in our new abode for about a year and then finally made the move to a bungalow in Pinner, where we were to reside for some time.

As I said earlier, we produced so many shows in those days the list is endless. The light entertainment output was phenomenal. Joe Brown, Roger Whittaker, Rolf Harris, Tommy Steele, Stanley Baxter, Russell Harty and even, dare I say, Simon Dee all passed through the studios of LWT at some point, and I worked on many of their shows. The best bit about *The Simon Dee Show* was Maynard Ferguson and his orchestra, who had a musical spot each week and I can still remember his rendition of 'Macarthur's Park' to this day. It was sensational but the band rig was a nightmare, because the director wanted to track his cameras three hundred and sixty degrees right round them. Try working out where to run the sound cables from the microphones faced with that little puzzler. The answer was straight up into the lighting grid and that is where the nightmare began because sound cables near lighting cables never get on, there was always an induction between the two, that caused a hum on the audio output.

Another memorable moment was when Eartha Kit was a guest on *The Roger Whittaker Show*. It was my job to take the microphone from her at the end of her song. During rehearsals, she finished the song and just stood there and stared at me, so that I was forced to climb onto the platform she was standing on to get our microphone back. As I got down again, she purred, 'Stay there.' She then promptly climbed on my back and made me give her a piggyback back to her seat. An even greater shock was a security man appearing to announce that Roger's car was blocking someone's car in the car park. Ken O'Neill happened to be near the whistling singer and Roger simply said, 'Can you drive?' Ken nodded and Roger chucked his car keys at Ken and asked him if he would move it, as he wanted to carry on rehearsing. Ken obliged having proudly passed his test some three weeks before. He was gone for a very long time. When he finally came back he looked a little shaken and the reason was that Roger had failed to tell Ken that the car he had volunteered to move was a brand-new Rolls Royce. Ken, terrified at denting it, had taken a long time manoeuvring it out and then back in again to the car park. I suspect the keys might have been thrown in someone else's direction had Roger known Ken had only passed his test approximately three weeks before!

Ronnie Barker was eventually given his own comedy series called *Hark at Barker*. Ronnie played a Lord of the Manor character whose gardener went under the name of Dithers. He didn't say much. He was a stooped, bearded, grey-haired old man who would mutter strange ramblings in a thick accent, often culminating in the word ''olly 'ocks', which became his catchphrase. Under that amazing make up was a very young actor called David Jason, who was not even recognised by the crew the first time he went onto the studio floor in that disguise.

The parlour maid in *Hark at Barker* was a very attractive, young, long-legged, blonde actress called Moira Foot who we would fight over giving a lift home to after the show as she too inhabited Pinner and only two streets away. Nothing ever happened, but we made the rest of the crew jealous as we said goodnight and left the building together.

Barry Cryer often did what were referred to as 'warm-ups' for many of the light entertainment programmes at LWT. This is the chap who comes out about half an hour or so before the start of the show and, as the name implies, warms the audience up with a few jokes and stories so once the programme starts they are hopefully in a relaxed and laughing mood. It may, at first sight, appear to be a very easy job but a warm-up man could often make or break a show. How? Well, if you failed to get the audience in the right frame of mind they would then sometimes go on to find the actual show itself not funny, having been suitably unimpressed for half an hour by an un-humorous moron. We saw a few of those over the years, but they never lasted long. We saw a lot of Barry because he was funny and professional. And along with a chap who was also a master of his trade, Bill Martin, they were LWT's main warm-up men for quite a few years. I can remember standing behind one of the booms listening to Barry doing his usual warm up for *Frost on Sunday*, which although we had heard it many times always amused me. But that night, on the punch line to one of his jokes, I laughed in a manner that sounded like a groan.

'Who groaned?' he enquired. 'It was you, wasn't it?' he said pointing at me.

'No, no Barry it was an inward laugh,' I said hurriedly, defending myself.

'Come on then,' he said grabbing me by the collar. 'If you can do any better, tell a joke.'

He then thrust the microphone into my hand and stood to one side. Fortunately, I have had a sense of humour for many years and I do pride myself on the fact I can tell a joke. I decided to tell the joke about the golfer who slices a shot, which disappears into the woods and he can't see the ball anywhere so decides to knock three off his score and play another ball. As he is about to play the ball, a policeman comes running towards him out of the woods and says, 'Did you just hit a golf ball through those trees?'

'Yes, I did,' says the man.

'Do you know what it's done?'

'No, but I've got a funny feeling you are going to tell me.'

'I'll say I am,' replies the policeman. 'It went onto the main road and hit a motor cyclist, causing him to swerve and come off his motorbike in front of an oncoming car, which plummeted down an embankment onto a railway line and was then hit by an express train, which was derailed. There are about two hundred people dead out there.'

'Oh, my goodness,' replied the golfer. 'What do you think I should do?'

'Well,' said the policeman. 'The next time you play the stroke, put your right thumb parallel with your left thumb.'

And here you demonstrate someone holding a golf club correctly, which is why the gag doesn't work too well on paper as it really has a visual tag! There was a huge laugh from the audience and a round of applause. Barry very quickly grabbed the mic back from me and shoved me out of the way. It was all done to get another laugh and I know he had just been fooling around!

The only time I ever saw Barry get somewhat unnerved was once doing a warm-up for *Frost on Friday*, for which David Frost was nearly always late. I know this because we had to find him to put a radio microphone on him. Quite often we decided there was no way, when he finally arrived in the studio, you would have time. We would seek him out in make-up and if he was late getting in there you often were trying to put the damn thing round his neck and the small power pack that went with it in his pocket while running down the corridor. One night, Barry, as usual, was doing sterling work with the audience and the floor manager, as usual, signalled for him to stop as the opening music was about to be played. Sorry, I forgot to say this was live television. The music started and there was no sign of David. Barry looked a little apprehensive, to say the least. The director was screaming, 'Where is he, where is he?' and in a flash of inspiration yelled, 'Keep the grams going, keep them going.' And then yelled at the cameras, 'Keep panning round the audience, keep panning.' And so, a series of

41

very pleasant shots of the audience clapping away appeared with the theme music still going underneath their applause and after what seemed a lifetime he finally gave in and said, 'We will have to put Barry on.' The floor manager quickly imparted this information to Barry who went a little ashen and just, as he was about to walk on and say, 'Good evening, you're probably wondering what the hell I'm doing here,' David Frost appeared in the studio doorway; rushed past Barry, took a bow and started the show. I think from memory he wittily said, 'Hello, good evening and welcome. My thanks there to Barry Cryer, who so nearly became a star.'

I know Barry never mentioned me in his autobiography, but I won't hold it against him. David Frost always joked that Barry had a sign in his front garden which said:

LAST COMEDIAN BEFORE THE M1

Barry lived in Hatch End, and I think he still does. If you have read his book, you will know he has never driven, so on a few occasions after hospitality, when *Hark at Barker* had finished, and Barry had done the warm up, because he knew I lived in Pinner, which isn't a thousand miles from Hatch End, he would scrounge a lift. Little did he know how sometimes that put my nose out of joint because one of the other lads would jump in and offer the aforementioned Moira Foot a lift home to Pinner without going via Hatch End first. Damn you, Cryer, my life might have been completely different if you had learned to drive. Only joking, we had some great times, especially one warm up gag the whole crew knew by heart, so they would all join in and yell out the tag line which was, 'The last two were mine!'

42

I can remember a young girl called Lulu, aged about twenty, doing a programme called *Lulu According to Freud*, which starred her and Clement Freud, an unlikely combination. I know myself and Graham Thor-Straten, the sound assistant A on the crew, fought constantly over who should be pushing the foldback speaker on the floor in order that we could get close to her and just gaze with a stupid grin on our faces. A foldback speaker was a big box on wheels from which the orchestra or backing track emanated and your skill was to get it as close to the singer as possible while keeping it out of shot. She was an engaging lady, full of fun and laughter and I have no reason, from what I have seen occasionally on the television, to doubt that she hasn't change one jot from that lovely girl we both fought to oggle over at such close quarters. Graham nearly fell over when she came and stole one of the sweets he was eating. I'm sure he would have gone out and bought a jar full just to get another smile and cheeky wink like the one that she gave him as she scuttled back to centre stage.

By now, sharing the bungalow with myself and Ken was another sound colleague called Rob Loyd. We called it our own 'cirrhosis by the sea', based on Errol Flynn and David Niven's name for their abode when they lived together. Unfortunately for us, Pinner, for that is where we were located, is land locked.

The bungalow had an enormous hall because it was originally built to house a huge organ that the original owner possessed. Please do stop making your own jokes up! The organ was no longer there but for us it frequently made the establishment a marvellous venue for a party. There were four bedrooms so we also shared with a variety of other male lodgers who occupied the fourth bedroom. We decided to rent it out to someone outside of the business. At the time, it was felt this would give our various conversations a bit of variety!

One of the unluckiest men I worked with over the years in the sound department was a sound supervisor by the name of Mike Fairman. He seemed prone to the adage that if something could go wrong, it would – and with Mike it invariably did! His hobby was glider flying and with his incredible streak of bad luck, we always wondered why he pursued this hobby but I guess enough sufficiently went horribly wrong for him during most weeks on the ground for him to feel reasonably safe at the weekends in the air. He is the only man I know that had the sound desk catch fire on him just before a live religious phone in called *Answer Back* one Sunday teatime. It was in fact a small bulb that had overheated and melted its plastic covering but it was enough for him to rush over to the mains switch and kill the power to the desk, thus taking the programme off the air before it had started. A maintenance man was summoned and the programme did go on the air some ten minutes or so late. One of Mike's other staggering tales was related to us one day after we noticed that he was walking with a bit of a limp.

'Ah, yes,' he replied, when asked how it had occurred. 'I went for the train last night, as usual at the station. It was close to its departure time so I opened a door fairly near the end of the platform and got in. The train is often a corridor train and I just planned to walk down the corridor and further along to find a seat. I opened the door on the far side of the compartment and fell straight out onto the line. You see, what I thought was a corridor, was in fact another train parked alongside the one I stepped into.'

44

There were about five of us around a table in the canteen listening to this and I know we gasped as one person. 'What happened next?'

'The people in the compartment were a bit staggered.'

A bit? Can you imagine being a happy commuter, reading your newspaper, when a man gets into the compartment walks straight through opens the door and falls out the other side?

'They helped me back in and luckily, I suppose, because I didn't have time to tense myself, I was so relaxed when I fell out, I didn't really hurt myself at all, just a couple of bruises. The worst insult was that I dropped one of my gloves on the line so I had to let the train go before I could get down, rescue it and wait for the next one, which wasn't for another forty minutes.'

I travelled home on the train from London to Newbury as often as I could but one exceptional journey I took was one November evening on bonfire night. With your weekend, not always Saturday and Sunday, in fact as the station was called London Weekend it figures that my weekend off was rarely to be Saturday and Sunday, if it did happen like that you sometimes found yourself with Monday and Tuesday of the next week as your weekend so with four days off in a row I would invariably head for home. This journey seemed slow and tortuous with lots of trackside works but for once I was happy with the slow progress because the displays we travelled through were wonderful. Just that slight elevation meant that not only could you see the Catherine wheels and roman candles in the back gardens by the trackside but also observe a travelling cascade of spectacular colours and sounds in the sky and all for the price of a return ticket to Newbury.

I gradually began to travel a fair bit on the work front covering such things as racing from Newmarket and Kempton, motor bike scrambling from Yorkshire, football from a variety of grounds, including cup finals at Wembley stadium, which for me I am afraid has terrible memories. Firstly, I was never that taken by football, I could take it or leave it. The sight of twenty-two grown men trying to get a ball between two sticks and a bit of net, very like my physics experience, had always left me cold. I never have been able to understand why so many people get so hot under the collar about it all. Still, each to his own and if it gives so many people such pleasure, then why not? It never did me any harm, well almost. What did upset me about my first visit to Wembley stadium and my first cup final, please don't ask me who was playing and what the score was, came at half time when we were able to wander away from our position on the touch line, which I know many people would give their right arm to be in, and toddle off in pursuit of a cup of tea. As I came around the corner by the outside broadcast vehicles, it started to rain, which I thought was a little peculiar as it was a bright if not slightly cold sunny day. I looked up to see if I could spot the rain cloud and to my horror I was greeted by the spectacle of lots of men leaning over the concrete walkway above and urinating onto me and the cables and the vans down below. That probably is the main reason that Brian Moore, that lovely and brilliant football commentator who's sadly no longer with us, and I never quite saw eye to eye over the romantic vision he held of Wembley Stadium and its place in football history. To me, it was the most appalling place of human depravity and has forever remained so. A very sad footnote is that Brian having retired was so looking forward to watching the world cup in the comfort of his own home. Unfortunately, he was denied that joy.

Chapter Three

South Bank Life

In February 1972, David Frost decided to tackle the Irish problem head on and an outside broadcast was mounted from Belfast. We did the Catholic side of the story first in Londonderry on Saturday and then did a debate in the Belfast studios on the Sunday. The programmes were then transmitted about an hour after they had been recorded and edited. We then got the hell out of there fast!

We had about six vehicles with us and when we set off on the Saturday morning there was a healthy half hour gap left between the first three and the second three travelling in convoy, just in case. We had finished recording in the studio on the Friday night an episode of *Budgie*, starring the late Adam Faith, together with the wonderful Georgina Hale, Lynn Dalby and Ian Cuthbertson, who played the memorable Charlie Enwright. The director Mike Newell, who went on finally to achieve the acclaim he so richly deserved for *Four Weddings and A Funeral,* had at one point shouted so hard and loudly at me for getting the boom in shot, I had collapsed to my knees with the shock. He apologised almost immediately and said he shouldn't have been so horrible to someone who was about to leave for Northern Ireland. The cameraman looked up at me and mouthed the word 'sorry' as it had been his fault because he had framed the shot higher than ever before, but kept very quiet.

After the recording, those of us heading towards Ireland briefly had time to go to the bar to forgive and forget before being rushed off to the airport to have a few nerve-steadying drinks before the flight. Upon finally entering the hotel on the outskirts of Belfast, the body search was so thorough that the male vision mixer, a wildly camp and very witty creature, wanted to join the back of the queue and have another turn!

After dinner, and a briefing on how things had been planned for the next two days, a small group of us fell into a discussion with the bar man about Protestants and Catholics and about everyone looking the same, it not being like fighting a proper war where people wear different uniforms, so how could they tell one another apart?

'Well, different things but he's obviously a Catholic,' said the barman.

'Why?' I queried

'Because you're wearing a St. Christopher round your neck.'

I stared down in horror at my open neck shirt. Mary had given me the saint just before I left, in the hope that it would keep me safe. I realised it was now about to label me a Catholic and terror raced through my body with the thought that it could cause me to get my head blown off. From then on, I kept it hidden in my pocket and only replaced it round my neck on the flight home, giving thanks that even in the depths of my trousers, its magic had worked and it had afforded me a safe passage. If anything untoward had befallen us, our lords and masters had seen to it that we were going to go to meet our maker well pickled. There was a mini bar in the hotel room, that under normal circumstances you would pay for, but on this occasion, we were told it was all free. So, a very likeable man Graham Walbrin, who was by then my crew boss, brought all his drinks into my room on a tray and we exchanged the ones we liked with each other. Swapping Vodkas for Gins and Brandies for Whisky and so on.

49

We left in the coach the following morning with slightly sore heads and then looking at the back seat of the coach to our amazement we discovered it piled high with beer and lager. When we got to Londonderry, a group of nuns made us cups of tea in the hall we were filming in and treated us with such marvellous hospitality and friendship that you could only surmise that if we were all like that, what a wonderful world it would be. I stepped outside at one point to see the generator driver with a tin of grey paint covering over the slogan on the side of his vehicle that read:

YORKSHIRE TELEVISION
FROM THE NORTH OF ENGLAND

'Well, you can't be too bloody careful,' he said.

'Shush, the nuns might hear you,' I hissed, with my stomach turning over, not from alcohol, but from fear. I then came crashing back down to earth with a bump, realising that unfortunately the entire world was not solely inhabited by nuns.

A slow and contemplative journey took us back to the hotel only to discover that the good fairy had been round and all the drinks had been re-stocked in the mini bars in our rooms and Graham and I once again played swap the Martini miniatures into the wee small hours of the morning.

Sunday in the Belfast studios was unbelievable now I look back on it. We recorded the show in the early evening and then had to wait while it got edited a tiny bit and transmitted from the outside broadcast truck back to LWT. Why not from a videotape machine inside the complex? I have no idea! All I know is we waited and waited. We had to because we had all travelled in the coach together. I stood in the yard with

50

the transmission controller from Belfast and enquired what the lights in the sky were that I could see.

'Of course, you haven't been here before, have you? They're tracer bullets.'

'Jesus Christ,' I blasphemed.

'Oh, don't fret about them old boy, they're at least five or six streets away. It's when they come whistling over the top of your head, that you want to get worried and start thinking about ducking.'

I didn't reply, my mouth had dropped open butterflies circled in my stomach and I realised this was a very, very serious place to be in. For the first time in my life, I felt real fear and both vulnerable and incredibly small all at the same time. The vision mixer leapt out of the truck and rushed passed me heading for the coach.

'Looks like we're off. Good luck,' I said to the controller.

'Don't worry about us old boy, we're used to it.'

I contemplated long and hard and decided that I personally could never, even given a month of Sundays, get used to it. I boarded the coach, the vision mixer was in a right old state, nervously twiddling a piece of blue tack in his hand at a ferocious pace. 'Come on, come on. Where the bloody hell are they?' He meant the director and a couple of others who were still yet to appear. We wanted to be as far away as possible when the programme was transmitted on air, because of the undoubted controversy its showing was about to cause. They finally arrived and once more we departed into the black night to our country hotel retreat and the whole team hit the bar running, flushed with success, adrenaline and a job completed.

At about half past midnight, a medium sized group of those who were left had retired to a room with a piano in it and were singing a few of the old songs when the owner of the establishment appeared in the doorway, the room fell silent. However, she was not in a steaming rage, as we had all first suspected, but was armed with two members of staff and under their arms were about ten bottles of champagne.

'Jesus, if you're all going to have a party, I'll show you how to have a party and you are certainly not going to have a party without me.'

She made a short speech thanking us all for being such wonderful kind guests and for making her laugh. In the odd dull moment, it still puzzles me how twenty or so drunken, terrified people achieved this and I have never quite come up with a satisfactory answer. But I suppose a bit like the Sixties slogan, if you can remember it, you weren't there. I'm afraid after one o'clock that evening I have no idea what happened but like almost every Irish person we met over that long weekend, the owner was a warm and generous soul, with a love of life and fun.

We travelled the next morning very slowly on the coach through the heart of Belfast and down the notorious Shankhill Road. We were stopped at a roadblock and a young soldier, who looked no more than a boy, climbed on board. He was armed to the teeth and very slowly walked the whole length of the coach gazing at each parcel or bag on the floor and each occupant in their seat. I had never seen a loaded gun at such close quarters before or a young man look so serious at such a young age. Not surprisingly, the butterflies from the previous evening began to return as huge moths. Having thankfully reached the airport, we walked towards the plane. But there was yet another shock in store for me. I looked up and stared at the vehicle in disbelief.

'Oh lord, now look, this bloody thing has got propellers.'

'It's the same as the one we came out on, dear,' said the vision mixer.

'Oh, blimey, I must have already been drunk when I got on the damn thing last Friday night because I would have noticed those propellers and been just a little afraid.'

Despite now feeling very afraid, I more than happily climbed on board and could not wait for it to transport me away from this conundrum of an Isle. Northern Ireland had defeated me utterly and completely. I just could not see as to how on earth it could be at all possible for a place to contain so many lovely, generous, gregarious, life loving people and yet to have been so troubled and so tortured for so long.

A few days after our safe arrival back we all received personal letters thanking us for our contribution to the broadcasts. Mine read very simply:

Dear Malcolm,

Thank you for volunteering to work in Ulster last weekend. It is not an exaggeration to say that the programme would not have been possible without the hard work and dedication of everyone concerned.

Thank you,

It was signed by the director, a great bloke called Bruce Gowers, who was the man that revolutionised the pop video world with Queen's 'Bohemian Rhapsody', and the producer of the programme, a certain Mr John Birt.

London Weekend Television's drama output was phenomenal. To be honest, I can only skim the surface here. *Manhunt*, starring Peter Barkworth, Cyd Hayman and Alfred Lynch, went on for something like twenty-six episodes featuring those three staggering through France, to the sound of Beethoven's Fifth. Philip Madoc, of course, famous for playing another nasty German Officer in *Dad's Army*. Resulting in giving Arthur Lowe the now historical reply to his line of 'And what is your name?' with 'Don't tell him, Pike!' None of them ever crossing the channel once to make the show, they all staggered mostly in the studio and through Burnham Beeches, as I recall. Oh, and there was one brief excursion to a railway siding at Stonebridge Park, just off the North Circular Road, where given a mirror on a stick from the administrative offices in Station House, the executives could see the workers hard at it down below. This was the famous episode where not one sentence of dialogue was spoken, the odd gasp was heard as they were shot and an occasional 'schnell, schnell' from the Germans, but that was about it. A film crew had also been let loose filming sequences without sound, which were then edited into the final show. The poor grams' operator, one Paul Faraday, such a sensible surname for a technical chap I always thought, was faced with about twenty minutes of totally mute film to which he had to add footsteps, gunshots and explosions from humble old 78" discs and quarter inch tape to bring the piece to life. Without the technology of today, how he achieved this was a minor miracle and he really should have been given some sort of award for bravery above and beyond the call of duty. It was one of the best pieces of sound dubbing I ever saw, and indeed heard, at LWT. However, due to being a perfectionist, Paul was not happy with his work on the programme. The series was also famous for the first full frontal female nude in a television drama. Again, that was the era I was working in, programmes were being made by programme makers, people who cared, people who were constantly pushing forward the frontiers of the industry and not driven by ratings and percentage shares of the audience and dictated to by accountants. They were simply there to try and make good and entertaining television programmes.

Enemy at the Door was a Second World War saga set in Jersey. The exterior scenes were mostly filmed over on the islands and the interior scenes were taped in the studio. I know the producer at the wrap party at the end of the final series said it just could not go on any longer because in historical date terms, which they vaguely did try to stick to, it was about to go on longer than the war itself! What was more, if it did continue apace, there was a severe danger of the Germans winning this time!

I had been the grams operator on quite a few of the early shows and in the office of the German Commandant, played by Alfred Burke, which was supposed to be in the port of St. Helier, I had added seagulls in the background, which seemed like a good idea at the time. The problem was that after about episode six the sound got on everyone's nerves, especially if there was a tense dramatic moment about killing someone by firing squad. I am afraid that the squawk of one of those wretched birds in the background rather detracted from the moment. Over the next few episodes they gradually became replaced by light dock work noise going on outside the German Commandant's window, so that it could be stopped if necessary, should the drama of the scene require it.

Other highlights included *Helen a Woman of Today*, which starred Alison Fisk and featured the famous theme tune of 'She', sung by Charles Aznavour. *Wicked Women* was a series about female killers with a different lead character each week. It featured some wonderful artistes including Billie Whitelaw. *Bouquet of Barbed Wire*, which starred Frank Finley and Susan Penhaligon, and *The Guardians* were also major drama successes. *The Gold Robbers* saw Peter Vaughan, as Detective Chief Inspector Cradock, trying to outwit and catch the baddies. A clever idea, where they were all seen in the opening title sequence, was the heist itself of the gold from a plane filmed at Blackbushe Airport, by about six robbers, I think. Each episode concentrated on the story of one of them, with a different guest star each week such as Patrick Allen, Roy Dotrice, Joss Ackland and once again Alfred Lynch. Lynch played the character that the storyline had homed in on. *Diamond Crack Diamond* starred Alan Dobie, who at one time was married to that wonderful actress, Rachel Roberts. *Black Beauty*, I suppose, was really a children's show but shot beautifully on film and co-produced by Paul Knight and Sydney Cole. Knight eventually went on to produce many notable one-off dramas for LWT, then *Holding On,* a series about an East London docker which launched the late Michael Elphick's career. From there, Paul continued to produce *London's Burning* for ten years and the customs and excise series *The Knock*, by which time I had moved on to be a location manager – but more of that later!

I will tell you about one quick little snatch of life on *London's Burning* to wet your whistle. We were filming a train fire at the Nene Valley Railway near Peterborough for a week. The crew had been billeted in various hotels dotted around the area, but the cast had mostly all been accommodated in The Haycock Hotel, just north of the location off the A1. I came across Richard Walsh, who played 'Sicknote' in the series, being dropped off in the car park on the first afternoon fresh from his hotel. The whole sequence we were about to film was set at night so we were girding our collective loins ready to embark on five long night shoots.

'Hello,' I said. 'How's the Haycock?' He had obviously been dying for someone to ask him this all day because the reply was immediate.

'The Hay is fine,' he said. 'And it's Mr Walsh to you.'

A big grin slowly began to stretch across his face as he wandered off in the direction of the make-up truck.

I can remember the announcement, that London Weekend International had been formed, which would sell our programmes far and wide across the world, being greeted by Graham Walbrin with the comment, 'Just think Malcolm, boom shadows over five continents!' What is difficult for me is to place where we made certain programmes because eventually LWT made the move from their Wembley studios to a new complex on the South Bank at Waterloo. As each studio set was similar, in so much that it was full of bright lights and done in a completely created environment, placing it in Wembley or on the South Bank gets a bit confusing. In some cases, programmes like *On the Buses* were made at both complexes. Incidentally, when we moved to the South Bank they realised the studio dock door was too small to accommodate a double decker bus, as it had done at Wembley, and so a single decker had a false upper deck added to it, rather than have Reg Varney suddenly driving a single decker!

Michael Aspel joined us for quite some time making the chat show *Aspel and Company* and a show called *The Six O'clock Show*, which launched quite a few people like Danny Baker, Janet Street-Porter and Russell Grant onto our screens. I have a very funny picture, a cast and crew one, of *The Six O'clock Show* in which most of the sound crew are stood hopefully at the back of the assembled group, a lot higher in the picture than those in the front. What a shame then that the photographer neglected to tell us we were not lit. Still a silhouette can be as dramatic a portrait as the real thing, I suppose. Strangely, I guess as an omen of things to come, in centre stage on this black and white image is not Michael Aspel, the director, Noel Green, or the producer, but a very pleasant researcher who would often pop into the sound control room during the pre-rehearsal period, asking for bits of music or a sound effect. He seemed reasonably mature to be a researcher, but we thought nothing of it. However, we later discovered it was none other than Greg Dyke.

We worked as a crew on a whole variety of programmes. Each day was different, which is what made the world of television so appealing. In the early days of LWT, situation comedy was almost second to none, although Thames also began to produce some classics. A young actor appeared in the studios playing opposite the late John Thaw in a series called *Thick as Thieves,* which Graham Walbrin wasn't too taken by as it almost glorified being a crook. I must admit I thought the balance was a bit out but Bob Hoskins was a funny man and the two of them bounced well off one another. *Minder* came along from Thames a little later and got the balance just right.

We were sat by the Thames near Richmond one day filming an insert for one of the episodes of *Thick as Thieves*. In the script, Bob was required to fall in the river. Although he was relatively unknown at the time, he was a lead actor. This resulted in a stuntman being booked to 'double' for Bob when the vital moment came to take the plunge. For some reason, the stuntman never turned up. I was just happily collecting sound with my 'fishpole', which was basically a long stick with a microphone on the end of it. So, the stage manager bravely volunteered to go where no man would normally dare. He donned the wig and took a dive for the sake of proving that the show must go on! He was quite poorly for a few days after the event, the Thames certainly not being as clean back then as it is today, but I am pleased to say that he did make a full recovery.

What has always stuck in my mind of that day was the trip to the pub at lunchtime where a new machine had been installed. Graham and I were each fascinated with playing with a bat on an electronic machine and a bouncing ball in between us, which you could vary the speed. Heady days indeed and the pre-cursor to space invaders. In the twinkling of an eye, look what has happened to those machines and computers. The mind does indeed boggle at times! It seems like only yesterday, but in another way, it was a lifetime ago and an age gone by and lost forever.

I can remember vividly standing at the end of a runway at Heathrow with Graham during a pause in the recording of *Thick as Thieves*, with me holding the microphone. I had been asked by Paul Faraday, who had now become a sound supervisor, to go and do what we called 'wild tracks' of some planes taking off and then identify them verbally once they were out of microphone range. He would then use some of this material for the sound transcription library back at LWT. Now neither myself nor Graham were very good on planes, and all we could muster once they had passed overhead were inane comments like, 'That was a blue one,' or even more detailed, 'That was a green one, with yellow stripes,' and even, 'er, that must be one of those Air Canada ones, it's got that pretty leaf on the side.' Paul, monitoring our conversation in the OB truck, came over our headphones loud and clear.

'You pillocks! I meant 'identify them'. For instance, 727 and Tri-Star. You know, that sort of thing!'

'No, I'm sorry. I'm afraid we don't.'

'Oh Christ, well do the best you can then.'

I turned around to face the runway to do the best I could but I swear the next jumbo was coming directly at me. It looked as if it was about to take my head off. Graham was already making a dash for it!

'Get the hell out of here, Malcolm, I can see the whites of the pilot's eyes!'

When we played back the recording you could hear the screech of the plane's engines, the thump as the 'fishpole' and our headphones hit the grass and then the sound of two pairs of boots running away into the distance. Perhaps we had strayed a little closer to the runway's edge than we should have done. You certainly would not get those recordings today for I am sure health and safety measures would never permit anyone to be that close to one of those monstrous beasts.

The other time that Walbrin and I struck danger was at Newmarket racecourse. The day had started off as cheerful and bright, but gradually the clouds had built up and gradually it became obvious they were storm clouds. Graham and I were testing a new radio mic for use on remote starts, where the cable run was prohibitive just for one microphone. Over a long run the signal got weaker, so in came the radio mic to the rescue and we had a huge long pole of an aerial we were carting about. Well, the storm struck with quickness and ferocity. Lightening flew everywhere. John Rickman that splendid commentator, who would always doff his hat as he bid you good day, was taken aback as one of the strikes went straight along the mic cable and tingled his chest. He said, 'Oh! Cripes!' live on air and out loud. The language could, I suppose, have been a lot worse had the man not been a gentleman. One of the cameramen, Colin Price, was knocked to the ground after his metal camera tower was struck, but he was all right and survived to fight another day. Walbrin and I looked at the lightening flashing all around the grandstand from way down the course and pondered on the outcome. Now, for anyone who doesn't know Newmarket, it is very flat and very open. We were soaked to the skin, the storm was heading our way and Graham suddenly looked at me and said, 'Give me one good reason why we should continue to hold this bloody great metal pole, when a batch of lightening is heading our way?'

I mused, 'Er, well I…'

Graham interrupted me, 'Put the damn thing down.' He yelled, wrestling it from my grasp and literally threw it as far as he could.

'Now come on let's go and find some shelter.'

It was like a scene from a Laurel and Hardy film. I gazed around at the miles of flat, empty countryside and then gazed back at Graham the rain pouring off the end of his nose.

'All right, stupid idea,' he said.

I was just waiting for him to say, 'This is another fine mess you've gotten me into,' when even though the force of the rain was stinging my eyelids, I saw that salvation was at hand. The riggers, who knew we were out there, came to our rescue in their American Chevrolet that had a camera on top that would travel along with the horses during the race. Gratefully, we pushed the offending pole into the back of the vehicle and both absolutely soaked through climbed aboard the truck and headed back to the main base. It was a thankfully relatively short, but a nonetheless terrifying journey. If you have never been in the heart of a thunderstorm in the open, and I do not recommend it, you really have never felt the awesome power that nature can throw at you. It is true about the hairs on the back of your neck standing straight up, mine most certainly did – even though they were completely sodden! When we got out of the truck one of the riggers fell about laughing and told us to go and look in a mirror. We found one in the washroom and we both collapsed in absolute hysteric; it wasn't just the hairs on the back of my neck and Graham's that had stood up, we both looked like we had just put our hands in an electricity socket. We looked like Michael Bentine with our hair, because of all the static in the air, I suppose, sticking out at all angles.

Supersonic burst onto our screens in a bid to rival *Top of the Pops*. It had been sometime since ITV had tried to have a go at a pop show, but they did and it was crazy. Directed by Mike Mansfield, the show was just a succession of foam, balloons, fireworks, streamers, dry ice and any wild effect the designer could think of. All this together with hundreds of screaming girls and, somewhere in the middle of all this, the music. Everything was glitter and silver and shiny. We were taping an edition of *The South Bank Show* in Studio 1, which was being directed by Bryan Izzard, and the whole thing was mostly set against black drapes, with very moody lighting. During rehearsals, we discovered we needed an extra foldback speaker because the artistes were having difficulty hearing the playback. I rushed to the sound store, dragged one out and wheeled it into the studio. Our foldback speakers, as I described before, were basically a huge wooden box on wheels; this one was bright silver. It had been covered in the stuff to be seen in shot on *Supersonic* and the previous sound crew had not removed it. We were all creeping around against the black drapes wearing black shirts and black trousers and here I was pushing a great big silver box, which I must admit did show up slightly. Bryan Izzard took one look at it on camera and yelled, 'Is there not one piece of technical equipment, in this building that hasn't been ruined by that white-haired lunatic!' He was referring to Mike Mansfield, who sported a fine head of shocking silver hair, and had all sorts of things painted and changed. Even the camera crane had been covered in glitter one week! A voice came from nowhere, 'I'm afraid not old love, you will just have to put up with it.' It was the voice of Mike himself, who had been editing upstairs in a video tape editing suite but at the same time watching Bryan's pictures and listening to the director's talkback. Luckily, Mike couldn't see Bryan put his hand over his mouth and mime the word, 'Ooops!' Bryan quickly thought on his feet and rallied, 'Look love, do try and stop it will you, some of us our still trying to produce quality programmes.' We all laughed, it was a friendly rivalry and that was just one example why LWT did for many years possess a warm and cosy atmosphere to work in.

The camera crane in those early days was a burley piece of kit that required a driver and a swinger as well as the cameraman and had an awfully big loom of cable protruding from the rear end. I once saw one of these beasts slowly make its way into the set of a live *Frost on Sunday* and systematically take the floor covering up as it lumbered towards a singer set deep in the bowls of the studio space. The floor covering was made of sheets of thin plywood and the cable loom had caught a turned-up edge of one and then managed to tear up the subsequent ones it encountered. The cameraman, driver and swinger were all blissfully unaware of the carnage that had been wreaked behind them. The main problem was that unless the floor was fixed swiftly the crane would be unable to return along the same line that it had majestically travelled along. We all rushed from different directions, the audience must have enjoyed the spectacle as grown men panicked to either remove the wretched flooring or re-lay it. We did finally triumph just as the song was about to finish and the crane reversed back into its prime position down an isle specially made to accommodate it in the middle of the audience.

The other time one of these pieces of kit got horribly out of hand was doing a special edition of *Aquarius*, directed again by Bryan Izzard, featuring the Swingle Singers. The set was a clever design of square blocks of various sizes upon which the vocalists of the group, who numbered seven in total, stood at varying heights. The crane I think was called a 'Titan' and had been brought in especially for the occasion from the film world. During a pause in the recording, the crane had been left unmanned and suddenly started to move all on its own accord, gently colliding into one of the blocks, which sent the singer on top tumbling to the studio floor. The block then knocked into the next one and so on like a huge domino game; several crashed to the floor projecting their unfortunate occupiers off into mid-air. Luckily, by some miracle, no one was seriously injured but several people were very shaken by the incident, not least the crane driver, who double-checked the brake constantly thereafter every time he left the machine for even a millisecond.

When Mary and I moved to our first house in Ash in Surrey, after living in a maisonette in Harrow and

Wealdstone, I became a commuter into London on the train from Ash Vale station. I found myself falling in occasionally with a bunch of guys from work that belonged to the 'W' club. They were all from various departments within LWT and thank God, because of my strange shift pattern hours, I didn't travel home from Waterloo Station with them very often. They always caught the same train, at the same time, that was fast to Woking with a buffet car, and that is where they always stood. However, whenever I did catch that train I was always made most welcome. We would gather in the buffet car for the journey to Woking, where we all went our separate ways or some stayed on to go on further down the line. Meanwhile, myself and a sound colleague Keith Green would do what we called the 'coronary run' over the bridge from platform two to platform one and hope to catch our connection onwards on another line. Now it was called the 'W' club for a very simple reason: every time the train passed through a station beginning with the letter 'W', someone had to buy a round and that was had to buy a round not would or sometimes but a definite had to. Not too bad you would think, until you board that train and realise the first station is Waterloo, obviously, but then they come at you thick and fast. Wimbledon, West Byfleet, Weybridge, Walton on Thames, etc. By the time you got to Woking, believe me, you were hard pushed to see the station name in focus out of the window, let alone to see if it began with a 'W' because, yes you guessed it, we all were drinking doubles. How those regulars survived that every night of the week, I have no idea. The die-hards would buy another round at Woking and then followed quickly by one at Worplesdon before alighting at Haslemere, which is where most of them lived. I dipped into their world occasionally and it was not unknown for me to deliberately miss the train because I knew they would all be on it, if I was feeling rough or even more probably a little poor. I am afraid I would sometimes watch the 'W' club special leave the station from the safety of a WHSmith bookstand, which was alcohol free and easier on the pocket! They all know who they were, so I do not need to mention any names. They were a lovely bunch of people and we shared some very funny moments that made commuting an enjoyable experience.

When I travelled on the train on my own, I had my own method of raising a few eyebrows and laughing inwardly. I came across three small paperback books in a sale at a local bookshop, they had originally been five shillings each but were here being sold for sixpence. I couldn't resist buying three for the titles alone were just wonderful. They were entitled *How to Keep An Elephant*, *How to Keep a Gorilla* and my favourite of all – *How to Keep a Man-eating Shark*. They were small enough to drop nicely in your pocket but the titles were in big print on the front with a suitable picture of the beast that was contained within. Now once a journey has started, and the railway carriage is full of happy morning commuters, if you slowly withdraw from your pocket *How to Keep a Man-eating Shark*, open it up and pretend to start reading, keep your eyes peering over the top of the book on the assembled company, you will derive much pleasure from the startled looks on their faces. It was such a hoot that Keith often borrowed the books so that he could have a bit of fun on the way in to work in the mornings too. He just loved the copies of *The Times* and *The Guardian* getting ruffled by people wondering what sort of maniac had joined them on the seven forty-five from Farnborough Station to Waterloo.

Chapter Four

A Bittersweet Win

The worst thing that eventually happened in sound, purely from a personal point of view, was the invention of the radio microphone. Up until this point, all presenters were either covered by the boom or a cabled microphone. This had come about when Rex Harrison, while making *My Fair Lady*, had refused to mime to his own pre-recorded sound track, saying that every performance was totally different. So, the Warner Brothers sound department went away in confusion but came up with the solution of the radio microphone. How big this was back in the day; I would love to have seen it, but they did slowly get smaller and smaller. Interviews on *World of Sport* in the studio were often covered by a 'fishpole' but slowly radio mics became more reliable and stand microphones did not need to be nursed and comforted into working. Ask any sound person who can remember that far back about the C28, the C29 and the C30, which were valve driven, and, honestly, they did have to be talked to very gently before a show to make them work! So, over the years, although still operating a boom on occasions, which was still my main skill, I slowly found myself becoming a highly-paid battery changer, a job that I was sure given enough peanuts a trained monkey of three could have done. If you were working on the studio floor on *World of Sport* you literally spent all day waiting for either the batteries in the radio microphone to need replacing or the ones in Dickie's earpiece, on which he could hear the director. Sometimes it was not the batteries that had died but the fact that there had been a build-up of wax in the 'deaf aid', as we used to call it, and you nimbly whipped out the TCP and a cotton bud and removed the stuff. This was kind of akin to Dudley Moore and Peter Cook as Derek and Clive and the story of Jane Mansfield and the worst job they ever had. I was becoming bored and boredom had never been a word in my vocabulary. I knew I didn't want to become a sound supervisor as it was a thankless task. You were not only very much under pressure with your life and career in the hands of the boom operator if you were doing a drama, but also liable to be sat in a dubbing suite for days on end, which as a grams' operator I had experienced and hated with a passion. The same piece of music being played repeatedly, no window to look out of and long twelve-hour days was never my most popular piece of scheduling. In the winter, it would be dark when you came in for work and dark when you went back out again. Also, you just sat there all day, no fun in that and certainly very little exercise. So, what to do? I examined the alternative jobs in the industry I could try my hand at and thought I would have a bash at being a floor manager. It looked straightforward to me. You waved your hand and cued somebody and you only had to carry the script around, rather than great chunks of technical equipment.

I got a placement with the floor managers' department for two months and hated almost every minute of it. The job was much easier, there was no hard rigging, and when the director said, 'That's a wrap' at the end of the day, I simply had to take off my headphones and head for the bar. In one way, it was fine, but the one thing I hated was looking after lots of background actors. I always swore I really needed a border collie to do the job properly! There were always one or two who just when you had rounded them up to take them into the studio would go missing. They had usually had hours to go to the loo, make that all important phone call to their agent prior to your herding them together but they always managed to disappear just as they were needed on set and who got the bollocking because they were not there? You guessed it, not them but me for not looking after them. That was kind of the role of an assistant floor manager but even as a floor manager, you didn't seem to have much to offer because apart from yelling at everybody to be quiet all the time, the only other thing you did was cue the programme off and once that happened it rolled along merrily on its own without any input from you. Having been in sound and been part of the action, as it were, for almost thirteen years suddenly to be standing on the side lines watching it all happen didn't fit comfortably. So, I went back to sound and manual labour and looked for another more suitable opening.

It was around this time that I was hit by that flush of late youth thing – how to better myself. I decided I wanted to learn a language, study for a degree, go to dance classes or go to night school and learn something. I did not like my school days and the problem in taking up, say, learning French, with the job I had, was that you could not guarantee that you would have every Monday or Thursday night free for whenever the French lesson might be. I had for a long time been interested in magic and I had bought a book by John Wade called *Do Get the Name Right*, in which he recounted some of his amusing stories as a magical compère. At the back of the book were listed a whole host of magical dealers that you could send off for their current catalogue of magical effects. I think I sent off for three of these. That was it, the bug bit deep and hard. I sent off for some tricks and then would practise and bore everybody at work by showing him or her my

69

latest acquisition. I joined the Magic Circle in August 1976 and have been a member of that celebrated body ever since. It fitted in perfectly with my work pattern. They hold their meetings every Monday night and that was the one evening I usually had free. It was either a rig day for a show, a maintenance day or a day in the sound transcription unit any of which meant I could be outside the headquarters near Goodge Street by seven o'clock just as the evening's lecture or competition or whatever commenced. Also, if I did miss an evening, it didn't matter as much as it would if I had taken up the language idea. Even though I was still a little uneasy in the sound department, I did at long last have a hobby, which was to delightfully distract me for the foreseeable future. I am pleased to report it still does.

We had a little charity group at work called *The LWT Roadshow* and we would go around to various places and put on a kind of old time music hall show. Ellis Ashton, who was at the time the chairman of the Music Hall Society, was our chairman and he would introduce, a group called The Singing Waiters, made up from painters and chippies, and a drag act from men's wardrobe called The Dolly Sisters. Mary sang a few old music hall songs and Pam Rhodes would sometimes join in with singing a selection of First World War songs. Then I would perform a few magical miracles.

The drummer with the small band that accompanied us sadly died. To mark his passing, and to raise a few quid for both Cancer Research and The Heart Foundation, LWT held the first and, as it turned out to be the only, *Len Fraser Award Show* for charity entertainers in April 1977. It was held in Studio 1 at LWT's South Bank complex with an audience of six-hundred people present, which is a big crowd to walk out in front of, I must say. People were asked to compete from all around the ITV network and from the BBC, and I was pushed into the line-up. There were thirteen entries including a comedian from the BBC, Mike Meys, Pam Rhodes, the Thames Television Big Band and yours truly, who staggered on about halfway through the show. I was very tired and a little hung over. I had worked on *World of Sport* all day as the grams operator with the aforementioned hangover and now, after a concentrated ten-hour day, had a thumping headache. In short, I just wanted to go home. What had happened the night before to account for this I cannot remember now. It was not the 'done thing' to go drinking the night before *World of Sport* for your own good, as much as anything else. Rosie Field, one of the many beautiful make up ladies at LWT, applied my make-up and I sort of got my second wind while sitting in the comfortable chair in the make-up room. I walked onto the stage and within thirty seconds I knew I had the audience eating out of my hand. It is a funny feeling when it happens but, for whatever reason, they thought I was hysterical. I swear I could have coughed and they would have found it hilarious. I picked a young lady from the audience to help me with the second of my three tricks and they thought she was wonderful. She was so funny that everyone swore blind she was a confederate and was secretly part of the act. I honestly had never met her before. There was one point where she just had to blow some notes on a wooden flute I had given her to make a card rise-up from the deck – and she could not do it! She would put the flute to her mouth and hesitate, the audience would laugh this would make her laugh and hesitate even more, which made the audience laugh more. This made her hesitate more and it just kept on and on like that. At one point, I shouted, 'Come on play it for goodness sake, you never

71

know you might win the ruddy competition.' And that, as they say, brought the house down.

I came off flushed with success and started packing for home. Mary was ill in bed and I thought well I've done my bit now I'll be off.

'Where are you going?' said Graham Walbrin, who along with Adrian Rodger had volunteered to do the sound.

'Home,' I replied.

'You can't go yet you twit,' he replied. 'You'll have to stay to the end to see who wins.' There were still six acts to come and I plunged into a fit of depression and wandered off to phone Mary to say I was going to be later than I thought because I had not realised we had to hang about for the grand finale.

The chairman of LWT, John Freeman, announced the winners in the usual reverse order, selected by the panel of judges, which included amongst others Hannah Gordon, Janet Brown and Jack Douglas. The Thames Television Big Band looked a bit upset when it was announced that they had come third. To give them their due, they had played brilliantly. The BBC comedian, Mike, came second and blow me down the winner was announced as Malcolm Treen! The Thames Television Big Band were still looking upset – and all thirty of them were now looking upset in my direction! I shook hands with John Freeman, produced a cigarette from his ear and tried once more for the exit door.

'Where are you going?' asked Mike Conway-Toms, who had produced, directed and compared the evening.

'Home?' I replied.

'No, no, no, you,' he said. 'You must come upstairs to meet the judges and have a drink in hospitality.'

I put the bag back down and off I went to be patted on the back, told what a marvellous career I would have in front of me, if I went professional, and discovered what a charming lady Hannah Gordon is. Of course, I eventually ended up in the bar with Graham and Adrian telling me it was the safest place to be until the Thames Television Big Band had all left the building and climbed on board their coach. I agreed with them, having this uneasy feeling I could end up with a trombone wrapped around my head at any moment. I made my way home with my prize statue in my hand. I told Mary I was very sorry I was running so late. I explained that I hadn't meant to win, it just sort of happened!

Graham Walbrin had a wonderful sense of humour, which sometimes left you wondering why he had decided just to be a boom operator and not a stand-up comedian. We had a young man join our crew from Channel 7 in Sydney; he was young and like most Australians had never been abroad before. Although being fairly intelligent, Russell in the early days, believed every word that Graham said, which was his first mistake. We were sat in the canteen at the outside broadcast base at Wycombe Road one morning, discussing the vagaries of the English language. Sure enough, it being breakfast time, the curious phrase of 'bubble & squeak' came up. Graham extolled its virtues to young Russ and then, straight as a die, said, 'Of course, if you want something really special, try asking for a plateful of mungo and poet.' As expected, Russ was off, having fallen for it hook line and sinker. 'I think, they're havin' a laugh sir, at your expense,' said the canteen lady. Russ looked at us with an expression that said, very funny but don't worry I will get you back. He was a great addition to the crew and only stayed for a relatively short time before returning to Australia because his father was taken ill. He did leave us with the legacy of the pub stunt of being able to drink three pints of lager quicker than someone can eat five cream crackers. You can see how usefully we filled up our leisure time!

Slowly we enriched Russell in the art of boom operating and one memorable moment was when he was operating a mini fisher boom in a corridor. The mini boom was used sometimes instead of the fishpole if a scene was in an awkward place or was also a little too long for some poor unfortunate to holds his arms up above his head for what seemed like forever. These mini booms were robust little pieces of equipment but a bit hazardous if you forgot to extend the wheels, which gave it a bit more stability. Sometimes, because of the confined space, extending the wheels was not always possible but as Russ was about to find out, extending the wheels should always be at least attempted if only for safety's sake. Whether he got carried away swinging to and fro between artistes, we shall never know, but halfway through the scene he somehow lost his balance on the beast and toppled sideways. There was a hell of a thump and a crash. Luckily, being well over six foot in height, as the floor approached, he and the boom parted company. Russ simply stepped backwards off the machine, held it at an angle of forty-five degrees and carried on operating. Mike Fairman was the supervisor in the control room blissfully unaware of the chaos ensuing out in the studio. 'Try and keep it a bit steadier if we go for another take. There was a bit of rumble that time,' he had said over talkback at the end of the scene. Russ failed to hear him as he was too busy trying to get the mini boom back on its wheels and help the stagehands restore a portion of the corridor set, which he had accidentally managed to demolish.

Michael Lindsey Hogg was a very well-known director who had shot the famous pop video of The Beatles on the top of the roof of their company Apple in London. He also directed drama and helmed a period piece at LWT called *Affairs of the Heart*. It starred Diana Rigg, Jeremy Brett and George Cole. It also boasted the wonderful Frank Nerini as the designer. Of Italian descent, he was never without a glass of something wonderful in his hand. The series seemed to have been in the studio for days! On this last day at seven o'clock the recording would stop – whether it was finished or not! Someone upstairs had decreed this and the production manager had been told that at seven o'clock he must go into the control room and stop the show. It had cost too much in overtime already and no more could be afforded.

At about four o'clock that afternoon, Diana crept round the back of one of the sets and caught Jeremy's attention and gently whispered in his ear, 'Darling, there is no way I can get through the rest of the afternoon without champagne,' her eyes widened and I would defy any male to have resisted her seductive charms as she drooled, 'Be a darling, won't you?' He grinned and disappeared, returning some five minutes later with a bottle and two glasses that he secreted behind one of the scenery flats. As the hands on the clock grew closer to seven, the atmosphere in the studio could be cut with a knife. We all knew that there would be a show down between the production manager and Mr Hogg if he had not finished and wanted to go on. It was like a modern version of *High Noon*. The clock was at one minute to seven, they had just said cut on the last scene. Michael wanted to do it again but it ran for three minutes. The floor manager removed his head set thanked the studio and walked off. The camera crew

75

were completely behind the director and, for once, so were the sparks, otherwise the lights would have gone out. While the production manager argued in the gallery with Michael, he began to get upset and threw a chair at the monitor stack, a voice came over talk back and said, 'Roll VTR.' The actors began to act, the vision mixer began cutting the scene and by the time people realised and stopped arguing we had done the scene again and it was in the can. We began to de-rig the studio and the main question on everybody's lips was who the hell was the brave, mystery person who had said, 'Roll VTR'?!

As we struggled to become professional boom operators, we did have some hair-raising moments. That seven o'clock cut off on a Friday night on a drama was the rule that could not be broken and as you edged towards it with time running out you could sense the urgency and cut the atmosphere in the studio with several knives. Ken O'Neil was perched high on his boom in the studio set of a hallway in a rather grand house at 165, Eaton Place, where an episode of *Upstairs Downstairs* was being recorded and the lovely actress Lesley-Anne Down playing the daughter of the Bellamys, owners of the house, was about to be married. It was a difficult scene sound wise because I was in there with him sharing the stress on another boom to his right. The lighting was such that I could put shadows on people standing on his side of the set and he could put shadows all over mine. Over the years, we had got used to that in the morning room set, where whenever David Langton, playing Richard Bellamy, came in and would say, 'Marjorie, the most extraordinary thing has just happened.' It was a line which he seemed to utter every other week. The boom on the left-hand side of the set had to go way up in the air or it cast a shadow on the wall to the right of the doorway as he entered. I used to hate that morning room; it was always a struggle. The vision mixer had your life in his or her hands, in that if they cut too early to the shot of the door, you saw the boom shadow flying up the wall and it was always a battle with the lighting director because nine times out of ten you could end up with something like seven or so people in the place, some sitting, some standing. It was not easy to light – and even more difficult to cover successfully for sound!

The clock was ticking towards that magical seven o'clock time and Herbie Wise, the director, was under pressure. Gordon Jackson had been offered some drops for his eyes by the make-up department to make him appear all tearful and emotional on this romantic occasion. In fact, they stung like hell, his eyes ran like buggery and we had to stop recording while water was sent for and his eyes rinsed out to normality. They went for the scene again. Lesley-Anne Down descended the staircase in her beautiful wedding dress and walked straight into a boom shadow from Ken on her veil. 'Keep it still. Keep it still,' yelled Herbie, which really defeats the object of being a boom operator, because the idea is that you put the microphone over the head of the person who happens to be talking. But Ken, as requested, froze and all our mouths went dry. The microphone at the end of the boom has a little bit of curled wire coming out of it before the cable runs back down the boom arm and this we always called the pigtail, and there on her veil was a pigtail shadow. You only tend to notice boom shadows if they move like bats flying around in a barn. But if you keep it still, sometimes it could be anything, a chandelier shadow perhaps? So, Ken having frozen, we did get the scene in just before seven. The shadow is still there, and can be seen if you watch a repeat of that episode carefully, and so are the teeth marks on the bar that we hit with some speed to unleash the tension, after hurriedly de-rigging the studio!

It wasn't always the people on the studio floor that made mistakes. No, the sound supervisors were sometimes responsible for the odd calamity too. We taped a series of *The Dickie Henderson Show* with a big band, dancers, lots of singing and a few odd comedy spots and even jugglers. Yes, that is what we used to call entertainment! One bright idea that someone had come up with was that as Dickie was singing, his microphone would suddenly go dead and I think Lionel Merton, one of the regulars on the show, would rush onto the stage with headphones on pretending to be a technician and begin to follow the microphone cable, which headed off into the band. He struggled through the trumpet section feeding the cable through his hand and the gag was that as he got to one end of the orchestra and then back out again he was following the cable that lead straight back to the microphone that Dickie was holding and at that point the microphone would begin working again. Good visual gag that would have worked had the microphone not really died because of finger trouble on the night from the sound supervisor. To have run the whole gag a second time in front of the audience just wouldn't have worked. Why? Well, audiences never laugh as much the second time round because obviously they know what's coming next.

I loved those big shows because there was always a live orchestra. Although I do remember the trumpet section (and it may have been on the same show) having celebrated a little too long in the bar before the recording and two of the players having to help the third player to his feet because unfortunately for them at one point the trumpet section had to rise to their feet in a little solo spot. Luckily, this most badly affected member was in the middle of his two colleagues and was helped to rise by a steadying hand on either side, which they nearly got away with, but unluckily it was his sway, having arrived in a vertical position, that rather dramatically demonstrated that perhaps there had been a little over indulgence!

There were other major productions that sometimes took days to record. *Jacques Brel is Alive and Well and Living in Paris*, was one example. Starring Mort Shuman, Elly Stone, Shawn Elliot and Alice Whitfield, it took days of rehearsal and some very skilled boom operating by Graham Thor-Straten, but the audience were treated to a superb show in the setting of a large nightclub. I rushed out and bought a double album of the show to remind me of the occasion and foolishly lent it to someone sometime later and never got it back. I spent many, many years looking for a replacement copy, only to find it had been deleted from the catalogues. Then, just when I had given up all hope, I finally stumbled upon a replacement copy in a little shop in Brighton.

Weekend World was a very popular Sunday morning current affairs programme. The series had several presenters over the years, but my favourite was Brian Walden, the ex-Labour member of parliament. My main reason for this was that he had a slight lisp and to hear him pronounce 'rank and file', as would Jonathan Ross these days, as 'wank and file' on a Sunday morning in the middle of a very serious political debate was well worth the journey in at the weekend. These were the heady days before the technology for those graphics on the screen we now take for granted were invented. The captions that were 'animated' were usually some of the stage hands pulling pieces of cardboard situated on a caption stand to one side of a bigger piece of cardboard on the director's cry of 'Reveal!' They sometimes wobbled, they sometimes got stuck half way and they sometimes fell off the stand altogether in a huge heap on the studio floor and the crucial order they had been placed in was destroyed. It was a live programme and much sniggering could be had while standing around waiting for Brian's radio mike batteries to fail!

I seem to have rushed through thirteen years in the sound department at LWT rather quickly, missing out the tale of Don Chapman, a sound supervisor, asking Fred Varley what the sticker in the front of his car was and Fred replying it was to show he was an advanced motorist, who then nearly crashed the car we were all travelling in. Don tore the sticker into neat quarters and replaced it on the dashboard. He had not been enjoying the experience as a passenger with Fred for some time and decided revenge had to be taken. Also, the tale of rigging some cross-country motorbike trials in a raging blizzard way up north somewhere and my feet and hands being completely frozen and rendering me useless as part of the rigging team. I just lay there on the floor of the commentator's box totally incapacitated as further down the course one of the outside broadcast number ones, a guy called Ted Flack, tried to tie a frozen microphone cable to a fence and it was so cold it just snapped in two. I thought the weather was so bad they would be bound to cancel the live broadcast the following day.

'No chance,' said one of the course stewards. 'They love these sorts of conditions.'

I stood there with my teeth chattering, looked at him in disbelief and said, 'They would wouldn't they!'

The only time I ever did a bit of moonlighting, don't ask me how or why I got involved, a favour for a mate probably, but I ended up mixing the finals of a talent competition organised by a brewery. All the entrants were acts that had won various heats in pubs and the final was to be held at the Astoria Theatre in London. It all went quite well. Rolf Harris was to be the cabaret after the show and then a big band was to play through into the early hours for dancing. Before I go any further with this story, I would like to make it very clear that I only ever found Rolf to be totally professional. I was, of course, incredibly shocked and appalled when he was later charged and imprisoned for a number of historic sex offences.

The competition was completed, the winners announced, trophies and prizes distributed and on came Rolf. The tabs were pulled and just Rolf and his pianist Barry remained in front, while behind them a relatively quick re-rig of microphones went on to prepare for the band. This is where it started to go horribly wrong.

I was happily up in the sound box mixing Rolf and the piano, when thud and Rolf's microphone 'died' – that's the technical term for it! Shades of Dickie Henderson, but this time I was in-charge of the faders. Adrian Rodger, who was helping me down on the floor, reported that the crew of the theatre were in such a rush to re-rig everything that Rolf's microphone had been accidentally unplugged in the fracas. There was a splat and it came back to life and Rolf laughed, apologised and carried on with his act. If I had known at that point I was to lose that microphone six more times before the end of Rolf's spot, I would have left the theatre right there and then. Embarrassed is not the word for it. My

81

temper was at breaking point, the air was blue and I wanted to kill someone. At the end of his somewhat interrupted delivery, someone else took over from me to mix the in-house band and I rushed down to apologise to Rolf. He was as calm as a cucumber, such is the professionalism I personally experienced of the man, it hadn't fazed him at all. I didn't know where to put myself and he said it just didn't matter these things happen. A phrase he often used to people when we did his show in the studios instead of 'thank you' was 'your blood's worth bottling' and I can only say how very true it is of this man. Barry his pianist said afterwards, 'Don't worry, he loves it when the microphone dies, that's half his act.' I have a strong feeling everyone was trying to be very kind to someone who strangely enough never went on to be a sound supervisor and having the responsibility of mixing shows. Now I wonder why?

Oh yes, and I have forgotten to mention my fifteen minutes of fame being the magic advisor on *Thomas and Sarah*, a spin-off series from *Upstairs Downstairs*. It starred John Alderton and Pauline Collins and the lovely Maria Charles. Chris Hodson, the director, knew I was a member of the Magic Circle and asked if I would oblige with a little bit of input, which I duly did and got paid the princely sum of one hundred pounds for my trouble. I was operating the boom as well as teaching Andy Ho how to be a magician. Pauline Collins very kindly agreed to be my assistant at the Theatre Royal, Drury Lane, at one of our larger charity events and she took to it like a duck to water bravely letting an amateur saw her in half with an electric saw.

The series was destroyed by the network strike, which lasted for thirteen painful weeks. But more of this anon: suffice to say that being on picket line duty was a bit odd because Mary, who by now was working in the press office at London Weekend, and was, of course, management, was crossing the picket line and going into work. Thank God she was though, otherwise we would have been in desperate financial circumstances. Work did finally resume but that strike did an awful lot of damage and I really don't think life was ever the same afterwards.

And I haven't mentioned that one time I sat in the audience of an edition of *The Russell Harty Show* with Mary watching David Niven being interviewed. What a gentleman. I remember Russell asking him how he stayed so trim and David replying he was lucky enough to have a very big bath in his home in Switzerland, which he could fill with water and do press ups in. At one point a lady in the audience started to have one of those tickly coughs that just will not stop. An usher arrived with a cup of water and there was a commercial break. Immediately, David Niven rushed to the women and said, 'How awful. Isn't it embarrassing when you get a retched cough like that you cannot control. Are you alright now?' He was already my hero but at that moment became a true gentleman and a star.

More and more of the programmes, especially drama, began to be made on location purely because of cost. Scenery was becoming expensive, and so was studio time. To hire someone's house for a day and have it already full of props, for example the chairs, the tables, the carpet etc., which normally would have to be hired in for the duration of a series, became a very attractive proposition to the accountants who were gradually beginning to establish their presence especially in the drama department. For a unit to go outside and film, you need a location manager to find the locations, set things up and look after the unit while it did the filming.

LWT had one location manager – Mr Brian Kelly – and various location production managers. It turned out that the one location manager was finding that he was beginning to get a bit busy. So, they decided to have someone seconded to the department and I applied and was given the job for yet again a two-month trial period. I trailed Brian for a while and was then given my own little project. I had a company car, a parking space in the underground car park and a car phone – what more could a man want? The phone was literally a phone in the car in those days. You got connected to various numbers by an operator. You couldn't dial the number yourself and you pushed a button on the handset every time you spoke, a bit like on a walkie talkie, and at the end of every sentence you had to say 'over' so that the person the other end knew that it was their turn to talk. As a result, I became known as 'over man' in my household.

I was working with a director called Paul Annett on a series called *Partners in Crime*, which starred Francesca Annis and James Warwick as the Agatha Christie characters, Tommy and Tuppence. It was a period piece and we wanted a spooky old house in the country. It was my first job on my own in the locations department at London Weekend. I had my company car, my Polaroid camera and my Polaroid picture of a house that Paul and I had dug out of the locations office files. It was a house he liked but was either in Barnes or Putney, I forget now which, but wherever, it was underneath the flight path to Heathrow and Paul wanted to get outside London to avoid the planes. I was instructed to go west and try the two pretty villages of Great Tew and Little Tew and the surrounding area, while he went east and hunted around the Cambridgeshire area. I looked around the villages and they were ideal. I drove down a hidden drive to see what was there. Sure enough, it led to a large detached rambling mansion; it didn't look quite right, not spooky enough. Well, I mused to myself, I've got the Polaroid, and so I will knock on the door and ask if they know of anywhere round here that might fit the bill. Remember this was my first day out on my own, my first house and my first door knock. Finally, a lady, I would guess in her late fifties, answered the door with a lit cigarette in her mouth. She looked me hard and straight in the eyes.

'Yes?' she growled.

I stuttered and said in my best Hugh Grant voice, although he hadn't been invented then, 'I, er, I, er, I'm sorry to trouble you but I'm from London Weekend Television.'

'We haven't got one,' she replied quickly and looked about to shut the door.

'No, er, no, er, I'm a location manager working on an Agatha Christie drama series and I am looking for a spooky house to use for some, er, some filming.'

'Ah, right.'

'Yes, er and although your, er, house is quite large, it's not quite right. So, I wondered if you knew of anywhere round here like this?' I proudly held up my Polaroid picture.

'Like what?' inquired the lady.

'Like this,' I replied, nearly shoving it up her nose.

'Like this house?'

'No, er, no like this one.'

The picture was now practically an inch from her face.

'I'm sorry,' she said. 'But what are you doing?'

Oh, blimey, I thought. I've offended her by shoving it too close.

'Sorry, what do you mean, what am I doing?' I asked.

'Well, what are you doing?'

I was on the verge of losing my temper. But I remembered that I was representing London Weekend Television.

'Sorry,' I said, 'but I'm showing you this Polaroid picture.'

I was talking very slowly and deliberately, thinking dear God she's thick.

'Er, in the hope,' I continued, as though I was talking to a four-year-old, 'that you may know of somewhere that looks like this house in the picture, round here.'

The reply came like a bolt of lightning, 'Ah. I'm sorry, I'm blind.'

At that moment, the world stopped and I wanted to sink into the earth. My stomach did hand stands. Thank God, she never saw the look on my face or how bright red my skin went and how far down my jaw had dropped to accept my clenched fist, which I bit on long and hard. No television, now it made sense. I just didn't know what to do. She probably didn't even know what her own house looked like, never mind her neighbours. I froze. I stood looking at her in disbelief. After what seemed liked at least ten minutes.

'Ah. Sorry, sorry to have, er, er, troubled you.'

She looked straight at me, drew on the cigarette, flicked the ash off and turned into the house and closed the door. I stood looking at the photo in my hand. What a bloody rum job this is I mused and suddenly the voice of my mother was echoing in my head and I was back on the front doorstep in Newbury.

Strangely, and goodness knows why, this incident did not put me off continuing my pursuit of the job. Finally, after returning to sound and then another attachment and then an interview, I became the second location manager LWT possessed. I loved the independence, driving around most of the time on your own and, as luck would have it, I do enjoy driving. There were bad days when you found nothing and they can be terrible if you're on your own for hours on end and return empty handed. But the bad days were offset by the good days when you found somewhere unique and everyone had said yes and they would love you to film there. There were no set times of clocking in or being on site and every single day was different and every single day you met someone new within a whole range and spectrum of people, from the managing director to the toilet cleaner. The various people I met each had a different story to tell and all had a different take on life. I had always been gregarious and liked meeting people and so this job was ideal. You got to go and see places that ordinary folk didn't and you weren't looking at the same four walls and the same desk day in and day out. The really great thing about being a location manager for LWT was that in the early days you were given a script, you went and found as much as you could but then handed the project on to a location production manager and you went onto the next project. My conversations tended to go along the lines of, 'I found the church, I've got the hospital and the shop, and sorry didn't have time to find the house and the stables.' And that would be that. You never saw the actual filming; it was wonderful never to see the moment when sixty odd people came along and caused havoc all over the property of the people you had become firm friends with.

Chapter Five

Blue Money

While I was happily ensconced in the locations department, a television film came along called *Blue Money*, which starred Tim Curry and a beautiful and talented actress, Debby Bishop. Also in the cast were Billy Connolly, Dermot Crowley, Tony Scannell, later to star in *The Bill*, and George Irving, who eventually was to play the senior surgeon in *Holby City*. My faithful companion, Brian Kelly, was supposed to be teaching me all about being a location manager. The plan was that I was to work shadow him throughout the shoot. However, he was whisked away to set up a new series called *Dempsey and Makepeace* while we were in pre-production. These days most productions of this size would have security men, a unit manager and a location assistant, but on this there was just me, shooting sometimes three or four locations in one day. I was very young, very inexperienced and very stupid! It was a ninety-minute film, which was to be shot over a period of some five weeks in London, Liverpool and Dublin. Out of those five weeks came some wonderful stories and characters! Most fun often came when checking into hotels, on the early recces, with David Fitzgerald (who kindly wrote the foreword to this tome) and Brian Kelly. The reception person would say, 'Ay, Mr Kelly room 5; ah, Mr Fitzgerald room 7 and Mr Tren, er, Trew, er Tron, er; it just wasn't Irish enough, was it?'

They were two plain clothes policemen that the production manager David Fitzgerald had engaged to look after us while we were filming on the streets of Dublin. They were armed, wore plain clothes, mingled with the crew, but who in their trilby hats and long overcoats, stuck out a mile and a half from the rest of the gang. But two nicer guys you could never wish to meet. Those early recces in Dublin, when Brian was still on board, were very funny. I had got back to the hotel very late after doing a letter drop on an estate warning them of our impending arrival. The cast and crew were happily ensconced in their hotel and had been fed and watered by the time I wandered in, knackered, fed up and pissed off that the restaurant was shut. It was just like the time you arrive late at a party and everyone else is drunk and you must decide whether to catch up fast or stay sober and enjoy the fun of watching everyone else drunk as skunks. I was so grumpy and anti-social I went straight to bed, without drink or food.

The following day I got up at the crack of dawn to see the caterers into a supermarket car park and wait for the crew to arrive. My head was killing me. Jim and John appeared around about eight thirty and greeted me in their usual friendly manner.

'Malcolm, how are you this morning?'

'Well, to tell the truth a bit tired really. I've got the mother of all headaches and I am not a headache person and my neck is killing me. And before you ask, no I did not stay up with the crew last night, bloody well enjoying myself.'

'Oh, dear, dear, dear. John, we have something that will cure this, do we not?'

'Oh, Jayzus indeed we do Jim. Malacam, come away to the boot of the car with us.'

I was led to the rear of John's car. The boot opened and the classic bottle in the brown paper bag was removed. A very small quantity was poured into a polystyrene cup and offered to me.

'What's this?' I inquired.

'Just knock it back all in one go and I bet your headache goes, won't it, Jim?'

'Oh Jayzus, yes John.'

I did as I was told. And just like a scene from a *Carry On* film, my eyes widened, my nostrils flared, I gasped for breath and I thought for a moment the end had come.

'Good God almighty, what the hell was that?' I wheezed, when at least my power of speech had returned, if not yet my complete vision. I looked at the blurred bottom of the polystyrene cup, hardly believing that the clear liquid had not gone straight through it onto the car park and melted the tarmac.

In a very low whisper came the reply, 'It's Poteen.'

'Poteen? Poteen? But,' I stared at the two police officers, 'but that's illegal, isn't it?'

'Oh, highly,' said Jim, quickly surveying the car park to see if anybody was watching us. 'Highly, indeed, but it comes from Wicklow where they make the best stuff,' said John, hurriedly putting the demon liquid safely back in its brown paper wrapping and quickly closing the boot lid. After about fifteen minutes, the two quietly approached me and Jim gently whispered,

'How's the headache now, Malacam?'

'Well, er, completely gone,' I replied. 'And the neck ache. Thank you.'

'Our pleasure,' said John.

We spent two days filming in Howth Harbour, which was about four miles or so outside Dublin. I savoured the fresh sea air as I was still recovering from my attack of food poisoning, received from the English caterers that had made me miss the whole of the second week of the shoot. My doctor was eventually coming to see me twice a day and by day five he threatened, given twenty-four more hours in the same condition, that I would be off to hospital because I was just so dehydrated. Luckily, the condition slowed down the day after and one week later I could return to work. If you want one little bit of culinary advice from me, it is never eat re-heated pork off a chuck wagon on location. About seven members of the crew had gone down with the same thing, none as badly as myself I'm pleased to say, and there was a minor inquest, which resulted in the dismissal of said caterers.

I very slowly drank pints of Guinness for medicinal purposes, of course, and did my PR job with the harbour master. He was a lovely man, very laid back, in complete control of his job and had an old Alsatian dog that followed him everywhere. His office was full of pale blue pipe smoke, which billowed up to the ceiling being highlighted by the late autumnal sunshine beaming in through the window. The dog was always in the same position under his desk by his master's feet and only when the old man moved would the dog also stir himself into action and without a lead, stuck closely by his master's heels. I asked him, the harbourmaster not the dog that is, if he would care to come over and have a look at the filming. He seemed flattered that I had asked, but a little dubious that he would enjoy the experience. However, I assured him that if, after ten minutes or so, he was bored, we could always slip away for a medicinal drink.

The following day, I duly arrived outside the Harbour Masters Office at the appointed hour and he climbed into the passenger seat. I opened the back door. 'What are you doing?' he asked. I looked at the Alsatian who was poised, ready to jump in.

'I'm, er, putting the dog on the back seat,' I said.

'Let him walk,' came the terse reply.

91

Now, as I have said, the dog was knocking on a bit, and we were filming way out on the point that had to be a good half-mile from the office.

'It's okay, I don't mind really,' I replied.

There was another full attack but louder, 'Let him walk!'

'Really, it's not a problem, it's a company car, I get it cleaned, I...'

'Jayzus, he has twice as many legs as we have, will you let him walk.'

It was a wonderful Irish observation that I had no answer for; it was a twisted logic that I could not dispute. I closed the door laughing and started the car up and sure enough the dog dutifully trotted along behind us, all the way to the location.

The Harbour Master was such a sensible man. He got bored after less than ten minutes and we retired to the pub. Half the time, the Irish just have that way with words and it is always delivered in a completely serious manner. I was walking around Dublin once with my Irish friend John McEvoy and he was describing the distance a building was from us that we could not see.

'It really is only about fifty yards straight down that road.' He paused, pondered then delivered, 'Sure, if the road didn't have that bend in it, you could see it from here.'

He looked blankly at me as I laughed and I just didn't know if he was serious or not. Perhaps that is one of the keys to the Irish problem, you can never tell when they are being serious or just making out they are serious to get a laugh.

Anyway, back to *Blue Money* and a strange thing happened when we shot in London in Kensington High Street. The location was a jeweller's shop called Henry Hall Pyke, which is still there, for both interiors and exteriors. It was supposed to be a jewellery shop in Dublin and obviously, the interior could have been anywhere but to give the exterior that touch of authenticity the designer, a young man by the name of Mike Oxley, who sadly died at far too early an age for any of us to comprehend, decided to put a green Irish post box outside on the pavement. This rather heavy but beautifully structured piece was made of fibreglass and was worth about five hundred pounds, which in 1984 was a lot of money, and let's face it is not an inconsiderable sum even today! We finished the filming, which only took half a day, and then we were off to film a sequence outside Royal Oak tube station. This was a rather funny piece near the end of the film where both characters dressed as nuns are chased by the police while losing money from underneath their clothing. Back at base, having completed the day, the construction crew realised the post box was missing. A van was despatched back down to the location, after all who would steal a green post box that almost needed four men to lift it? But alas, it was no longer on its marks on the pavement.

A huge search was implemented the next day, which also involved me having to telephone the police, wait for it, to see if such an object had been handed in or spotted anywhere. The policeman who took the call was very polite but with an enormous tongue in his cheek, said he would make a note of the incident and keep the description on record, but it may be best that I didn't hold out too much hope for the return of the said prop. He feared it was already probably upside down in someone's garden with a few plants sticking out of it. This suggestion mortified the construction manager, who spent days afterwards searching down on tube lines, in tunnels and passageways but to no avail, the

93

post box was gone forever. Even now, whenever I pass by that jewellers, I still throw a passing glance in the hope that I might spot that post box strangely positioned on a balcony or in a doorway.

I always had a romantic theory that Michael Winner may have moved it because he complained to the authorities that I had parked the kitchen and dining bus outside his premises. We were only there for half a day, so by the time anybody came along to get upset we had already gone. Besides which, you couldn't see his premises from where we were parked in the road by a very long brick wall. How was I to know that behind that wall was where Mr Winner resided? There wasn't a sign on the wall saying, 'Filmmaker lives here, no film making'. So how was I to know Mr Winner didn't like film crews? And how was I to know he especially didn't like them outside his house?

One of the early sequences after the opening titles was George Irving being dropped off by Tim Curry at various places you assume collecting protection money of some sort. The first port of call is a sex shop. The camera has a high angle shot on the 'Peek-a-boo Shop Club' as we see George get out of the car go into the shop and then come out again. Instead of getting an empty shop, and having to dress it, Mike Oxley and I decided it would be just as cheap to use a real one. We didn't need the interior, so simple use of the outside for about an hour was all we needed. We found one near Paddington Station run by a couple of charming girls who said they would have to ask their boss if it was alright and their boss would want money but they wouldn't want 'nufink' as I wouldn't be interfering with their trade. A couple of days before hand, I popped in to make sure they were still all right for the horribly early Monday morning start time of seven thirty. I was to learn the address I had to take the money in cash to after the filming, which was in deepest Soho somewhere. As I stood there, talking to Mandy, I was aware of a customer sliding past me and accompanied by the other girl Sharon. They both disappeared into the back room, an area into which I had never ventured. I continued my conversation about dates and times and after what seemed no longer than a minute, the cry went up from Sharon, 'Mand, Mand have you got a tissue?' My mind raced into overdrive, as I am sure yours just has. It may well have been a perfectly innocent statement but the mental image that was conjured up by that one sentence was all too much for me. Sensing it was time to leave, I said, 'See you on Monday,' to Mandy and left.

When we got there, we discovered the shop had had a nasty fire over the weekend. Luckily for us, the outside was fine but the interior, unfortunately for the girls, was pretty trashed. Mandy apologised profusely but I said it was not a problem we could still film the sequence. It took no longer than the hour I had promised and we left with everybody happy. But what still annoys me to this day is that I had yellow bags put over two parking meters outside the shop, with police permission, to make sure no one parked there, thus allowing room for my 'hero' car to pull up and park immediately outside the premises. I had failed to get a key so that I could remove the bags at the last minute for the shot because it looked so wrong to me to have someone pulling up on a bagged off meter that said no parking was allowed. It really doesn't show on the small screen but having eventually gone to the cast and crew screening at BAFTA, and seen it some years later at the National Film Theatre, when they showed a season of films made for television on a normal cinema sized screen, the moment still jars. However, it was to be first of many practical lessons I had to learn.

If you look closely as Tim is driving around Liverpool on his way to the ferry for Ireland, you will see him pass a hotel with a sign outside which says:

TONIGHT: BOXLEY AND COXLEY IN CONCERT

The reason for this is that returning from one of our many recces to Ireland, the director Colin Bucksey, and were sharing a car because they lived close to one another. As they came out of the customs area, there, holding up a sign that should have read 'Bucksey and Oxley' was a man with a piece of card in his hand with the names 'Boxley and Coxley' displayed. They asked me if I could persuade the hotel to put this sign up for a couple of hours one afternoon so they could film it as part of the driving sequence as it had made them laugh so much when they arrived at the airport. The hotel kindly agreed and a very in-joke was committed onto celluloid forever.

There is a boat featured in the film that ends up being blown up. The interiors were done in St. Catherine's Dock in London and a couple of shots of the wheelhouse, a 'build', were done in a room in the unit base, which was an office block near Paddington Station. The exteriors were done in Howth Harbour and the final explosion was a mock up on a pontoon in Poplar Docks in London. Yet I would defy anybody to spot the join!

After the end of filming *Blue Money*, we went back to the locations office and I was given two weeks R and R. This meant because you had flogged yourself to death doing a least a ninety-hour week for six weeks, the company, or at least those in charge of the department, realised that rather than booking leave, which would be unfair as they had asked you to work those crazy hours in the first place, you would not be too heavily put upon for a fortnight or so. You could stroll into the office at about ten, stroll down to the bar at about twelve thirty, stroll back to the office at about two thirty and then wait to stroll at a respectable half past five or so to the 'Stage Door', the watering hole I have already mentioned, which nestled at the back of the Old Vic Theatre. Jim, the landlord, always gave us a warm welcome and we would drink, nibble on the odd pork pie, verbally put the world to rights until around seven to 'let the traffic die down a bit' and then proceed home. I have just read Michael Buerk's autobiography and his early television days seem to have been very reminiscent to mine due to the rather alarming amount of alcohol taken. I am sorry to say that it was the norm in those days, however appalling it seems now.

Chapter Six

Dempsey and Makepeace

I was drafted down to the bowels of Southwark into deepest Bermondsey and the *Dempsey and Makepeace* base to help Brian Kelly out on the new series he had now swung into full production on. The series was being made 'out of house' and starred Glynis Barber, Michael Brandon and a wonderful Welsh actor called Ray Smith, who played 'Spikings' their boss. As you may recall, he appeared in *Gareth*, the first drama I worked on at LWT when I had started way back in 1968. A whole army of people were in offices and a sort of studio away from the mother ship on the South Bank. An old warehouse and office complex had been taken over and the corridors and some of it was used for filming the police headquarters and to build other sets and to also house accountants, producers, script people, wardrobe, props and the whole village that supports the making of a production drama series. The rest we filmed on location working out of that self-contained building. It was like a little rebel army detached and on their own and with limited reference back to H.Q., save to say that the first commissioned series of ten episodes would be in the can on time and on budget. It was here that the pressure was so great that I slipped very easily into a wonderful Hamlet cigar and Whisky Mac diet!

Our watering hole near the Old Kent Road was to be The Barnaby public house, where the good folk of Bermondsey eventually came to terms with the invasion of a bunch of 'showbiz' people and 'luvvies' in their local hostelry. We used the Barnaby for celebrations, for commiserations, for birthdays, for anniversaries and sometimes we used it simply to drink in. The landlord,

Carl, and his wife, Jo, made us comfortable and at ease. The bar was very long and made up of old pennies stuck side by side under glass and I suppose I did get used to it but it never ceased to fascinate me every time I entered the premises. You could eat there, you could sleep there, you could play darts there and it did, I guess if I am honest, for many of us, including myself in this list, become nearly a second home.

'If only' is a well-worn phrase and used many times in television. Filming the opening sequence of one of the *Dempsey and Makepeace* episodes, with Tony Wharmby directing, we realised 'if only' the van containing the masked armed robbers and their shotguns had not parked outside the bank around the corner waiting for the cry of 'action' before driving into shot, the resulting visit from four very young, angry and armed plain clothes policemen would never have happened. And the bank manager calmly looking out of his office window wouldn't have thought 'My God a raid!' and hit the alarm button. The scene was supposed to be an armed raid on a petrol station that then blows up, but the police who looked like they were fresh out of an episode of *The Sweeney*, were not very impressed by any of us and our futile attempt at making an entertaining programme on their patch. They threatened to shoot if we tried to film it again, which even now looking back on it does seem a little over the top, but Tony managed to persuade them that one more 'take' wouldn't distress anybody, especially if the actors promised to keep their weapons hidden until they arrived on the forecourt. The police conceded and Tony and his charm won the day.

Crime did pay off certainly in my direction the day some complete idiots decided overnight to break into the mobile kitchen and take it for a joy ride. The caterers were agog to discover at half past five in the morning that it was missing from its parked position. We were filming in Covent Garden and I really wasn't too convinced I had enough parking spaces for all the attendant vehicles, as I had found out the day before that we were doing quite a big 'crowd' scene in Stringfellows' nightclub. I also had an additional dining bus to add to my collection. I paced up and down before anyone had arrived and tried to work out where to park what and, more importantly, how. I had a security man with a load of cones on duty overnight but as always, not everywhere was clear and there were two cars still parked up spoiling a complete and uninterrupted run. My pager went off and I read the message with joy, 'Kitchen stolen. Organise local breakfast.' A nearby café owner was staggered when I wondered in through the door and asked him if he could start a tab for me and then serve people as they came in and said the magic words *Dempsey and Makepeace* with bacon rolls, sausage rolls, tea, coffee and whatever and I would pop back and settle up with him later. Oh yes, and there would be about seventy of them. His eyes rolled to the back of his head and I thought he was going to faint! Quite early on came another message that no replacement kitchen could be found at such short notice and everyone would be given a cash allowance and an hour and a half for lunch to make their own arrangements. I rushed round the corner and dismissed the extra dining bus and pondered on the fact of what a marvellous day it was turning into!

We should have been out of Stringfellows not long after lunchtime. We weren't. Also, because we had the hour and a half for lunch, we began to get more and more behind. We had to be back in Penarth Street our base to complete the last scene of the day and I knew if

100

we went on much longer, we would incur the wrath of the club because they had to set up for their evening trade. Luckily, I had told Tony he had to be out an hour before he had to be, but as he was now eating into the time, I had to keep up the pretence of concern and anxiety that his overrun was allegedly causing me. I wandered into the club and stood on the stairs until I caught his attention through the crowd, amid the racket of playback and dance music. He gazed up at me with a fixed stare and mouthed the words 'go away' very slowly at me. In response, I shook my head and mouthed back 'no' to him. He grinned looked at his watch and mouthed 'don't worry' at me. I mouthed back 'I am already' and then frowned. He just dismissed me with a big grin and waved his hand. He did wrap within half an hour, so he thought he had got away with about an extra three quarters of an hour, which I knew he already had so everybody was happy. If only all the days could have ended that way!

As we tumbled into the third and last series of *Dempsey* with Ranald Graham now producing, who had written some of the episodes, the scripts began to get later and later and the preparation time got even tighter and tighter. David Fitzgerald was now the production manager. I can remember not being allowed to see one of the scripts because the content hadn't been discussed properly with some of the artistes and they didn't want them accidentally catching sight of it. I wrote a stinging memo, just to cover myself, saying that I had never heard such nonsense as the location manager not being allowed to see the script and how for goodness sake was I supposed to start preparing the damn thing? Scenes would be written with no heading above them. Normally they would say something like 'Exterior Park' or 'Interior Pub' for example. But now they were coming with just dialogue and no reference as to where they might be set. I can remember saying to Ranald, 'Where is scene twenty-seven supposed to be?'

His reply staggered me, 'I don't know, just get me something visual'.

Now this really didn't help. Tower Bridge, Buckingham Palace, even the Red Lion public house were visual inside. The list was endless and by golly you could sit at a desk and ponder for an awfully long time as to where you might set the scene.

I am sure there are many stories of *Dempsey* that I have long forgotten. Indeed, there seemed to be a host that came back from Chilham Castle where one of the episodes was largely shot. I didn't work on that episode, so perhaps as I wasn't personally involved that's the reason they haven't stuck. Well, except for one. John Conroy reminded me of this. John was a carpenter with the construction crew and they had gone down to Chilham as an advanced party to prepare the location for the arrival of the filming crew. John was up a scaffold rig working at a fairly reasonable height on something and trying to negotiate his task with only one plank to walk on. The rest of the chaps had passed by down below for a chat. Among them was John Carman, who later went on to be construction manager on *London's Burning*. As they departed, and as an afterthought, they yelled up to him, 'Anything else you want John?'

The obvious response came back at them, 'Well another plank might be nice.'

Carman yelled back, 'Blimey, what do you want, a dance floor?'

The construction crew always were very dry witted!

The day that they swapped scripts on me still sticks glutinously in my mind. I had been happily plodding

102

along preparing an episode when I was told that was not the episode to be filmed next but another one which would be on my desk later that day. It was about eleven thirty in the morning. I was a good way into finding most of the locations for the script I had, so now I would have to start all over again and with a lot less time. I was so angry I couldn't talk to anyone because the pressure I was about to be put under seemed very unfair. I stormed out of the front door and headed for the sanctuary of the Barnaby. Just arriving was Tony Wharmby, probably fresh back from some ghastly script crisis meeting and he stopped his car literally in the middle of the road. He leapt out and leaving the driver's door open and the car ticking over rushed towards me.

'Malcolm, I'm sorry, I'm so sorry.'

He held me by the shoulders and looked me straight in the eyes.

'You were the first person I thought of, when we decided to swap the episode. You were the first person, truly, truly you were.'

I stood there doing what can only be described as a passable impression of Stan Laurel just opening and closing my mouth with no words coming out and raising my eyebrows.

'You'll be okay, really you will. If it gets behind, we won't blame you, just don't worry, it will be absolutely fine.'

He had his back to his car but I could see over his shoulder a small but orderly queue of cars beginning to form, with their occupants probably beginning to speculate if the tall bloke with the grey hair was about to knife the younger guy with the moustache.

'Great, you'll be okay seriously, you will.'

'Sorry, I was just off to the Barnaby.'

103

'Fine, absolutely fine. It's my fault we just couldn't go with that episode in the state it was in. You'll be okay, really you will.'

I pointed behind him at the queue.

'Ah! Yes, better get on. See you later. Sorry, really I'm very sorry.'

He ran back to the car and I felt better and no longer angry. Such a simple thing to make me feel wanted, but it worked. Like the production manager Peter McKay, Tony's people skills were immense. I wandered off to the Barnaby but just had the one and went back to the office. When I had walked out I had contemplated staying in there all day and drinking to forget the nightmare I was about to embark on, deliberately becoming very miserable and wallowing in self-pity and alcohol abuse. However, knowing that Tony was fully aware of my predicament, and had apologised so vociferously, suddenly took all the pressure away. Man management at its finest.

The turnaround was relentless, which held me in good stead for the six years on *London's Burning,* which was yet to come. It was two weeks' shoot and two weeks' preparation. A script arrived on a Monday and you had a week and a bit to find the locations (assuming they didn't swap the damn thing on you halfway through!) before a technical recce was needed about halfway through week two. Then the following Monday you started to film for two weeks from seven in the morning until seven at night. By that time, you needed all the permissions, all the parking permits, all the residents and neighbours on your side and a whole stack of paperwork of licenses and facility agreements to be sorted and in place. Looking back now, I don't know, and I am not too sure we knew then, how the hell we did achieve in such a short space of time what we did achieve. That is also excluding night shoots, which did crop up and often threw a spanner in the works for the production manager, Peter McKay, or Mac as he was affectionately known, to then get the crew back on course for normal shooting days.

We had just finished filming a caravan being blow up, not an unusual occurrence on that series and in fact my second explosion in two weeks. The explosion was invariably the last shot of the day and this one had been no exception. 'That's a wrap,' someone shouted and the crew were off. So, by the time the sirens had reached me, most of them had long gone and I was left alone to face the music. On this occasion, I had two police motorbikes, three fire engines, an ambulance and two police cars to face all arriving and asking for the person in charge. The crew, what was left of them, had very kindly pointed in my direction as the last silver box was packed into the back of the last estate car and they fled. With hindsight, we discovered that Mac, who had very kindly offered to distribute my residents' letters on his way home the week before, telling the locals of our intended invasion and use of pyrotechnics, had lettered the wrong street. So, not only did I have the emergency services to deal with, but also a rather large number of members of the public who had been rather surprised, to say the least, by the explosion and were very keen to show me where various plates had fallen off various walls due to the shock wave from the unexpected bang.

I went back to the office ready for a row with Mac, not about the letter drop, we all make mistakes and we only put two and two together at another later debrief, no it was about my life in general. I wandered in quite late and there he was alone writing at his desk.

'I've had it. I don't want anymore.'

'What, what don't you want?'

'I can't take the stress of those bangs, Mac.'

'What, what stress?'

'Mac, I have had two bangs in a fortnight.'

He peered over the top of his glasses, 'Well, consider yourself lucky, some people don't get one in a month.'

I laughed and so did he, all my rage dissipated by one sentence. And that was the essence of this man.

'I'll see you in The Barnaby in ten minutes.'

My father had died many years before but there was something about Mac that reminded me of him. Like my father, Mac drank a bit, had a wonderful sense of humour and I'm afraid did smoke a little. You could walk into the office sometimes and realise that Mac had a cigarette behind his ear, one in his hand and one in the ashtray. There was one terrifying occasion when I wandered in and saw this usual condition but noticed that all three cigarettes were alight at the same time!

One of the most dramatic moments I have witnessed while filming was in Limehouse Basin, not looking at all like it does today. It had a swing bridge, where you could cause the most enormous traffic jam if you kept it open long enough and get mentioned on the local traffic news, which we did manage quite successfully to do. But no, that wasn't the dramatic bit. We were filming a sequence in which Richard Johnson, playing the baddy, goes off the rails and drives his Jaguar car into the dark and murky waters of the basin. After the initial shots of him driving and being chased by Dempsey, we came to the final sequence where the car plunges into the water.

The car had been rigged on a special ramp, which would fire it off into the water courtesy of the special effects team led by Tom Harris and the biggest rocket in the world. I can now freely confess that at the time I hated Tom with a passion. Over the three series the explosions, the bullet hits, the cars blowing up were all

106

a giant learning curve for him as well as my fellow location managers and me. Something like five cameras were set up to cover the action at various points round the jetty, and even one in a boat bobbing about on the water. As the tension mounted over the last shot of the day, as always, yours truly was to be found near the catering wagon, telling them it was nearly all over and any second we would release them to go home.

The cameras rolled, a man yelled 'action' in that over-dramatic way many first assistants often have: if you weren't worried or concerned before, you sure as hell were once that cry had gone up. There was a thud as the Jaguar car moved about a foot forward and then slumped back onto the ramp; then an almighty whoosh as what looked like an Exocet missile flew out of the radiator, across the water, over the camera boat (where panic nearly broke out but the damn thing was moving so fast no one had time to react until it had passed overhead), and splashed into the drink behind them. The caterer said, 'I don't think they got that quite right,' an understatement if ever I had heard one. Stunt arrangers rushed about, special effects people rushed about, the grown-ups couldn't rush about because most of them were in the boat. But they soon got back to shore and then joined everyone else and rushed about with the others.

I realised that they had only one go at the rocket business, which was now many feet down in the basin. The only other alternative to get the car into the water was to get another car and push the Jaguar at speed off the end of the jetty. To my horror, I realised the stunt arranger, a wacky Yorkshire man called Roy Alon, was not going to do this – but Tom himself! It had been his failure so he felt duty-bound to get the production the shot they wanted. I gazed in disbelief as Roy described to him in detail what speed, what gear and, more importantly, when to brake, so that he didn't end up in the deep end as well as the dead Jaguar.

'My God!' I said to the caterer. 'It's all gone horribly wrong and the special effects guy obviously has a death wish.'

'Oh dear.'

'Oh dear, indeed. You haven't got anything to drink, have you?'

'Yes, we have, but only gin, I'm afraid dear Malcolm.'

'That's fine, thank you.'

I lit a cigar and bit my lip and watched as the two cars began their run up. Remember this was a long time before 'health & safety' was invented and bravado and the show must go on were the buzzwords that we worked by.

'Sorry, I don't seem to have anything to mix it with.'

'It doesn't matter. Just please give me the bloody drink.'

'Neat Gin?'

'Yes, for Christ's sake, yes. Give me the bloody drink,' I hissed in a stage whisper.

As the cars began to pick up speed, I took a huge slug of the clear liquid. The Jaguar plunged off the end of the jetty, not quite at the jaunty angle it would have flown at with the rocket up its arse, but not bad. The entire crew held their breath as Tom in his car screeched to a halt and stopped just before the lip of the jetty. I took another huge slug and breathed out very slowly.

'Cut,' yelled a voice.

The customary round of applause followed and Roy galloped to the car and ruffled Tom's hair.

'Well done, old son. Well done.'

'Well, that wasn't too bad, was it?' said the caterer. 'How long will it take them to get the car out of the water?'

'I've no idea, I'll let you know tomorrow.'

'More gin?'

'No, thanks,' I sighed. 'For you, that's a wrap.'

Many years later, dear Tom, who I eventually came to like and warm to, told me he had never been so shit-scared in all his life, but with eighty people stood around looking for a solution, he had had no alternative than to solve the problem his own mistake had created. Hero or fool? Answers on a postcard to....

Quentin Annis. Now, Quentin was what they called the third assistant on the series and was a character and a half. One memorable moment was when Glynis and Michael were filming a scene in the police headquarters corridor, the usual walking along and musing over what to do next moment. Suddenly, halfway through the scene, from a side corridor, comes Quentin blissfully unaware of the filming and walks straight into the back of the shot framed nicely between the two actors. He sees the camera dead ahead and freezes brilliantly imitating a rabbit caught in the headlights glare. Realising his predicament, he then turns full circle and walks back out again.

'Cut. Quentin,' shouted the director. 'You were in shot. If you had carried on walking instead of standing still, it would have been fine, you pillock.'

'Sorry, sir,' said Quentin. 'I was mesmerised by the acting!'

Another of the enduring memories I have of Quentin Annis on *Dempsey and Makepeace* was on a Friday evening on the last day of filming an episode when Quentin was off back home to Wales. We had a weekly raffle in those days, which consisted of writing your name on the back of a pound note and all the notes went into a bag and the one that was drawn out won all the money contained therein. All comers were welcome to contribute both cast and crew and the 'pot' could sometimes be a sizeable amount of say eighty pounds or so. One Friday, Quentin won and celebrated with a few drinks and then departed in a taxi. It was just the sight that tickled me of a few colleagues helping him on his way into the taxi. There was Quentin, wearing his big Australian type hat, with money tucked in all around the rim like a mad hatter on speed and every other pocket he possessed stuffed with pound notes sticking out of them. He waved madly out of the window, like a wild drunk festooned with money, which, of course, was precisely what he was. As he sped past me off to the station, I had a moment of severe panic and wondering if we would see him bright eyed and bushy tailed the following Monday. I need not have worried because thankfully we did.

Michael Brandon finally got to direct the very last episode of *Dempsey and Makepeace* and the opening sequence called for a set of feet walking mysteriously along an old cobbled street in the fog.

'Not many cobbled streets left in London, Michael,' I said at our first meeting to discuss what sort of locations he had in mind.

'You know de way I see it, it's one of those narrow-cobbled mews dat you have over here,' replied the thick New York accent. 'Yeah a really narrow mews.'

I sighed, 'A mews. Right I'll get looking.' I did a lot of sighing on that series.

So, I went off with my trusty A to Z and my camera. I took a few shots of one or two cobbled ones but very few were what I would call narrow. After a day on the road, I rushed into the office, clutching my Polaroids.

110

No, it's not a social disease, it's just these were the days before one-hour printing and digital cameras and so the Polaroid was king. Anyway, as I lay them out on the table Michael was not impressed.

'Nah! Nah! It's got to be narrower, Malcolm, I want a really narrow one.'

I went back on the road, pouring over the map, when by sheer coincidence a man is interviewed on the radio, who has just published a book on London Mewses. Unbelievable, but true. I thought, if anybody knows where to find a really narrow cobbled mews, this is the man who will. I quickly phoned LBC and it turned out he was an estate agent in Kensington. I phoned him and before you can say, 'Is that a magnum under your coat or are you just pleased to see me?' I was sat opposite him in his office and we were going through his beautiful book. I noted down a few names he recommended but at least I now had an expert witness to back up what I had already thought, that really narrow mews didn't exist. Why I never actually bought a copy of that book for future reference still eludes me to this day!

I photographed as many possibilities as I could. I had spent nearly three days on finding this one location and I had to move on. As I have said, it was about an eight-day prep for a two-week shoot on *Dempsey*, meaning you had about eight days to find an average twelve or so locations per episode, so there was no time to hang about.

An hour later and I was back with Mr. Brandon. His brow furrowed.

'You know I hate to say dis, I really hate to say dis but it's just got to be narrower. Really, really narrow.' He held up his hands like a fisherman describing the length of a stickleback.

'But Michael, they just don't exist. Most mews you had at least to have been able to get a horse and cart down it.'

There was a long pause that you could have driven an awfully wide horse and cart through. The disappointment on his face said it all but slowly his head lifted and his brow smoothed out.

'Wait, wait, a grin broke out on his face. 'Maybe mews is de wrong word.' Now my brow furrowed. 'Alleyway, dat's de word, you call it an alleyway, right?' This now of course makes it our fault. 'Get me a narrow, cobbled alleyway.'

'There's one by the Mayflower pub in Rotherhithe Street, Michael. A narrow, cobbled, *passage.*'

'Yeah, passage, passage, an even better word. That's real cool 'cause dat's where we did de first scene for de very first episode of de show in series one. So, we'll finish back where we started, kinda romantic, don't you think?'

'Yes Michael, bloody wonderful.'

I was already heading out of the office. My fine collection of mews Polaroids hit the metal wastepaper bin with a loud 'clang'. 'Bloody language, bloody American language,' I muttered under my breath. I now had five days left to put together the rest of the locations needed for the two-week shoot and had no idea I was experiencing a magical moment that I would 'dine out' on for years to come.

The real irony of the mist covered cobbled street story was that the shot that they eventually did indeed film down by the Mayflower Public House in Rotherhithe was never featured in the final cut version of the episode. All that energy, all that time expelled for no apparent reason. I can remember spending a long Saturday driving aimlessly around the area with the designer Rodney Cammish and both of us getting more and more depressed because we just couldn't find a site for the opening of that episode. After the cobbled street shot it settled in a monumental stonemason's yard, don't ask me why, where there was a shoot-out at the start of the episode. We stopped at a pub for lunch and vowed that if we survived this torture we would play a game that Rodney knew. It consisted of flicking a coin at the optics behind the bar and taking a drink out of whatever bottle the money clanks against. He never did say how long you go on doing this for, but presumably, it was until the first person fell over. Luckily, we never remembered to play it even when the depression lifted after finding a series of disused arches into which Rodney simply dressed a whole load of statues and gravestones, which, as if by magic, became the monumental stonemason's yard.

Chapter Seven

Heady Days

We made the three-series run of *Dempsey and Makepeace* between 1984 and 1986 and after being involved in something like ten or so episodes, and watching the other twenty being made, there is a problem that unfortunately they do all tend to blend into one another. That last episode that Michael directed was in fact the one that featured the jaguar car going backwards into the dock. We were also the first drama crew to be allowed into the Natural History Museum, a moment I was proud to have achieved. They asked for a credit on the end and were given it, 'British Museum (Natural History)', it read, and I can remember punching the air as the credit flashed onto the screen.

I've just revisited that episode on video and decided that really that whole series should be shown as an historical social history of south east London. We blew cars up and chased them along quaysides that are now Canary Wharf and its environs, half the derelict buildings we filmed in are now flattened, the big warehouses have gone and the road systems have changed beyond recognition.

Perhaps this may be a good time to explain the pecking order of seniority on a production and who does what, some of which I have touched on, but I thought a reasonably comprehensive breakdown might help you dear reader understand the hierarchy. First comes the producer, who may have an executive producer above them, but for the sake of argument, let's keep it simple. So, the producer is the person who puts the whole thing together, gets the script written, gets the money in place, gets the artistes, and appoints a production manager, these days called a line producer, to sort out the nuts and bolts for them. The line producer gets on board in collaboration with the producer, a director, and then someone called the DOP, which stands for director of photography, who basically is responsible for the look of the piece working closely with the production designer. Underneath the designer will be an art department consisting of art director, assistant designer, storyboard artist, prop master and then prop boys and then sometimes a construction crew. The DOP will have a bunch of lighting operatives to place and position his or her lamps.

The first assistant answers directly to the director and carries out his or her instructions and usually schedules the piece and allocates how many days it will take to film a scene. Therefore, so many directors always work with the same first assistant because over time, they not only trust one another, but also one knows how fast the other usually goes so that the daily schedule is always achieved, circumstances permitting. Underneath him, he will have a second assistant director who makes sure transport is arranged for artistes and makes sure they all know what time to be on set and daily works out a 'call sheet', which is issued to everybody. This information is attached to a 'movement order', which tells everyone where to go and how to get there and where to park, and is issued by the location manager. Under him/her there may well be a unit manager, who, as the name suggests, looks after the unit, i.e. all the vehicles, and makes sure they park properly and get from one place to another and have access to water and power if necessary. Also, there may well be an assistant location manager, who helps with the movement order, also distributes resident letters and generally helps the location manager.

Beyond this, is the make-up department, the wardrobe department, the catering department and various unit drivers. There are also chippies and painters and a script supervisor, who works closely with the director on notes and changes and keeps an eye out for continuity problems. Then, to finish off in the office, you will usually have a production secretary, a coordinator, the casting department and lastly, but by no means least, an accounts department.

On most of the major series I have worked on you are looking at somewhere in the region of sixty to seventy people, or so, all combining to make that one-hour programme of drama that you will sit there and watch completely unaware that such a huge army has been responsible for bringing this into your living room. On one episode of *London's Burning*, with stunt drivers, additional fire-fighters over a three-day period doing a big motorway crash, we managed to boost this figure to a healthy one hundred and forty people or so to be fed, watered and deployed in the right area at the right time. It can, and frequently does, become a logistical nightmare.

That learning curve of Tom Harris' pyrotechnic art was not just practised on me. Peter Pearson was also a location manager on the series and he suffered with a memorable 'small bang' in a phone box that took out most of the windows in a derelict block of flats nearby but made a local glazier's financial year. Also, a truly memorable explosive destruction of three cars in a big hanger during late evening that we all felt was a little bigger than anyone had anticipated. A whole convoy of blue lights thundered towards the scene and all Peter can remember is a man with a peaked cap and an awful lot of pips on his shoulder angrily approaching him and with an unflinching stare and pointing his stick slowly uttered through clenched teeth those immortal words, 'They tell me you are the one in charge here,' after which the ensuing bollocking left Peter a frail and shattered man. This was way before terrorists as we know them today had been invented but the words IRA outrage were on everybody's lips. I went back with him the next day to visit the scene in daylight and found it hard to believe that such thick heavy metal doors could have been bent and buckled by such a force from just a 'special effect'.

The moment that Tom redeemed himself for me was the day he had to blow a van up in mid-air. Houses almost completely surrounded the bit of derelict land we had chosen as the location, so it wasn't really the best place to choose to do something like that in. Tom designed and thought, and designed and created, and designed and finally came up with a van that again, similar to the jaguar, would be fired into the air off a ramp (rocket permitting) and simply explode in mid-air with a big gas flame effect and specially rigged fall apart sides. We would have to put the bang on later. I didn't believe it until I saw it on the day. At the moment of destruction, I was talking to one of the locals leaning out of her window, when the van sprang into the air, silently split apart and a huge ball of orange flame ballooned upwards into the sky. 'Oh! Was that it?' said my host in a very disappointed tone. 'I was expecting a much bigger bang than that.' At that moment, I knew it was a peaceful success, there would be no repercussions, no distant sirens approaching at speed and Tom had suddenly shot to my number one all-time favourite special effects person.

Strange things do happen and a stunt person if asked by a director, 'What do you think, can you do that?' will never, never ever say no. In one episode, a crook was supposed to fall into a huge vat of acid. Well, we had a huge vat that looked like a mammoth industrial oil drum and we filled it full of water, of course, not acid, but the problem was it didn't look particularly menacing. Step forward someone with suggestion of why not throw a load of dry ice in there to create a sinister mist on the top. This was the perfect solution because through the camera lens it now looks dangerous and threatening. Roy Alon stepped forward with a little weighted belt round his waste to help him stay under the water and look as though he has sunk without trace before someone bangs on the side of the tank to let him know the cameras have cut and he can pop back up. The cameras roll, in goes dear Roy, cut and bang and sure enough he came up. But the layer of mist on the surface of the water was now quite thick and he found himself taking a big gulp of not oxygen to revive him, but carbon dioxide gas, because that is what dry ice turns into when mixed with water. So, Roy gets no oxygen and went down again. While under for the second, time he removed the leaden belt and popped up again but frighteningly with the same result, in that he once more filled his lungs with carbon dioxide. As he went down for the second time, now exhausted and to say the least, a little short of breath, one of the camera team, who happened to be hovering on the edge of the tank, realised that there was a problem. So, as Roy popped up to the surface for the third time, our hero camera lad jumped in and managed to pull him out and saved him. Roy in his usual dry Yorkshire manner, although standing there dripping wet, mused, 'I should 'ave bloody thought about that, but you don't at the time, do you?'

I met Roy many years later in the bar at Shepperton Studios, while I was working on *You Bet!* He was pleased to see me but was bemoaning the fact he had just agreed to work on a BBC children's programme, only to find out the day after that he had missed the opportunity to do a big feature film. He hadn't signed anything but said in his wonderful Yorkshire brogue, 'That just isn't me. If I agree to do something and say I will, then having given my word, that is the end of the matter.' Roy sadly died in 2006 but by that time he had been awarded a place in the *Guinness Book of Records* after appearing in more than one-thousand cinema and television productions. For example, he was in almost all of the James Bond films made since the mid-seventies as well as the Superman films starring Christopher Reeve.

We often used the old British Gas works down at Greenwich for filming. Once again, we had an open derelict site with a small road system where we could play silly buggers without interfering or being interfered with by the public. It now houses the O2 Arena, of course, but once employed one thousand five hundred people. The old men on the gates used to tell us tales of the sight of trams and all those workers arriving at six in the morning.

One day, Roy Alon decided he would 'roll' an open top car for the excitement of the viewing public. We were in the Greenwich Gas works and Roy told the director, who I have a funny feeling was again Tony Wharmby, where to put his cameras.

'By the time I cum down that road thur, I'll be doing about thirty. I'll hit the ramp and it'll turn in mid-air and land thur. So, you can put a camera thur and a camera thur.'

'Will they be safe?'

'Oh aye. I'll never get further than thur,' he said pointing at a spot on the ground.

Roy had an amazingly complicated rig in the car which necessitated him as he took off skywards, to pull a lever that flattened him across the passenger seat so that when it landed upside down, (the theory went), he would still be inside neatly tucked up and safe. Once more the cameras rolled. The far camera, which was well away from the landing spot, had a man stood behind the camera holding the operator and a man stood behind the focus puller holding him. The car came hammering along the road, hit the ramp, flew through the air, turned over, as described, but kept flying past the mark it would never get to. When you are looking through the lens of a camera, you are strangely remote from the action in front of you but, thank God, the two holders were not. The cameraman, to his surprise, was pulled backwards, and so was the focus puller, just nicely in time to clear a space for the open topped red Camargue to land exactly where seconds before the camera had stood. The cry of 'Cut' ascended from the middle of the stunned onlookers, the car was rolled over and out came Roy all in one piece, a round of applause from the assembled company and he entered the history books as certainly the first and, I don't know, maybe the only person to have ever turned over an open topped car for a stunt. The cameraman had a drink later when he realised after seeing the 'rushes' just how horribly close he may well have come to a rather sudden and sticky end to his promising career.

We were due to film yet another scene at the Gas Works but for some reason it was cancelled the night before. Everyone was told to go to the studios and shoot office scenes instead. Even so, I went to the Gas Works simply to double check that they knew we were not coming and to make sure no stragglers turned up who had slipped through the net and had not been informed.

Only one artiste arrived in the wrong place at the wrong time, a chap called Nick Brimble. He looked at me with a resigned look on his face of, 'It's all right, this really is the story of my life. I would be the last person they would tell, it is always happening to me,' and off he went. I could sympathise because I have always felt that too. Anyway, he obviously made a huge impact on our production secretary because they have been together for many years now. I had, for a time, a desk opposite that delectable creature and I shall save her any embarrassment by not naming her. However, I must admit trying to work with such a gorgeous vision facing me was a very onerous task. I would often just blatantly gaze at her stunning features and had to shake myself vigorously to step out of my daydreams to continue with the job in hand. Nick has gone on to act in many feature films and television and I firmly believe he has the most impeccable taste in women of any man I have ever met.

Tony Osoba, a delightful actor who played one of the regular sidekicks in the series, found out I had a small collection of dinky toys, which he made me bring in one day then offered me money I couldn't refuse for some of them! I keep thinking one of these days he will appear with his collection on the *Antiques Roadshow* saying, 'Oh yes, and these three I bought off a simpleton location manager in the mid-Eighties who just didn't realise what the hell he was parting with!'

And back to Ray Smith ('Spikings') who often gave the impression he didn't seem to want to be in the series. 'I can quote Dylan Thomas, I can quote Shakespeare, tell me why am I here?' he would say when a little tired and emotional after a long days filming. I felt he constantly had an inner battle raging within himself as a 'real' actor being in a telly series, very like Alec Guinness seems to have had after his appearance in *Star Wars*, which, having recently read some of his diaries, seemed to haunt him for the rest of his life. Ray had a beautiful rich Welsh voice, which quite often put me in mind of Richard Burton. I only ever met Burton once, and didn't really meet him just hovered in the background, when he came into the studios on the South Bank when I was still in the sound department. I was in the sound transcription unit, STU for short, for the day and Mr Burton was booked in to do a voice over for, I presume, *The South Bank Show*. I was just the humble bloke who operated the tape machine to record his voice. It was about eleven o'clock in the morning and this presence swept in and seated himself in our humble recording suite. Many flunkies were present. I know not who, but before many minutes had elapsed, Burton had summoned one of them into the cubicle where he sat alone with a microphone and a table and whispered in their ear and they departed. He coughed a little, did a few practise lines for a sound level and then the dispatched person returned armed with a bottle of Teacher's Whisky fresh from some booze cabinet he had raided. This was duly placed in front of our guest with a glass and some water. The tape was rolled and the session began. The coughing stopped, the voice became as mellow and as smooth and as rounded as any voice could ever be. Just to listen to those words coming from a speaker was a total joy and of the finest quality you would ever hear because the speakers in your television sets in those days were very, very small. The lines were read perfectly without any retakes, with only slight guidance about this inflection or that pause, because whoever they were standing there listening, they didn't dare 'push' a master too far. Within half an hour they were all happy with the outcome and departed. He thanked us all as he left, which is all any technician ever needs to make his day. The real joy came when we discovered he had only drunk half the bottle of Whisky and the whole group had left leaving such a marvellous gift behind them. We didn't bother to go to the bar that lunchtime. Little things!

Towards the end of the last series, it was clear that Ray Smith was not a well man and if you watch episode one of series one and then the last episode of series three the change in him is hauntingly obvious. Ray was a very talented performer who left the stage much too early on 15 December 1991 aged just fifty-five. There's no-doubt that he should have gone onto far greater roles.

On a lighter note, one of the most amusing expense claims I ever heard at LWT was the occasion where a location manager working on *Dempsey and Makepeace* had happily parked his make-up and wardrobe vans outside a normal suburban house in a normal street. About two hours or so into the shoot, a lady accosted him from number thirty-seven. 'I've got a business to run here dearie. You're interfering with my clientele,' was her opening gambit.

The location manager said, 'Sorry, didn't you get the residents letter I sent round?'

'No, I did not.'

'Oh dear. My apologies, you should have got a letter. Obviously if you're losing trade or customers then...'

'Yes, of course I'm losing trade,' she interrupted. 'They park here, outside my premises, when they want to come and see me.'

'Well for how long?' By now he just wanted her to go away.

'For about half an hour or so.'

'Right, so what have you lost in terms of earnings?' he said, trying to be as diplomatic as possible. You're probably already ahead of me here, but you would be wrong with your nasty, rude minds! Mind you we all thought that at the time!

'Well, about one hundred and fifty pounds at the end of the day,' she said.

'Right well, I'm sure we can compensate for that,' he said, removing his wallet from his jacket pocket.

'Oh, that's fine ducky,' she replied.

And then he decided to cut to the chase.

'So, er, what kind of business exactly is it that you run from here?'

'Oh, I'm a fortune teller dear; they all come here to know what the future holds!'

So, of course, he could not resist writing on his expenses form:

Gratuity of one hundred and fifty pounds to clairvoyant, who didn't know we were coming.

As the series unfolded, it was obvious that Michael and Glynis were getting rather fond of one another. What really upset me was that they continued to have separate Winnebago's, which are those mobile home things that artistes 'rest' in between 'takes'. So instead of having just the one vehicle, which they could have shared, I was still forced to find parking for two of the damn things. Little things! They nearly both left the show, and indeed the country, after the Chernobyl disaster because Michael was convinced that we in Britain were all going to be covered in nuclear fallout or dust. Someone, I presume Tony Wharmby, persuaded them to stay and they have been together in this country now for many years and have two children,

I believe. The show is still shown all over the world at all hours of the day and night. Nigel Payn, Kevin Holden, Dave Currie, Martin Bond, Peter Cotton and, of course, Brian Kelly, who did many of the episodes, and, as I mentioned, had got the ball rolling, were among the other location managers who got thrown onto the merry-go-round and somehow survived and were spat out at the other end. A very strange time of stress, which was a word that had not been invented then anyway, and sometimes absolute elation of a job well done, superb viewing figures and a huge fan base. Heady days of work hard and play hard and, 'I'll see you in The Barnaby.'

Chapter Eight

Dutch Girls

Dutch Girls was an interesting project. It was a television film directed by Giles Foster and starred Timothy Spall, in one of his first ever television roles, and a very young man by the name of Colin Firth. The story was a love story about a group of boys off to play hockey in Holland and one of them falls in love with a Dutch girl. Upon hearing the title, most people I spoke to thought I was making a blue movie of some sort!

I became so short of time for any logical preparation for *Dutch Girls* at one point that when the production designer, a wonderful character called Bryan Bagge, who's sadly no longer with us, said to me, 'Molcom, this is going to cost you a few bob,' as we gazed at a row of derelict houses he had fallen madly in love with as a double for the red-light district of Amsterdam, I am afraid I replied, 'I really don't give a damn about the money any more Bryan.' At this reply, there was a sharp intake of breath, his eyes lit up and his face glowed, as a broad grin broke out across his lips. He held me by the shoulders and looked me straight in the eyes, 'At last my dear boy, at long bloody last,' he chortled. 'You're beginning to embrace the ephemeral concept of design in television.'

'Baggy', as he was affectionately known, and I had some good times together. Although I never quite knew why he always pronounced Malcolm as Molcom, but he was the sort of guy you could forgive for lots of things. He loved his craft, if he approved of the project; his enthusiasm was second to none. Only if the show was run of the mill, did he get bored and his attention wander; he'd been there and got the t-shirt. He always loved a challenge and 'scale'. It was a shame he never got to work on cinema films, he would have loved the scope, grandeur and not least the 'budget' he would have been able to play with.

The technical recce for *Dutch Girls* was something of a marathon itself. We had caught the ferry from Harwich and were on our way to Vlissingen in Holland. The ferry was to be part of the filming, so we were travelling and doing a recce at the same time. I can remember, and it may have been half serious, because life was like that in those days, someone trying to find a clause in the rule book that would answer the question as to whether travelling and eating lunch at the same time did not incur some sort of additional union overtime payment! Anyway, some people did have lunch but most of us were saving ourselves for the meal in Amsterdam that night. The production manager had gazed at a map before we sailed and spoken with contacts in Holland, and had assured us that the train journey we were about to embark on to Amsterdam was probably half an hour or so at the most.

We waited at Vlissingen railway station for quite some time and a few clever ones (hindsight being a wonderful science) had decided to have a quick beer and a bowl of soup at the station buffet. I declined, saving myself for the wonderful meal I had already started in my mind, with lashings of wine and fresh bread. Idiot. Somehow, and I don't remember where or how, the information got to us but as we boarded the train, we became horribly aware that the journey time we were about to embark on was something approaching four and a half hours. Now Baggy did smoke and Baggy did drink and Baggy usually did both of these together and he certainly did them after seven o'clock in the evening, which was the time the station

127

clock was showing as we slowly pulled out of Vlissingen. We were in a very modern train and it was no smoking throughout, which just goes to show you how ahead of the game the Dutch were even then. This 'ahead-ness' did not impress Bryan. He disappeared forward to find somewhere hopefully not only to smoke but also to drink.

I gazed out of the window. Four and a half hours did seem a very long time. That put our arrival in Amsterdam at around eleven thirty, if not midnight, depending on how far the hotel was from the railway station. I began to visualise that montage sequence from *The Train*, which starred Burt Lancaster, where you see the black line going along the railway map, the wheels of the train spinning around in the background and all the name signs of the stations zipping past. The signs and stations were zipping past all right and so was Baggy. The door crashed open from his forward recce and he rushed past going the other way this time. Having completed his voyage of discovery to the front and obviously, from the thunderous look on his reddening face, found nothing, he was heading full pelt for the rear carriages. I know *The Train* was set in France and we were in Holland but it's all Europe isn't it and it was all occupied? The production manager was looking a little uneasy; he squirmed in his seat like a young corporal waiting to be roasted by the head of the Gestapo. I had seen Baggy lose his temper only once before and it hadn't been a pretty sight. Perhaps just sheer lack of food and water has set me off on this World War Two tableaux. The noise of the wheels got faster and faster and that diddley de, diddley da reached a crescendo and the door burst open from the adjoining carriage and there stood Obergruppenführer Bagge, resembling a bull on heat, fresh from his sortie to the rear of the train. We all as one man raised our eyebrows in a quizzical fashion.

'F**k all,' he declared to the assembled throng. 'Three fifths of f**k all.'

'Ah, no luck then?' asked the production manager, David Fitzgerald.

There was an almighty pause at this point and Bryan just stood there his face visibly swelling and his eyes looking ready to burst from their sockets. Timing, it really is all to do with timing this game, and to say that I felt this might have been the wrong thing for the production manager to say at this point, is an understatement.

'No luck? No f**king luck?' Bryan launched into him. 'Do you seriously expect me to sit on this train for four and a half bloody hours, with no food or drink? I came on this recce in all good faith to make a television programme and you, you are telling me that we have no food, no water and that no provision has been made at all?!'

It was this Hancockian outburst that even he began to realise was over melodramatic and more of a performance. Gradually he could no longer maintain the seriousness and began to crack and slowly but surely burst into hysterical laughter. If you had never seen Baggy helpless with laughter, you had never lived. His handkerchief came out and he mopped his brow and laughed and laughed and laughed.

'Brilliant, isn't it? It is absolutely, bloody brilliant. What a monumental f**king cock up. No one will believe this back in London, no one. In fact, if we tell them we got on a ferry at seven in the morning and at nine o'clock at night, we still hadn't got to where we were going, they will never believe us.'

The tears flowed down his cheeks.

'In fact, I'm not bloody well going to tell anybody this happened when I get back, so your career may be safe, David,' he pointed at the production manager with his hankie. 'There is no point, there is no bloody point. Who, who tell me who, in their right minds would believe it?'

He wiped the tears from his eyes.

'No one will. No bugger would believe a man in London.'

He paused for more laughter and by now everyone was enjoying the performance.

'A man in London looks at a map apparently having only ever been familiar with the A to Z.'

His voice was getting higher and higher and we were all now beginning to hold our sides.

'He looks at a map of Holland and says to himself, that'll take about half, half, half a bloody hour that will. When, get this, when it is actually going to take four and a half bloody hours because we are crossing half the bloody country.'

He looked like he was going to burst a blood vessel at any minute; he was just a red quivering blob, that had given the performance of a lifetime, to a captive audience, who were in the mood for such a showman. David now had tears of laughter flowing down his face and I was yelling, 'Stop, stop.' I had reached that point where you think you are never going to breathe again and your stomach aches and aches. Finally, the hysterics stopped and calm was restored. The train thundered on and at least Bryan solved the no smoking problem by leaping out whenever we did stop at a station and puffing away on the platform until the whistle blew. I kept a lookout in the hope that the odd spy would emerge from the shadows. To have a Robert Shaw look-alike, creeping about like he did in *From*

Russia with Love, would have been wonderful. I think tiredness had overtaken me and I was beginning to hallucinate.

Bedraggled, tired, hungry, thirsty and just plain knackered we stood in the brightly lit foyer of the hotel as the clock struck midnight.

'I'm afraid, er, that er, because you are so late,' stuttered the manager.

'Here we bloody go,' sighed Bryan.

'That, er, there are seven of you, no?'

'Yes. Seven.'

'I have unfortunately only got five rooms left. I, er let two of them go, er, earlier, as I had not heard from you.'

'No, sorry old boy, we were just a tad too busy starving to death on a train,' said Bryan a little louder. Then chuckled again.

The producer, director, director of photography, a rather grand name for someone who tells someone else where to put the lights, I have always thought, Bryan and his assistant took the five rooms in the hotel. The production manager and I were then driven, after a swift phone call by the manager himself, to another hotel. He left us with many apologies and an agreement that he would pay the difference between the hotel we now found ourselves in and his. Little did I know that I was about to become the proud possessor of one of the most exquisite rooms I have ever stayed in, in an hotel nicknamed the 'Grand Old Lady of Amsterdam'. It was now one o'clock in the morning and I had gone way past eating. The huge double bed beckoned and so did the mini bar – but not necessarily in that order! The room was wonderfully old fashioned but with an ensuite to die for, a writing desk where I could have spent many a happy hour and a room service menu second to none. What a waste. We left at seven the next morning to join the others for breakfast in their plastic hotel.

The street we chose to double for the red-light district of Amsterdam in London was called Rampart Street in the east end. The BBC later did a drama series entitled *Rampart Street*, but I got there first. This was the location that was going to cost me that money I no longer cared about. We couldn't afford to build the set; you couldn't film in the real place for fear of getting your head and the camera kicked in, so the only answer that Bryan and I came up with was to find somewhere that we could make look like the real thing. Not an easy task, but we did it. The houses were mostly unoccupied, the council were going to pull them down anyway, so I sought and got permission to knock out some of the windows in order that Bryan could create a Dutch street full of scantily clad girls in the windows, false shop fronts, neon lights and most importantly bollards. Amsterdam was, and still is I presume, full of these things and they are very distinctive so Bryan had proudly brought all the way back from Holland an Amsterdam bollard. It weighed an absolute ton but he struggled home with this damn thing so that a cast could be made of it and many more produced, which would then be placed down our street and bingo you must be in Amsterdam mustn't you? Such was Bryan's attention to detail and all this for just a television programme but that was the calibre of the people who I was working with in those days. We had flown back to England and the customs and excise officials at the airport were very intrigued with his bollard, carried very carefully in plain brown paper between his assistant Maggie and himself, forever known, of course, as Maggie and Baggy. They were probably convinced that it was full of all sorts of illegal substances until Bryan had explained that this was the sort of everyday chore that television designers got up to and please could he now be on his way as it was once again way past seven o'clock and it was cigarette and a very large drink time.

There was a sense of relief when having arranged the whole shoot in Rampart Street with the council, the senior police officer in charge, having had a site meeting with me, also gave his blessing to the project saying that he was going to assign a police officer to be with me for as much of the shoot as he could. This was a constable by the memorable name of Geoff Divine Jones, whose fluent Urdu I would have valued very highly some years later when I worked on *The Knock*. However, there was this marvellous moment when as I stepped out of the police car and the superintendent wished me well he turned to me and said, 'But remember, Malcolm, if this all goes "pear shaped" we never had this conversation.' I was never sure what that meant but as luck would have it everything in fact went smoothly.

When we came to do the shoot in London, the biggest annoyance was the weather – it rained solidly for the two nights that we filmed there. Also, whenever Geoff disappeared now and again to fight crime, which occasionally he had to because after all it was his real job, there were people demanding money from me. They hassled me constantly for cash, just trying their luck to get a little extra pocket money, I guess. As soon as he reappeared, the protesters strangely melted away into the night and denied all knowledge of having had a go at me at all. It turned out to be a hard couple of nights fending them off when he wasn't there on my behalf to say politely to them all, 'go away' in his fluent Urdu.

When we finally did the Dutch part of the shoot, we were in the coach, which was waiting to take us to the location, outside the hotel in Amsterdam. Two very old, very wrinkled, male and female Americans appeared at the entrance and began to slowly descend the steps; both very over dressed, both in fur coats and both dripping with gold jewellery. The stage manager turned slowly to me and said, 'Oh would you look at those two, dear. How wonderful, just held together by money.'

When the time came for the filming on the ferry, it was not too successful. They had run out of time and were unable to complete the sequence. Once again, 'muggins', was asked to find a cheat for the ferry within two weeks. We didn't have the budget to have another go on the real ferry. Bryan couldn't afford to build it, having spent a lot of his money from the budget in Rampart Street, and as usual I was asked to find it near London. Was I the only person who knew that the London Docks no longer existed? That phrase even appeared in a script for *The Knock*, it actually said 'The London Docks' and at that point you have to ask yourself has this dear writer ever escaped from the Fifties? Anyway, somehow, I discovered Purfleet Deep Water Wharf and discovered there Finanglia Ferries, God bless them, and they offered me a roll on roll off cargo vessel to use for filming. Baggy loved that it would be docked and empty on the day we wanted it in the schedule, which believe me happens once in a lifetime given the short notice. But all this, of course, was weather permitting! Because, after all, it was coming across the North Sea and into port just two days before we wanted to film on it.

I stood by the side of the ship with the skipper, the week before we needed it.

'You see, the biggest problem I have is the number of trucks that come with us.'

I was looking around the wharf, where strangely I could see that parking was at a premium. And then I mused on the fact that cameras, sound and especially lighting would all have to carry their gear up onto the ship.

'That won't be a problem, Malcolm,' said the skipper. 'Look, we can put all the vehicles actually onto the ship itself, we have a lift either side.'

'You're joking?' I said

'No, they take the weight of those huge paper lorries, so even your generator won't be a problem.'

'And the mobile kitchen?'

'More than welcome, if some of my crew, who will be helping you, can have a cooked breakfast.'

'That, sir, will not be a problem.'

I had cracked it and once again in a very short space of time and it was to turn out to be one of the best days filming I ever had.

On the day of filming, the first joy was that the ship was there. The second joy was that all the trucks did not arrive together. Many times, I have waited in the pitch black at seven o'clock in the morning, by the six bagged meters that Westminster Council have kindly allowed me, waiting for the technical vehicles to arrive and they have rounded the corner all at once. Knowing I can't get them all on six meters, a little thinking time between arrivals would have helped but the arrival of everybody all at once often denied me this luxury. However, on this clear morning, I could see them in the distance coming down the A13 and for once they were beautifully spaced out at approximately ten-minute intervals. True to his word, the Captain had each one lifted onto the deck as they arrived. The whole lot, caterers, make-up, wardrobe, mini buses, generators, lighting trucks et al. It was a wonderful image; they just drove on and took no more time parking up than they sometimes did in a car park. I was over the moon. Once they had parked, a stroll along deck two brought them nicely to the kitchen and they had their bacon roll in their hand before you could say 'Bright Lights'.

There had once again been industrial trouble brewing back at the studios on the South Bank and I had had a phone call from the ACTT union representative a couple of days before to say they were organising a mass meeting at the studios on the day of our filming. Obviously, because the crew could not attend, I would have to organise a room at lunchtime and a sound link for the 'brothers' who might be interested to hear the latest developments, should they be interested. As most of the crew involved were still staff members in those days, mostly all of them were interested. I had taken some kit out of the outside broadcast garage with me, my sound training having not been in vain, and I jacked up communications from the remote quayside back to the mother ship, if you will pardon the pun, at LWT. The 'brothers', and maybe even a couple of 'sisters', broke at one o'clock for lunch and came to the room and listened to the meeting and then returned to the ship, thanking me on their way out for my efforts on their behalf. On wrap, they all came off the vessel just as easily as they had gone on, if not quicker. I stood back and lit a cigar and mused on what a successful day from my point of view it had been. Filming of that nature was a potential nightmare waiting to happen but, as is so often the case, the day you think is going to be trouble goes swimmingly and the day you think is going to be a doddle, turns into a complete eighteen-hour shambles. Now why is that?

Chapter Nine

Scoop

It is 1987 and I am filming a two-hour television adaptation of Evelyn Waugh's *Scoop*, directed by Gavin Millar, for LWT, and we have just completed filming in Erfoud, a small town right on the edge of the desert in Morocco. The unit is packed up and ready to move for three days filming in Fez, only an hour away by plane, but something like a five-hour journey by road over the Atlas Mountains.

The generator, the lighting truck, the grip truck (a vehicle that carries all the camera equipment), the prop truck, the construction truck, a couple of cars and the minibus, all making an impressive convoy, are lined up outside the hotel, as the sun breaks over the distant sand dunes, heralding another typical hot and dusty day. Typical, because two days before we arrived in, 'it never rains in Erfoud,' the heavens had opened and the construction crew had been stuck outside the town for two days.

It is eight o'clock in the morning and I had decided not to fly with the rest of the cast and crew, who I knew would be tucked up by the pool-side in Fez by ten thirty with their first gin and tonic in their hands, but had opted to see a little of the scenery and travel in the minibus. Along with the young sound assistant, Mark, we plumped for what we hoped would be the ride of a lifetime little knowing it was nearly to be our last.

Our packed lunches are placed securely in the grip truck along with ample fruit; we have our own drinks and walkie-talkies and we in the minibus are tail-end-Charlie in case anything happens to the others en route. We are in the company of four of the Moroccan crew,

138

two of whom speak English. After only ten minutes of travelling, there is a quick exchange of dialogue between the Moroccans, we screech to a halt and one ashen-faced Moroccan leaps out and is promptly sick by the roadside. I should mention that the night before the village of Erfoud had given us one mighty departing party and send-off, after having filmed there for a week and obviously, our friend had over-indulged somewhat. The other Moroccans looked embarrassed, laughed and helped him back into the minibus.

There was much banter on the walkie-talkies; well, to be fair, generator drivers and grips don't often get to play with these machines. Ten minutes later we grind to a halt and more vomiting occurred. I was beginning to go right off my forthcoming egg and salad sandwich and kept trying to think of other things, if only to try and keep my own breakfast secure. The construction van driver was away, singing songs, telling jokes, but gradually the novelty wore off and for long periods radio silence was observed. We stopped another four times before the Moroccan finally succumbed to sleep and a closed mouth, but by now we had slipped further and further behind the others.

At last, the ascent of the mountains began and as the air got cooler and cooler the minibus engine got hotter and hotter until finally we stopped. I called on the walkie-talkie to let the others know we were in trouble but got no reply. There is no feeling quite like the despair you feel at having a piece of technical equipment in your hand that could help you out of the problem you are in but when no-one can hear you it renders the piece of equipment useless to say the least. Also, remember that this was long before the advent of mobile phones. So, we sat and eventually it cooled down and we topped it up with some of our drinking water (you can see it coming, can't you?) and once again we were on our way. Slowly we climbed and slowly the temperature gauge went up again and twenty minutes later we once more ground to a halt. Off again, and once more the slow ascent, every now and then calling on the walkie-talkie, hoping that we were closing in on the others and we would re-establish radio contact, but nothing. Another stop. They were becoming more and more frequent, until finally we stopped, lifted the bonnet, steam poured out and we sat and contemplated our future. After about half an hour, we tried the minibus but it was no longer playing even the 'I'll eventually start' game. We had little water left, it was about twelve thirty, the sun was high but the air thankfully, because of our altitude, was reasonably cool. The road went on for miles in a straight line both ways into infinity. After one hour, nothing had happened and no one had passed us. After two hours, I decided that if I was going to die I couldn't have picked a finer spot: scenery-wise it was breathtakingly stunning and thank God it wasn't SE1 in London. I had always had a sort of agreement with God that whenever I was to shuffle off this mortal coil it would not be in SE1!

Young Mark was philosophical; well he was young and probably more optimistic than myself, not for one moment believing his life would end at such an early age and all for the sake of a flickering image in the corner of someone's living room. It must have seemed to him grossly unfair and highly unlikely. I kept my eyes on the horizon for vultures, as my past life and lots of black and white movies slowly drifted before me. Had I really been that evil, so far, that it should all end here? Also, I have never experienced before or since such a resounding 'silence'. There was literally nothing

140

to hear, and if you wandered off (as you had to from time to time for a quiet moment in the bushes), the voices of those around the corpse of the minibus carried towards you as though you were two yards away. I did say to Mark that it appeared to be a sound man's Utopia, but after now three hours of waiting for just something to happen even his youthful optimism was beginning to give way to a slightly furrowed brow. I pondered where my egg and lettuce sandwich, so lovingly stored in the grip truck, had got to by now and gave into the thought that Gary the grip operator had probably already devoured it long ago. Gary started in the post room at LWT and now works as key grip, in charge of many others, on productions like the Bond movies and Star Wars and is still a really nice guy.

Then finally it happened. Like Omar Sharif arriving at the water well in *Lawrence of Arabia*, first we heard a distant noise, and then slowly out of the heat haze, along the tarmac road it appeared. What was it? We could see the dust cloud and its reflection in the shimmering road surface. It was big, it was moving and it had an engine. We all stood in the road to flag it down. Fortunately, it was the biggest empty low-loader I had ever seen, it could happily have accommodated two chieftain tanks. Now whether through lack of food, drink and nicotine, I don't know, but things now began to take on an almost surreal feel and look. We gave up asking the Moroccans to translate, why was the low-loader there, where had it come from? Who cared? All that mattered was that it was there and that is all we needed to know. The minibus looked like a dinky toy riding on the back of the huge vehicle, we all squeezed into the cab and it was like driving along in one of those lorries out of the very early American television series, *Cannonball*.

Our relief was short-lived. Two hours later, and at last seeing some sort of civilisation at the next village, where the road forked, the low loader went left and we and the minibus were abandoned to go right. The Moroccans went off to discuss repair details with a garage but at least we could now feed and drink. Only soft drinks, of course, I was beginning to hallucinate badly about clutching a large scotch and American with lashings of ice. The word came back that the minibus would have to be left there to be repaired. We could now take taxis the rest of the way, but as there was only one in the village, and only licensed to carry four people, and there were six of us, once again we had a problem. Location managers and sound assistants first was nearly my answer but through collective bargaining, we decided to catch the bus. As there was one due in about thirty minutes, which went directly to Fez it seemed the obvious answer.

We happily climbed aboard the bus as if just popping out for a short trip on a school outing, not realising that it was to be our home for the next six hours. When finally we arrived at our destination, I realised we should never have given up asking questions but such is the science of hindsight. I never thought when I had set out that morning I would see the sun go down over the Atlas Mountains and I would be spending part of the journey on a metal seat in a bus in the company of chickens and goats. There were women with their deep brown eyes that seemed to stare at you in disbelief through their yashmaks, as you looked back and tried so desperately hard to appear casual, as though you had quite deliberately intended to be on the bus, in the middle of nowhere and were really enjoying the journey in the swaying, bouncing, humid, hard-seated mobile farm shed.

What really staggered me was that occasionally the bus would stop in the middle of nowhere and people would get off and walk away into the distance. It was flat, there were no trees and there was not a house in sight; where were they going? At the same time people, would get on. Where had they come from? There was nothing at all for miles and miles and as night fell and people still got on and off, in total darkness. I really did wonder how on earth they knew where they were going. I had not seen one illuminated sign post saying Croydon five miles or whatever the Moroccan equivalent would have been.

Finally, at about ten thirty that night, we entered the outskirts of Fez. Nonchalantly looking out of the side window, I suddenly realised we were passing the grip truck pulled in by the roadside. I was still clutching my walkie-talkie in my hand. I yelled down it, 'Can anybody hear me?' There was a moment's pause before, blow me down, a voice responded, 'Treeny is that you?' It was Ken Sheppard the generator driver, who had gone back to mend the broken-down grip truck and minutes before had just got it going. It had been his second repair of the day. We later were to find out that earlier that afternoon, he had somehow managed to repair the brakes on the construction lorry, which had packed in at a particularly bad moment on a very winding road descending the Atlas Mountains, much to the terror of the driver who had apparently had a very alarming few minutes trying to stop the beast. 'Arête la bus,' I yelled running down the aisle, kicking animals and poultry out of the way in a desperate attempt to stop my present mode of transport and find freedom. 'Arrête la bus. Mark, wake up, come on, come on! We're getting off.' We dismounted and ran towards Ken and hugged him feeling as though we had been separated for weeks. We all jumped aboard the grip truck, my first and only trip in that mode of transport, and Ken drove us singing all the way back to the hotel.

We entered the hotel to be greeted by the production accountant, Mike Littlejohn.

'Where the hell have you been?'

'How long have you got?' I responded.

'Do you want a drink?' he enquired looking at my face and said. 'Sorry, you're right. Stupid question.'

But too late I was off, in full Lawrence mode.

'Yes, I'd like a beer for me and a lemonade for him,' I said pointing at young Mark.

'Piss off, I'll have a beer too,' he quickly chipped in.

We both downed them in one. I faced the barman, 'He likes your beer,' I said, in my best Peter O'Toole voice. He looked back at me blankly. The moment was lost, but I couldn't help gilding the lily: I looked him straight in the eye and said, 'We have taken Aqaba.'

The accountant raised his eyes to the ceiling, 'Just one more Treen, then time for bed, I think.'

'Yes, I suppose you're right,' I replied. 'It, er, has been a bit of a long day. Still, look on the bright side, Mike, the bus fare must have been cheaper than a seat on the plane.'

'Good man,' said the accountant. 'That's what we like to hear! That's just what we like to hear.'

The following day we were whisked away to film at a railway station some few miles on the city outskirts. By golly, we got there in style as we were given a police escort all the way to the location! Three motorbikes stopping the traffic at each junction with lights flashing and whistles blowing. It was just like being in the movies, or at the very least a member of the royal family, and we all felt slightly grand. At the railway station, the scene to be shot was of a train arriving, the

144

place swarming with extras, who had arrived very unceremoniously in the back of an old open top lorry. There was a band playing and I was put in charge of three of the background artistes, who appeared from around a corner on cue and mingled with the crowd. They each sported a fez upon their head and were wearing long white robes. I nicknamed them 'Wilson, Keppel and Betty' and we spent a very pleasant day between takes standing in the shade out of the warm sunshine, speaking in broken English to one another and smoking my duty-free Benson and Hedges.

We moved up the line to film a scene where the train has broken down. The old steam train we had pulling the coaches was none functional and was in fact being pushed from the rear by a modern diesel. To get a wide shot of the train in motion prior to it stopping, the problem arose that the sight of the diesel at the rear was a bit of a dead giveaway. So, the art department had camouflaged the engine with a tarpaulin to make it look like just a sort of guard's van travelling along behind. What they didn't realise was that they had put the wretched sheets over the engine vent ducts and sure enough the heat escaping from the engine was hot enough to catch them on fire. Panic. Buckets of water were lobbed at the tarpaulin and the fire successfully extinguished but in the process water had also been thrown all over the batteries in the main compartment and the engine was now dead. So, we carried on filming inside the carriages where the train had ground to a halt and once more the hero of the day Ken Sheppard was summand to get his generator as close as he could to the line to dry out and recharge the now extinct batteries. All this took to say the least a bit of a time.

Now, how we knew, I don't know but obviously, someone had told us that the line we were filming on although not greatly used was a real railway and occasionally trains did pass along it, as trains are prone to do. Most of us expecting an early wrap, knew that we had to be back in the sidings by four thirty that afternoon to let the suitably named four thirty express thunder by. Manfully, the crew carried on filming inside but I began to get more and more edgy about whether anybody had told anybody that we were stuck in the middle of nowhere on a single-track railway. Slowly over the period of the next half hour it was obvious that painters were finding a reason to move away from the stranded train and clean brushes up the hill; make-up ladies wandered away to take advantage of a sit in the dying rays of the sun and people appeared to just wander away a few yards knowing that if they were urgently needed, a call would come over the walkie talkie but at least they were not inside the stricken express. David Matthews, the stage manager, and I mused on the situation in hand. We were at the rear of the train gazing into the distance from where we thought the express might appear and wondering again if anyone knew of our predicament. We started to wander ourselves away from the train but staying on the line and headed in the direction of where we thought the express might come from.

'I'm sure they would have told someone by now,' said David reassuringly.

'Yes. Of course, they must know,' I wholeheartedly agreed.

'Except if the train is on the move how would they tell them?'

'Well,' I paused and thought hard. 'They would have told them at the last stop.'

'Yes, but only if it is an express. Where was the last stop?'

146

'Oh, David, I'm sure they will know. You see…,' I was interrupted by a blast on a hooter that sounded a bit like the QE2. We both stared at one another in disbelief. 'No, it can't be,' I squeaked.

'No, must be somewhere else,' replied David but with little conviction, as he surveyed the vast expanse of absolutely nothing in any given direction. A second blast sounded out but this time much closer.

'Oh, Christ,' I said. Then the vision of one of the most spectacular train crashes since Burt Lancaster starred in *The Train* appeared in my mind. We were now too far away to rush back and tell everyone to jump for it, so we began to run towards the offending sound. Then suddenly there it was coming around the bend at the base of the mountain, a single light shone out and behind it a huge thundering diesel engine that appeared at that moment to be at least the size of Harrods. The whole thing took on the memorable scene from *The Railway Children*. Campily announcing, 'I can't take my petticoat off, dear, I'm not wearing one,' David then nodded as I explained plan 'A'.

'Well, I suggest we both wave like hell and if it fails to stop, you jump to the right and I'll jump to the left. But for God's sake don't faint, remember this is real life and not *The Railway Children*.'

Now, I have had some heart stopping moments in my time, but this was probably well up in the top five I have experienced. For a time, it did look as though the shining beast was just going to glide straight past us, assuming we did leap out of its way but bearing in mind its size and a bit of hindsight, it probably did take a bit of stopping when suddenly surprised by two Englishmen in the middle of nowhere. I began to hope that this was a normal occurrence indeed, a bit like the bus to Fez and they would be only too familiar with people hopping on and off at will in remote places. Slowly it did appear to be stopping and David and I mopped the sweat from our brows and shared a 'woodbine' as he always called having a cigarette, while our Moroccan filming fixers appeared at speed and saved us having to stutter and stammer to explain the situation ahead to the driver of the now stationary vehicle. The police escort on the journey back meant that at least we were transported quickly to hit the bar running to calm our very unsteady and jangled nerves. Although David seemed to have recovered somewhat better than myself, as he could not resist waving regally at any spectators that stared up at the coach.

The hotel was quite out of this world and one of the many fine actors in *Scoop* was none other than Herbert Lom who had stayed there before on several occasions. For such a star of his generation he had, as they say, no side to him whatsoever. He was also very funny and would regale us with tales of amusing incidents that had happened while filming *The Pink Panther* film series with Peter Sellers, until the tears were running down not only his but everybody else's faces as well. We had all been told to call him Mr. Lom when he arrived and I happened to be passing by as his taxi dropped him off at Lydd airport on his first day of filming with us. I opened the car door, introduced myself as the location manager and he offered me his hand to shake and simply said, 'Lom.' We got on like a house on fire and after about three days, much to the producer's horror, but at his insistence, everybody was calling him Herbie. At dinner, the following evening, the day after my small adventure, he gathered a few of us together in the lounge of the hotel, bought a round of drinks and said, 'Now watch the ceiling.' He signalled to one of the ever-attendant staff who turned around and dimmed the lights, then pushed a button on the wall. As we looked up the ceiling slowly began to slide back, I looked swiftly round at the assembled company and to a man all their jaws had dropped wide open. It was like something out of a James Bond film and as the ceiling passed by, slowly your eyes adjusted and there straight up was the awesome sight of thousands and thousands of stars, twinkling, shining and dancing above you in all their glory as you reclined in your armchair and slowly sipped on your brandy.

Herbie's malaria tablet day was the same as mine, so we used to remind one another to take them. He was a charming man and I have a Polaroid picture of him in costume, which he signed to me from him, and I consider myself very privileged to have met and worked with him. He was a gentleman in every sense of the word. Mind you, so were the rest of the cast. It was a truly magnificent line up. Sir Michael Hordern, who seemed as mad as a hatter, used to mutter and sing to himself and sometimes roared up on a motorbike to the location but goodness what a lovely man. Denholm Elliot another complete charmer, who had travelled abroad so often, his tummy was continually upset. I went off down to the chemist for him one day to procure some kaolin and morphine. Upon my return, he offered me the money for the purchase. I was staggered that such a star should proffer the money, many I have met just expect everything to be provided for them, and quite often it is. I declined and said I could claim it back off expenses I was sure. What I am trying to say is that is the difference between a star and a complete pain in the butt. We were so lucky on that shoot there was not one bad egg in the barrel. Nicola Pagett was young, flirty and full of beans and I once saw her eating her lunch sitting on the tailboard of the props van and at that moment I fell completely in love with her. Michael Maloney, who had the lead as 'Boot', was very nervous; it was his first big break, but again a complete gentleman and has gone on to become one of our finest actors. Last, but not least, Donald Pleasance, again absolutely no bother and a joy to work with. I had an extra special reason for liking him because in his role as editor of the *Daily Planet*, he smoked some rather large and very splendid cigars. At the end of the day, when the scene had been completed, one or two of these items did tend to fall off the back of the prop van in my direction.

On the second evening, Mike Littlejohn suggested a stroll around the old town of Fez into the medina. I was quite happy to sit nursing my brandy but with the persuasive words of, 'Come on, you may never come here again and think what an opportunity you would have missed,' I agreed to join the adventurers' party. So off we went and were almost immediately accosted as we entered the old town by a young lad who spoke passable English and offered to guide us through the maze of streets and alleyways. For a while, we tried to ignore him but such was his persistence, and as the complicated geography of the place began to dawn on us, he eventually found himself employed. We passed all manner of shops that sold all manner of goods and our noses were assaulted by all manner of smells from spices to, well, I'm sure you can guess. You may well be eating a pleasant sandwich or roll as you read this so why should I spoil it for you?

One sight that startled us all completely was the image of four donkey's feet, we assumed them to be, parked outside a shop but with the rest of the donkey apparently missing. We gazed skywards in the hope of perhaps seeing the rest of it lurking on a roof somewhere. We pondered if it had, for some unknown reason, exploded and left its feet behind. It was straight out of a *Goon Show* script! Finally, we arrived at a carpet shop and the lad bid us enter. Now it suddenly all became very clear, he had been posted on the main gates by the proprietor to herd innocent passers-by into his shop and then the sales technique began and what a technique it was.

Now, we really had not started out on our perambulation with the intention of buying a carpet. In fact, I could state solidly that it was the last thing on anybody's mind as we left the hotel. However, here we now were and there were four of us, being given tea and a comfy seat and a dazzling display of carpet selling the likes of which I have never witnessed. Every time we said no, another design would be placed before us. 'Is it the colour that is wrong?' We explained that we just didn't want to buy a carpet and that was the reason for our negativity. 'You cannot come all the way to Morocco and not buy a carpet,' we were told. 'You may never pass this way again and think what an opportunity you would have missed.' These words sounded a little familiar and I looked at Mike, 'A distant cousin of yours perhaps?' Mike shrugged his shoulders and smiled. The owner was showing us carpets of a size that would have covered my local swimming pool. As the argument of 'we don't want to buy one' seemed to have failed, we fought back with how on earth could we get such a bulky article onto the plane? Apparently transport was no problem, they would ship them to us back in London. After explaining that the size was the problem, in that they were more than the whole of the floor area of probably our four houses put together, he began to scale things down a little.

151

More tea arrived and more but now at least smaller sized carpets. If ever you enquired about price, he would always say he would tell you later and then he would make you an offer you just couldn't refuse, but first you had to find one you liked. It went on like this for over half an hour. 'Look boys. Someone is going to have to buy something or we will be in here all night,' said Mike. So, we capitulated, broken by his sales technique that would have won him an award of honour from any self-respecting double-glazing firm and an OBE for services to industry. Finally, when I selected a very small one I liked, just to get us out of there, it didn't end there. Tradition dictated that we then had to barter over the price. It came down and down and down, until at length we agreed and I walked out into the night air with a carpet under my arm that I didn't want – and so did two of my other companions! The lad guided us back to where we had come in, we gave him a tip and he scuttled off to once again begin lurking, ready to pounce on another would-be customer who, I could guarantee, within forty-five minutes of his approach would be carrying a carpet they also really didn't want under their arm into the warm night air. I would have put it on my shoulder and said, 'Just smell those Tuareg camp fires,' but unfortunately the commercial was many years off being made so it wouldn't have got a laugh.

The flight back was an alcoholic aerial adventure. We had boarded the plane, Air Morocco, don't even ask me what colour it was, in a very happy mood. We all thought it would be a 'dry' flight so everyone had made sure they already had a little drop or two inside them to tide them over the journey. Also, many had ample provisions with them and I can remember a bottle of Vodka being passed along the line even before we took off into the unknown. There were three seats either side of the central aisle and I was with, shall we say, some of the more extrovert members of the team. 'Round up the usual suspects' is the phrase that springs to mind. The stage manager, who really should remain nameless but, unfortunately, I have already mentioned him, had been an airline steward in a previous existence and knew the type of plane we were on. So, when, somewhat surprisingly, we were given those small quarter bottles of wine to have with the lunch, and the one steward and stewardess that were serving us had both disappeared, David knew instantly where to lay his hands on extra supplies. The plane was also for carrying equipment and I had never seen an interior like it before or indeed since. It was not the usual straight isle it went to the side, along and then back out again, so we were kind of in the back section and a host of others were in the front. A human chain was formed and the bottles were passed along the rows. This was the first and again the only time I ever ate a meal at an angle of about twenty-two degrees caused by all the wine bottles between my back and the plane seat that were forcing me so dangerously forward towards my food and chronic indigestion.

One of the early scenes featured Nicola Pagett coming out of her house and being confronted by a huge traffic jam outside. The bedroom where we first see her was a room at the Moet and Chandon headquarters off Hyde Park Corner. The stairs she then wandered down and to her front door were at the Foreign Press Office in Carlton House Terrace and the street scene with the traffic jam was also Carlton House Terrace. I later went back to the Foreign Press Office for an episode of *Spooks* and blow me down it was still the same PR lady who I had dealt with all those years ago, but she didn't remember me at all! Such is the power of my personality!

The biggest problem I had with the traffic jam was that Nicola drove her car to avoid the congestion onto the pavement and round a statue pursued by a policeman. How I organised and got permission for that traffic jam looking at it today, I have no idea. All I remember is that the largest problem for the police and whoever controlled the statue she drove round, was the fact she was going to drive round the statue. Not her personally, of course, it would be a stunt driver. Anyway, I did win that point and we did do it. She then arrived, in the story, at a restaurant for lunch, which in fact was the Women's Club in Audley Square. I was hanging around outside on the day of filming, like most shoots, a lot of my time being spent on the tailgate of the generator. We had bagged all the meters for miles and my stomach tightened when up drew a chauffeur driven car and out stepped none other than Sir Lew Grade. Now I'm for it, I thought. His chauffer has got nowhere to park outside his own office. 'Morning boys,' said Sir Lew as he passed by puffing on a beautifully aromatic cigar and went into his office without so much as a pause of step. What a lovely man, I mused to myself. He really should meet Michael Winner.

During the filming of *Scoop*, we spent nearly a week at Chastleton House, near Moreton-in-Marsh in Oxfordshire, which played the part of Boot Magna, the family home in the story. There was a dreadful cock up with room allocations. I didn't 'hot desk' as much as 'hot bed' my room in the hotel with the night security man. An arrangement that baffled the hotel staff completely, I am sure. I would leave for work in the morning and meet the security man on site, ask if all was well and then he would head back and sleep in my room during the day, then I would hand over to him in the evening and I would sleep in it at night. A most peculiar practice, indeed, but the hotel staff did accommodate it and managed, somehow, to clean and service the room between incumbents!

There was a scene in *Scoop* in which Michael Maloney was seen to be crossing some stepping-stones in a small river. This scene was one of those that you quite often get on a production that for some reason follows you around all the time, if you understand my meaning. Someone would always say something like, 'If we finish early on Tuesday, we could get that stepping stone scene shot.' This would become a kind of weekly statement, with obviously a slight variation in the day of the week. So, on this occasion Monday had dawned, the phrase had been uttered, and off I went to find the nearest stretch of water. Gazing at the Ordnance Survey map I spied a small stream to the west of Moreton and headed off to find its source. It turned out to be on a huge private estate. It would be, wouldn't it?! But having looked and liked what I saw, I then bravely drove past it and onwards up to the huge mansion at the end of the drive.

Ringing the doorbell summoned nobody but attacking the huge brass knocker with a little more gusto than I had intended, the door magically swung open with a splendid Hammer House of Horror creak. I ventured inside, whistling happily and loudly and calling out, 'Hello, hello,' in as friendly a tone as I could muster. In a momentary pause, I realised I could hear the distant sounds of crockery clanking and following the noise down the hall, turned right and entered a huge sitting room. I could see in the distance two ladies and an old man taking afternoon tea in the

155

alcove of a window that offered a spectacular view onto the expansive lawn and countryside beyond.

'Sorry, to trouble you,' I said. They all turned towards me and looked completely unmoved that I had entered the premises, let alone the sitting room unannounced.

'Come in, come in,' the old man yelled. 'I'll never hear you from over there.'

I did as he bid and after apologising for the fact I had just so freely wandered into their dwelling. I then began to try and explain what I wanted and why I really was in a bit of a rush for an answer right away. At one point, one of the elderly ladies began to ask me something but was put down immediately by 'His Grace' with, 'Shut up he's trying to explain why he's here.' I completed my shouted explanation and there was a very brief pause.

'You'll be bringing a tripod, I presume?' queried the gentleman, presumably trying hard to impress his two companions with his knowledge of the subject. Momentarily a mental picture of the back of the grip truck flashed in my mind, packed full of tracking equipment, camera dollies, lens boxes and a multitude of gear for all occasions.

'Oh, yes,' I reassured him. 'We will be bringing a tripod alright.' I reassured him.

'Then yes, you must proceed at once,' he replied. 'Let me know how you get on.'

'Thank you,' I said. 'I will,'

I had a quick chat with the accountant and feeling a little guilty that no one had mentioned money, for example a facility fee, I returned that evening with two bottles of Champagne to present as a little thank you to 'oil the wheels' as it were. This time the ring on the doorbell did affect an answer and the butler opened the door with a huge pigeon feather sticking out of his hair. I tried to remain as stoical as the incumbents had done when I first entered the premises that afternoon, but admit I nearly lost it. There is a small scar on my lower lip, which proves the point. I entered the drawing room and one of the ladies was up and about and from a room beyond I could hear 'His Lordship's' voice bellowing forth.

'He's on the phone to London, my dear, he will take forever. How can I help?'

I proffered the bottles, 'Well I just came to give you these as a little thank you.'

'Have you done it?'

'No, no it won't be until tomorrow at the earliest, weather permitting but I just thought a little gift would be in order.'

'No, certainly not. No, no,' she said. She looked very stern and I was thinking I had blown it and that she was offended by my paltry and minimalist offer. However, relief flooded over me, as she said, 'No, not until you have success!' and she smiled sweetly. I insisted and she eventually accepted, bade me good luck and the butler, still sporting his jaunty feather, escorted me out.

The prop boys and myself descended on the stream the following day and placed our own stepping-stones in position. I am sure you will not be surprised to learn that they stayed there for the whole week and the scene was never shot. I returned once more to the house but alas only the butler was in, thankfully 'sans feather' this time (I mused that perhaps it was just for evening wear), and I asked him to pass on my thanks to the lovely owners and to tell them that unfortunately time had beaten us and we had not had the opportunity to use their stream. I felt on my way back down the drive I was leaving behind a small-time capsule and for many weeks after I wanted to rush back there and revisit the place, but sadly I never did.

On a couple of occasions, I had the pleasure of working with Barbara Jenkins, a production assistant full of life and one of the boys. While working on *Scoop*, Barbara was taken very ill for a couple of days in Morocco with a stomach bug, which did, at one point, 'down' quite a few of the crew. During this period, we all moved up a job or juggled sideways. David Matthews took over from Barbara and proudly sporting a clipboard and wearing a stop watch around his neck, took down film timings and roll numbers and sound rushes details and watched for continuity mistakes. I was upgraded to become bell ringer. Because television had aspired to become like film whenever the first assistant yelled out 'turnover', a voice would come back and yell 'turning' and another would call 'sound running' and a bell would ring to warn people in the vicinity that the film was rolling and to be quiet. When the first assistant yelled 'cut' the bell was rung again, twice this time, I believe, so that distant chippies or lamp riggers could proceed with their noisy duties. It was a very boring job but I entered it with great vigour and enthusiasm, but unfortunately, with such vigour and enthusiasm that before an hour had passed the job had been taken away from me because my bell rings were often longer than some of the scenes they were shooting! But at least I was told face to face to go and find something more useful to do. I still have a Polaroid in my collection that was taken by Barbara of myself, David and Kevin Holden beside the pool in Fez, which obviously, despite the dreaded journey described earlier, I had eventually made and all, of course, with the compulsory drinks in our hands raised towards the lens.

Barbara suffered from asthma, which was a condition my elder daughter, Laura, also had, but thankfully only in her younger years, and like my daughter Barbara's inhaler was always close at hand. She was going steady with Ian Coles from the sound department and I believe that marriage was in the air when she succumbed to a severe attack of the awful affliction and died. She was tragically young for such an occurrence and people just couldn't believe that someone could die from an asthma attack. Mary became secretary of our local asthma society, mainly because Laura had it and we learnt from her involvement that despite popular belief, yes indeed, it could and frequently was a killer. It was just so hard to accept, as I have said earlier, that whoever ordains or decides these things that they could be so cruel as to take that life away. Such an event does, I fear, test people's faith to the limit, in whatever God they may believe. Luckily, not believing in one, I don't have that problem but it doesn't make it any the less distressing.

They say that life goes round in circles – well, I often say that! The most bizarre thing happened in the summer of 2003. I once again met, after a long number of years, the director Gavin Millar on an episode of *The Last Detective*. It was so long ago that I had almost forgotten that he had been the director of *Scoop*, but what was even more co-incidental was that one of the guest artistes was Michael Maloney, which I just found to be an incredible thing to happen for the three of us to be together after all that time. One fascinating piece of information to come out of various reminiscent conversations during the breaks in filming was that in fact Peter Davison, the star of *The Last Detective*, had been up for the part of Boot in *Scoop* all those years ago but but had lost out in favour of Michael. Now, not many people know that!

Chapter Ten

Wish Me Luck

The funny thing about the first series of *Wish Me Luck* was that, as I progressed round London finding various locations and again it was a mixture of studio and location inserts, I seemed to be accidentally following in the footsteps of a feature film called *Plenty*, which starred Meryl Streep, Charles Dance and Sam Neil. I never mentioned this to the director and began praying that he would never watch the film when it was released. *Plenty* was the same period, the Second World War, and the story was about Meryl being a spy with the French resistance working for the S.O.E. (Special Operations Executive). It was in a way reassuring that I was on the same wavelength as a feature film location manager but a bit annoying because they had left a trail of very unhappy people in their wake. There was a particular street, called Caradoc Street, in Greenwich, which had been used quite a bit for period dramas, and I can tell you it required a lot of skill and persuasion to get them to play ball again after *Plenty* had hit the street for a few days and then departed. When I arrived and happily knocked on the door they were about to have no more filming there at all. Anyway, I managed it and afterwards the main protagonist praised the way we had conducted ourselves in a letter to his local paper. For quite a few years afterwards, Ron Diprose and I would occasionally bump into one another and have a few laughs over a pie and a pint.

Sometimes things and situations regarding locations were easy. I had set up a meeting with one of the chaps in charge of Black Park, which is very close to Pinewood Studios, because one scene called for a

Kubelwagen to be blown up. 'Now then,' he said. 'What's the problem that needed us meeting one another, face to face? I began hesitantly, 'Well, I'm working on a Second World War project that calls for a Kubelwagen driving through a forest being blown up.'

'Oh, is that all?' he replied, looking completely unphased, while my face must have been a picture, 'We've had two hundred horsemen galloping down that hill over there, in full battle gear, following Henry the Fifth and all you want to do is blow up a Kubelwagen. No problem.' My jaw was probably on the floor. 'Come on, I'll show you where you can have your unit base.' I should have, of course, realised that with Pinewood so close this was almost like the studios back lot and had been used on countless occasions for many films and television series.

In November 1988, the pint was about to be my undoing. I had been trying to find what could be a munitions factory in France, again for *Wish Me Luck*, but it had to be filmed over here, as a main chunk of the budget had already been committed to a block of filming in France and we just couldn't afford the extra time over there. Firstly, the factory had to be isolated. Secondly, we wanted to blow it up. Not literally, of course, but a certain amount of special effects would be needed. The other problem was I needed not only the outside but also the inside of the place and it obviously had to look like, or as near as we could get, to a real munitions factory. A tall order and I hunted high and low with the infamous designer, Bryan Bagge. We even contacted Fred Dibnah in the vain hope that he would know of an amazing factory 'up north' that was due for flattening – and that he was due to demolish the chimney of! We visited him at his home in Bolton and laid eyes on that back, and I use the next word in its loosest possible sense, 'garden'. It was full of engineering monsters from years gone by, very familiar to us both from his television series. But to stand in his garden was something else! Really, it was more like a back yard – but a very big one! The air was perfumed with the heavy smell of engine oil and grease. So much so, that I was immediately transported back to my youth and to the steam engine sheds at Crewe where I had smelt that exact same smell. He told it like it was and said that all those old factories and mills had all but gone. In fact, all the chimneys had been downed within the area and almost certainly by him. He mused for a while, complaining that the BBC series had not made him a rich man, despite what people may think, and was very annoyed that he had given up smoking; not, from what I could gather, in consideration of his health, but for monetary reasons. This was because he had recently acquired a new wife and a young nipper called Jack. With an, 'Aye right. Well, good luck in yer quest, as yer might say,' we were summarily dismissed and Fred wandered back into his outdoor workshop. Taking care not to go base over apex on the rather slippery surface, we climbed back into the car and ascended the steep slope out of his premises back onto the main road. 'Well that got us three fifths of f**k all,' said Bryan with his usual catchphrase.

'Yes, but a nice bloke,' I ventured.

'Nice bloke? Did you clock all that junk he is surrounded by? He's absolutely off his rocker. Mad as a March hare.'

'Takes one to know one.'

'Watch it, Treeny!'

Finally, Bryan and I had a breakthrough. A scenery company called Watts and Cory, who were based in Manchester and used to build a lot of LWT's scenery, had heard Bryan puzzling as to where this place could be found, had told him of a place in Rochdale that was a massive factory that built machines. Now if you are building machines with machines, it follows that they will be of some size and quite impressive. Bryan and I went to look.

The owner was a charming man by the name of Jim Marsh, who took us around the place and Bryan was smitten. It was perfect. We certainly couldn't use the outside for explosions because it wasn't isolated and as the filming would be a night, a large majority of the population of Rochdale would not have thanked us for keeping them awake, but at least we now had our interior. In desperation, I went onto an early morning chat show on BBC local radio and announced that if anybody had a factory they were thinking of demolishing, could they please get in touch. I got a call from a demolition company who said they were about to knock down a factory, subject to contracts and the timing being right, did I want to go and have a look? Bryan, of course, was ecstatic: he suddenly realised if the demolition company were going to blow it up, we could blow it up for real and save a lot of money on special effects. It really did suit the bill but nobody talked about money and nobody would talk about money for a long time. It depended how long we wanted to be there, what we wanted to do, how many days we needed for filming and so on. We were getting very close to the filming dates and it turned out that the factory would not be in the hands of the demolition company but they would strike a deal with the owners and let me know how much for the location and how much for the demolition.

We had done a technical recce, which is the last stage before filming, and by then both parties knew they had us because we had no back up and no-where else to film. Then the crunch came. By now I was back in London and waiting for the phone call with the price. It came and it was a lot of money. The company wanted nine grand to use the site as a location and the demolition people wanted the same amount for the pyrotechnics. I met Bryan, the production manager, and the producer in the bar. We simply couldn't afford it. Bryan went off to try and get a price for special effects and I went off to telephone the demolition people and say we could only afford the location fee and sorry we didn't need the real explosions. The answer I got sent me cold. 'Well, I'm afraid, Malcolm, it doesn't quite work like that. Even if you don't need us, I think you will find that the owners will raise their price to eighteen thousand pounds.' It was out and out blackmail and they knew I had nowhere else to run. We all met in the bar again and the strain on me was enormous, I had been drinking at lunchtime and had no lunch and here I was drinking again. I had never paid a figure like that for filming anywhere either before or indeed since. In short, we had been well and truly shafted. We had no alternative than to go ahead, except Bryan did decide to use his special effects. I felt terrible and totally responsible for the whole mess, having met all the people involved on several occasions, I had assumed they were all good and honest folk. I knew I had drunk too much and I did think about taking the train home but I was off back to Manchester the following day and to come back into town and then out again seemed crazy. So, stupidly, and I have no excuse other than I had had one of the worst days of my life, which is in fact no excuse at all for drinking and driving, I drove home. My car had just come back from a service and had been pulling to the left. Of course, as

164

it was late at night on the M3 motorway, and I was on the inside lane, there was very little traffic. I let go of the wheel to see if the fault was still there, it was and the car gently sauntered over to the left. I was so annoyed that it hadn't been fixed I tried it again to double check, with the same result, except that this time a blue light appeared in my rear-view mirror. I was caught bang to rights, and quite rightly so. It was a foolish thing to do and the thought of what might have happened driving in that state still makes me feel very queasy.

The case didn't come to court until January the following year. I had a clean licence and the solicitor I went to for advice said, 'No point employing me and costing you money. Obviously, you will get banned but it will only be for a year.' Despite a letter of mitigation that Peter Pearson the location production manager on the project very kindly submitted on my behalf, probably claiming complete insanity, the magistrate peered over the top of her glasses and, I thought, rather unfairly delivered with some relish in her voice that I was to get an eighteen month ban and a two hundred and fifty pound fine.

Although several years have elapsed since the incident, typing the events I described was terribly difficult and most unpleasant. The night I was stopped has come flooding back like it was yesterday and with it the guilt, the stupidity, the embarrassment of facing my family and friends and the gut wrenching feeling that I was going to lose my job. You see, what a location manager does most is drive and as someone who was about to lose that capability I felt the company would have little use in future of my services.

However, the company treated me exceptionally leniently. I think everyone realising at the time that it could so easily have been one of them and everyone looking to me as the classic example of there but for the grace of God go I. I must have single-handedly decreased the takings in the bar by a huge amount and at the 'Stage Door' near the Old Vic, where we would often gather after work 'to let the traffic die down', cough, cough. I was given the third series of *Wish Me Luck* to do, as a lot of it was to be shot in France and I would be driving around with a French location manager anyway. I was also given the deputy job of looking after the run up to the *Telethon '90*, which was to be staged at the London Arena. I covered many meetings in the Docklands with the London Docklands Development Corporation on behalf of my good colleague, Peter Hall, who would eventually come on board in overall command. I used to commute via the River Bus to these events that became weekly and enjoy the Thames in all its glory.

Going back to Jim Marsh, the owner of the factory in Rochdale, the one we didn't blow up but just filled completely with smoke, wore a toupee. I hope he won't mind me telling this story but he also had a canny sense of humour so fingers crossed I will be forgiven. The effervescent Bill Hays had remarked on this hair piece on several occasions, but obviously not to Jim's face, and pondering that Jim probably wasn't short of a bob or two, had wondered why hadn't he got a better-looking wig because it was one of those that was relatively obvious even at the swiftest glance. Anyway, Bill had a joke that he loved to tell at the time, which was a true story about his expedition into a restaurant toilet. As he approached the urinal, which was one of those long trough affairs, a man had just finished doing what he had to do and went to wash his hands. As Bill began to pee, the man hit the button on the hand-drying machine, there being no towels, but failed to notice the blower nozzle was pointing up. The fast blast of air was so strong it shot the guys wig straight off his head into the trough directly landing in front of Bill. 'Well, you know what it's like when you are in mid-stream love,' Bill was often heard to recall, 'you just can't stop can you? Well, men can't can they, not like women do? So, I just looked at him and he just looked at me. Not a word passed between us. Well there was no point was there, he could see what I was doing and I couldn't stop could I?' I heard Bill tell this tale several times but the first time I heard it I was doubled up. It had no tag because Bill just left the toilet leaving the man behind gazing forlornly at his sodden hairpiece languishing in the urinal.

On one of the recces to the factory we were staying overnight in an hotel and Bill thought it would be a good PR move to invite Jim to dine with us one evening. We said he could on the proviso that on no account did he tell the wig joke. Bill looked shocked that the thought would even cross his mind and scolded us for even thinking and believing such a thing might happen. 'Yes, but you know what your like when you've had a couple.' Peter Pearson had said as the voice of authority in the group.

'Peter, Peter please credit me with more sense than that,' responded a hurt looking Hays.

The evening approached and Bill was gently reminded again to be on his best behaviour. We had one of those long tables for us all to feast from and Bill had seated Jim next to him and they got on like a house on fire. Just after the main course, when the wine had flowed freely for a good hour and a half and the conversation ebbed slightly, Bill excused himself and toddled off in the direction of the toilet. He returned with a slightly mischievous grin on his face and declared in a slightly louder voice than up to now, 'Jim, Jim you've been to the toilet, haven't you?' The table went deathly quiet.

'Aye, aye I have,' Jim responded innocently. 'Isn't it unusual that they don't have a towel in there? It's just one of those drying machines.'

The whole table had stopped eating, talking, drinking, moving and probably thinking. We were all held as if on the edge of an abyss, with just one small footfall ready to take us over down into the black beyond. Bill very quickly flicked his eyes around the whole table just to reassure himself that everyone but everyone's attention was on him, 'Funny, isn't it? I just thought I'd mention it,' and he picked up his glass of red wine as if to secretly say cheers to us all, 'Now, what's for pudding? I do like a nice pudding don't you Jim?' We had all been got so skilfully by the master it wasn't true. I often wonder if Jim ever noticed not only the looks of relief around the table as the sweet menu emerged, but also the massive exchange of glances of fear at that moment that we thought Bill was about to launch into the gag and several brains went into overdrive wondering how the hell they would stop him.

All I can remember of the filming at the factory we did blow up, apart from my seething anger, was that I had two problems. One was the closeness of the railway line and the other was that somewhere to the south of the location were located the ICI brine fields. I didn't know an awful lot about brine fields – but I was about to find out! The answer to the railway line problem was solved by me agreeing to toddle down to the nearest signal box some ten minutes before the big bang and they would let everyone know it was happening; the last thing I wanted was a train to pass by and everyone on board looking out of the window having heart attacks as they watch huge fireballs ascend into the air. Why I couldn't just phone, I have no idea.

The brine fields were more complicated. They were used in the Sixties and Seventies to extract salt for chlorine and caustic soda. This process left a large hole in the ground. ICI took advantage of the space by stabilising the caverns for storage of petrochemicals and gases, including hydrogen. If a cavern was targeted for storage, the salt was extracted in a way to develop a large (thousands of cubic meters) cylindrical storage cavity. This storage system was shown to be viable because the underground strata of salt are three hundred and fifty meters to six hundred plus meters below ground, and twenty-thirty meters deep. ICI would drill a hole to the salt layer to extract the brine and increase the cavity. It is amazing what a little expert you become in this job on outside influences to your work. Their biggest fear, understandably, was earthquakes, not that we get many, of course, but we do get a few and from what I could gather these places were crammed with very sensitive measuring devices. They also seemed to be a bit 'hush hush' about it all and although it was in the public domain, probably from their point of view, the less people who knew that there were great caverns of hydrogen under their house, the better. A big explosion and resulting tremor from us would cause the equivalent panic and pandemonium to World War Three breaking out and I had long and protracted discussions about this with ICI. In the end, we decided that it probably wouldn't affect them and we could go ahead and they would keep their fingers crossed. 'Let's hope it's not a frosty night,' I think was the last statement I remember them saying. 'Because if the ground is hard the shock waves will carry further.'

I had, as a matter of course, informed the fire brigade and police of our plans and I mused that special effects are special effects, we were a long way from any habitation, only a few farms surrounded us, and I had letter dropped them all, so that they knew we were there. So, what could go wrong? Well, for a start the bang, correction, make that bangs, were a little bit louder and longer and bigger than either Peter Pearson or I had imagined. Bill was happily tucked up in a little outside broadcast truck directing away when the first explosion rocked the cold night air and also gently rocked the vehicle he was sitting in. The whole thing built and built to a huge crescendo and I imagined not only the monitoring equipment needles over at ICI bending a little but cracks appearing in the surface of the earth and masses of hydrogen being released into the air. Before I heard them, I saw them; their blue lights flashing along the main road down in the valley, which we overlooked, I counted three fire engines and two police cars. I went to the gate to meet them and as I was showing them where to park I was aware of Peter being rounded on by a very irate farmer. We had timed the explosion perfectly to coincide with the moment he was getting his cows in for milking and he had cattle all over the shop and was not very happy. The fireman, who had arrived in his own car, with his own blue light on, shook my hand, 'Well, I did say on the phone that I hoped we wouldn't meet, Malcolm, but now we have is there any chance of a cup of tea for me and the boys?' They were all very pleasant. It turned out they had received a phone call from someone saying they could see smoke and flames, so they were obliged to turn out, even though they know it was probably only the filming that they had already been warned about that had caused the alarm to be raised. I questioned him about

ICI. 'No, don't fret, Malcolm, I'm sure the Brine Fields are fine. Believe me we would have heard about it by now if they weren't.' Also, Peter seemed to be finally okay with his newfound farmer friend. Because the blast had blown out a lot of windows in the complex and we were obliged to re-glaze them, (don't ask me why when the whole place was due for demolition anyway!). When he eventually calmed down, we discovered that the farmer just happened to be a part time glazier and Peter had little choice than to offer him the contract of the year. So, all was well that ended well!

Lisle Middleditch was the senior cameraman on the series. One day, Bill turned to Lisle's assistant and said, 'I wish I had nicknamed you Tate, love.' The assistant looked back with a question mark above his head. 'Well it's obvious, isn't it? I could have shouted out when I wanted somebody, Tate or Lisle!'

Sometime later in deepest Kent, Bill and I had been waiting for about twenty minutes outside a big country house, the front of which was covered in roses, for the owner's daughter to turn up and show us the house as a possible location. She had the title of Lady and ran a pub – my sort of woman! Bill was very patient, but after thirty minutes he sighed, lit up a cigarette and said, 'Well, I suppose we could dead head the roses, do you think?' You had to be there, I guess, but he was a very funny man who really should have been in front of the cameras, not behind them!

With *Wish Me Luck* and then *The Knock* I have been lucky enough to have filmed in France and got to know several French colleagues, who have remained friends. The two main names in the frame are Jean Louis Xavier and Mathieu Howlett, simply because after working together we had stayed in touch.

Wish Me Luck meant that on the first series we spent two weeks filming in France. On the second series, it went up to four and I think series three we spent six weeks over there. The first series was directed by a man who appeared to be on the surface, at least, a dour Scot, who went by the name of Gordon Flemyng. He had contacted Antoine Sabbaros, a chap he had worked with before in France, and with him a little later came Jean Louis. We filmed in Normandy and Gordon had the idea that as France was occupied it should feel claustrophobic and enclosed, so he shot everything on long but very tight lenses. In England, which was unoccupied, he shot big wide angles of extensive scenery. The money men were not very pleased that we had expensively gone all the way to France and shot so tightly that it could have sometimes been done with a bit of a backing flat behind whoever happened to be talking and thus we had not really seen France at all. But, as Greg Dyke so eloquently put it recently, the trouble with money men is that they know the cost of everything but the value of nothing. I liked Gordon and he never, as they say, did me any harm but he did not suffer fools gladly and when he went for you, you knew you had been got at.

I was driving him to the location one morning somewhere in the wilds of Kent and we passed by one of those little stalls outside a house, down a country lane that announced they had homemade honey for sale. 'God,' he mused. 'I love homemade honey.' This little piece of information went into my head and later in the day, during a lull in the activities, I drove back to the house and purchased a jar of the nectar for him to take back home to Scotland for the weekend. He usually flew home on the Friday night, if he could, and I figured it would be a nice little gift that might creep me even further in his good books. Wrong. Monday morning dawned and a very hard faced looking Gordon headed straight for me.

'That f**king honey you gave me on Friday.'

'Oh, yes. Was it nice?' I asked innocently.

'It only had a loose top, didn't it? It only came off in my suitcase during the flight, didn't it? And it only went all over my bloody clothes, didn't it? The missus was bloody furious.'

So, not only had I managed to put the director out of salts, but also his wife. I maintained a very low profile for the rest of the week and vowed never to crawl in such a blatant way to a director ever again. I didn't keep that promise because Gordon was not a well man and towards the end of the filming was constantly coughing and always asking for water. We stayed in various hotels on that shoot but in one near Burnham Beeches I made sure that the staff had placed some bottled water in his room before he arrived, so he wouldn't have the fuss of ordering or finding it himself. He approached me the following morning almost with the same look he had on his face when relating the honey incident. I braced myself for the onslaught.

'The good fairy had been to my room before I got there last night.'

'Oh, really?'

'Aye. I have asked around and I can't find the culprit.'

I tried to look innocent.

'Thanks,' he said. 'I appreciate it.'

At least I got that one right I contemplated as he walked off coughing. Alas Gordon is no longer with us, taken from us while producing and directing *Ellington* starring Chris Ellison. I assume he must have enjoyed this because his one real hate was the people he called 'the front office' coming on location and watching him work. This covered everyone from producer, executive producer to head of drama. 'Just keep those bastards away from me,' he would say. But being producer on *Ellington* he now was a part of that front office, so I guess he at least couldn't hassle himself.

Bill Hays directed the second and third series of *Wish Me Luck*. Antoine was not available for our dates this time, so Jean Louis took up the French production manager position and Mathieu joined us filling the role of Jean Louis as French location manager.

On the first series of *Wish Me Luck*, because of time and distance, our recces were often based out of Biggin Hill in small aircraft, so that, a bit like the S.O.E., we could get in and out of the country quickly. We would catch a small plane, be dropped into enemy territory, be gone for about three days or so and return via the same route. Looking back, I should have appreciated those days more, a sensible production manager, a realistic budget and the one thing that nobody seems to have these days 'time'. Anyway, the Biggin Hill staff were an agreeable and friendly lot, who would write down your duty-free order before you flew out, with phrases like, 'You don't smoke? Well, you must know someone who does. With prices like these, how can you refuse?' They would cajole you into ordering anything and everything, and it would be waiting for you upon your return. And then to the flight itself. Don't ask me what sort of plane it was, as you will have gathered from earlier I am not very good on planes, except I know this one usually came equipped with a pilot and a hamper. The pilot had the unnerving habit of turning round and talking to you, the aircraft being happily on 'George', or whatever the aviation equivalent of cruise control is. The hamper had all sorts of exotic things like quail's eggs in it that I had never sampled. It also had Scotch, Gin, Brandy and beer. While the more adventurous members of the unit, such as the designer and director, tucked into the 'fare', I was quite happy with the liquid part of the deal. The one thing *Wish Me Luck* did teach me over the series was to be more adventurous with my food intake; by the end of series three I was vying with the best of them over the eggs and brown bread.

One memorable technical recce we took the same route but, because of numbers of crew, we needed two planes. On our approach back, the production assistant, Lynda Ostermeyer, who was nervous about flying anyway even in a jumbo, made me keep talking to her to take her mind off the flight. The return journey seemed worse but at one point her heart went in her mouth as the other plane flying happily alongside us, both teams waving at one another, suddenly ducked underneath, came back over the top, and resumed its position. 'Ho!' cried our pilot, 'that's probably given someone in traffic control a change of underpants!' Meaning that the two lights on his screen would momentarily have merged into one. 'Stupid twit,' muttered Lynda, looking at the other plane, and we all berated the other pilot for being well out of order. It turned out a few days later it was our plane that had performed the flying stunt. At that altitude, we had no points of reference; you cannot tell who is doing what to whom. The pilot in the other plane was our pilot's boss and he very nearly lost his job because of his tomfoolery. Strange what a planeload of television people makes other people do. I've often wondered if he would have done the same with a day trip of city bankers?

The best flight I ever had was a return trip from Lyon. I had been lucky enough to get dispatched to

France again on *The Knock*, the Customs and Excise drama series that Bronson and Knight productions made for LWT. I was sent out on the Monday with the following words from the production manager ringing in my ears, 'And remember, when you get out there, the most important scene is the one in the vineyard, where the car blows up. Your main priority is to find the vineyard.' I think he had to turn the light off in my office, such was the speed with which I left the building.

Well, the actual shoot is another story. I once again teamed up with my good friends Jean Louis Xavier and Mathieu Howlett. Jean Louis and I spent a very pleasant first week touring the vineyards, an exacting job but somebody had to do it. Of course, at every stop, such is the hospitality of the wine growers of France, we were forced to sample their latest vintage. I am happy to say Jean Louis was driving and I did a splendid PR job of nodding and smiling my approval as various glasses of red and white wine presented themselves to me. Lyon, which is where we eventually based ourselves for the shoot, is the gastronomic heart of France and for me started another learning curve in that area. I had led a very sheltered existence, well anyone who asks for 'Steak tartare, well done, please' must be from a humble dietary background. No, it was the flight back that, for me, was one of the highlights of the shoot. For reasons of economy, the production manager called me back a week early. I didn't argue, I had been away from home for over nine weeks and was happy to return and have a week at home; even if I wasn't to be paid. I flew from Lyon airport on a Saturday morning, my French chums took me to the airport to see me off. I was catching the eleven o'clock flight. We arrived in plenty of time for a couple of final glasses of Pastis, before I headed for the departure gate. I had had a marvellous time and was sorry to say goodbye. So, already a little tired and emotional, I boarded the plane. It was Air France, a blue one, as I recall, and I made my way to my seat. It was at this point I realised I was in first class, quite how this came about, I have no idea. Maybe the production coordinator had done a deal with the airline, I do not know and never did inquire. I was just grateful to whoever had organised it for the one and only time in my life I have ever sat at the front of an aircraft in such splendid comfort. I looked around me and realised that I was the only one in first class, and that there were only about six people in total on the plane. The steward ostentatiously pulled the curtains to avert my gaze from the poor folks behind or was it the other way round? And there we were, just the steward and me. In a charming French accent, he enquired, 'Would you like a drink before we take off, sir?'

'Pardon?' I replied. No one had ever said that to me before!

'Would you like a drink before we take off, sir?'

'Well, er, yes, I suppose, er, what have you got?'

'We have Champagne, Gin, Cognac, Whisky.'

'Er, I suppose, er, Champagne would be rather nice, thank you.'

I sipped the bubbles and mentally relived the six weeks of filming and relaxed. As the plane taxied to the end of the runway, he stepped forward, took my empty glass and bottle, secured himself in his seat and we took off. At this point it is important to remember that the flight from Lyon to Heathrow is only about one hour and fifteen minutes. As the plane levelled out, there was a click of a seatbelt and he was by me again.

'Would you like an aperitif, sir?'

'Well, that's very kind of you, what have you got?'

177

'We have Gin, Martini, Dubonnet, Ricard.'

'Thank you, I'll have a Gin and Tonic, please.'

I sipped the cool liquid and gently bit the lemon. Why does a drink you have been served rather than prepared yourself always taste so good? Within minutes, the real cutlery had arrived and I chose from the menu. Just before the meal arrived, came more words again in that soft accent, 'Would you like a drink with the meal, sir?'

'Well, that's extraordinarily kind of you. What have you got?'

'We have red wine or white wine.'

'Red, I think.'

'The Cotes du Rhone or the Macon?'

'Er, er, I think, er...'

'I tell you what, sir, I will bring them both and you decide.'

'That's very, very kind of you.'

The meal arrived along with the two half bottles of wine. I tried the food and then tried the Macon. It was very pleasant. I drank it and then I tried the Cote du Rhone and that was very pleasant too. I paused for coffee. The steward didn't.

'Would you like a drink with the coffee, sir?'

'That's ferry kind of you, what 'ave you got?'

'We have Cognac, Liqueurs, Rum.'

'I'll have a Cognac, please.' But I bet I didn't say it like that. I sipped the cognac, gazed out of the window and to my complete astonishment; Windsor Castle flew past going at an amazing speed in the opposite direction. Well, that's the way it looked to me. We landed and as I stepped off the plane the steward said, 'Thank you for flying Air France, sir.'

I replied, 'No, shank you for 'aving me. Thatsh the bestish flight I ever had.'

A car, thank God, was waiting to take me home. Unfortunately, the travel time from Heathrow to my house is only about thirty minutes so there was very little time to sober up. 'Hello, darhling I'm home.' I said after nine weeks out of the country.

'My, God, what the hell has happened to you?' said Mary, taking one look at me on the doorstep in total disbelief.

'I've jutshed had the bestish flight I've ever had,' I replied. There was a long pause, which gave me time to sway very gently to and fro at least twice in the doorway.

'Obviously!' she said.

Bill Hays, as a director and a man, was an extraordinary character. He lived in Kensington with a beautiful lady called Catherine Schnell, who was one of the Bond girls. Quite a few of our English locations for series two of *Wish Me Luck* were east of London, one of the places being Ongar, which was right at the end of the Central Line in those days. Bill hated the journey by car through the east end of London to the wilds of Essex. He used to say it was a most depressing way out of London that seemed endless and oppressive. So, whenever we needed to be 'Look back in Ongar' as he would always say, he would take the tube rather than journey with me in the car and I would rendezvous with him at the station. He would happily suffer the twenty-eight station stops along the way and have plenty of time to study the crossword before emerging with that enigmatic grin on his face at Ongar station, frequently still puzzling over twenty-two down. I can remember him getting really angry on a night shoot with a bunch of background artistes who were supposed to be a crack German fighting division. When they got to a scene where they had to run out of their billets and fire at our heroes, quite a few of them complained rather campily that the guns were 'rather heavy and were very loud.'

'I don't care,' yelled Bill. 'I don't bloody care. You're supposed to be crack German soldiers. Now go back and do it again and fire the bloody things like you meant it and don't hold them away from you so they don't go bang in your ear.' As he turned and walked back to the camera he looked at me, 'Christ knows where the hell they got this effeminate bunch from.'

Bill was much more pleased when we ended up in the Vercors region of France and did a spectacular parachute drop with the aid of the French Parachute regiment, who were to put it bluntly as hard as nails. They were dressed in German uniforms and did us proud with a drop in a valley high up in the mountains from their huge plane. I had gone along with Jean Louis down below to say hello to the team before they took off and thank them in advance for their help. Their commander stood them all to attention and addressed them and I turned to Jean Louis as he finished and asked him what the commander had said towards the end of his speech that had caused most of the assembled company to laugh. Jean Louis translated, 'Whatever happens, even if you land on the roof of a car, in a tree or break your leg, you lie there and do not move until someone yells 'cut' and then you can scream.' One did land on the bonnet of a car that had stopped on the edge of frame to watch the excitement but the car lost. I gained as a souvenir a sweatshirt, which says 602e G.I.A. on it and a picture of a soldier holding a gun and parachuting down. I probably swapped it for a *World of Sport* tie! But thank you again to all the men and women in 602e G.I.A. – whatever that stood for! We had used them earlier in the day for some walking and shooting sequences and it was so obvious visually that

180

they were 'real' soldiers and Bill was delighted. They joined us for dinner that night managing to drink all of us under the table, including Bill who was no amateur at this sort of engagement and were gone by first light the following day. I spent the day in a field with Jim, a lovely prop man, nursing my hangover and picking up empty cartridges so that the farmer could put his cows back there without fear of the stupid animals eating lumps of metal!

Bill got a lot more than he bargained for when we were filming in Le Puy in France for *Wish Me Luck*. He had cast his wife Catherine Schnell to play one of the roles in the series and on one of her days off, when Bill had enquired what she would do while he was filming for the day, she had replied she would probably go shopping. Indeed, she did go shopping – she bought them a house in the Auberge region of France! Bill said it was the last time she would get a day off and dined out on the story for ever after. We exchanged Christmas cards for quite a few years but finally they stopped coming and I often mused as to what became of Bill and Catherine. Then I read the news in the obituaries section of *The Stage* of the death of Bill in France on 2 March aged sixty-seven. Having realised that Bill had still been in France, I immediately wrote to the old address I once sent my Christmas cards to, proffering my sincerest condolences to Bill's widow, Catherine, hoping against hope that she would receive the message. A small miracle occurred and she did get my letter and replied by email that Bill had a stroke in 1998 and it had been downhill from then on until, as she put it, the morphine finally got him.

Many things happened over the three series of *Wish Me Luck* that I would never have imagined. I never thought I would spend my fortieth birthday dancing in a disco in Grenoble but low and behold there I was, as always, not dancing very well, really hating the music being very loud and thinking I should really have been sensible and gone to bed early. However, because the drink was so expensive my French chums had a whip round for my birthday and bought me a bottle of Scotch, which was the cheapest way to drink it and had it placed behind the bar with my adopted French name of 'Marcel' on it. And I certainly never for one moment would have imagined I would be trapped on the side of a mountain trying to get back to the wrap party at the end of series three!

We had been filming way up on the top of the Vercors region, which lay south west of Grenoble in two small villages and the only way for our larger trucks to get back to our Hotels in Villards de Lans on the other side of the mountain was via a forest track. The main road route along the Gorges de la Bourne had overhanging rocks and tunnels that certain of the vehicles just could not have made. We had got them over the pass the week before to film at two small villages called St. Julien en Vercors and St. Martin en Vercors, and now all we had to do was get them back again. So duly assembled at about eight in the evening, having wrapped, packed and stowed everything away, the happy convoy moved off. I was travelling in the generator having learned my lesson, or so I thought, from my Moroccan experience. Nearly at the top of the ridge, the convoy ground to a halt and I wandered up front to see what the problem was. It was the construction lorry, an amazingly large vehicle, which had ground to a halt with a burnt-out clutch. Unfortunately, most of the other vehicles were behind it and there was no room to pass, we were all well and truly marooned halfway up the mountain pass. Jean

Louis, who had been in the front of the convoy, drove hurriedly off into the darkening sky with farewell words of, 'I'll be back, with something, somehow, sometime.' Patsy, the lovely driver of the construction truck, who was the smallest person on the unit and drove the biggest vehicle, kept apologising for the event and felt guilty. We all gathered round and assured him it wasn't his fault and it could have happened to anybody. The wardrobe van, the make-up van, the prop van, the generator, the grip van, the lighting truck all were piled up behind him and we didn't even have the facilities to make a cup of tea. Back at the hotel, preparations were in full swing for the wrap party, as this had been our last day of filming. But as this was once again way before the invention of the mobile telephone all we could do on the mountainside was just sit and wait and this time I watched the sun go down over the Vercors. The surrounding forest began to get cold and damp and slowly began to become very dark and very sinister.

How we passed the time is difficult now to remember. I suppose the usual round of telling stupid jokes, singing, smoking Ken the generator driver's Benson and Hedges cigarettes and eventually sitting in the cab and falling into an uneasy sleep. We were jolted awake at about eleven thirty by a huge noise and blazing lights approaching us through the woods out of the darkness. It looked for all the world like some enormous menacing alien spacecraft approaching. 'Oh dear, that is never going to get past us,' I muttered to Ken. 'I'd better go and tell them the bad news.' But I was wrong in my assumption because there was Jean Louis looking triumphant standing beside the biggest JCB I had ever seen. Somehow, despite the lateness of the hour, he had managed as only Jean Louis could, to enlist the help of this amazing beast to come to our rescue. Obviously, it was used in the forest for logging and shoving great lumps of stuff about but tonight it easily towed the stricken construction lorry away into the distance.

We were almost back onto the proper tarmac road in an area where we could abandon the construction lorry, overtake it and make our way down into Villard de Lans, when we realised we could see lights and people and activity and tables laid out with food and drink. There, in the middle of it all, was Peter Pearson the production manager, 'Well, I thought, bloody hell they'll never make it to the party now, so I thought I had better bring the party to you.' A wonderful gesture of man management that lifted everybody, by a bloke who cared and had a far happier look on his face then than he would fifteen years later in September 2004 in Paris.

Jean Louis like a lot of Frenchmen, liked to smoke a cigarette between cigarettes. He developed the first signs of cancer in 2002 but with treatment, hope had sprung that it had been conquered and when I saw him in January 2003 in Paris, while working with Mathieu on an insert for the BBC production of *I'd do Anything*, although he himself wasn't working, the signs of a complete recovery were looking positive. Mathieu helped me out for three days or so and Jean Louis popped by to say hello. Apart from the lack of a cigarette in his mouth, and a severe lack of hair as a result of all the chemotherapy, he seemed much his normal self. Later, in the summer of 2004, I stayed for a few days at Mathieu's house in the southern part of France and we spoke to Jean Louis on the phone, but Mathieu had already warned me that all was not well and that a meeting with another specialist had been arranged.

On the 21 September, some two weeks after seeing him, Mathieu phoned me while I was on holiday in Cephalonia to say the prognosis was very bad and that Jean Louis had been given only two weeks to live. I received a text on the 24 September which said simply. 'JLX died last night, I'll call you later.' On the 27 September, both Peter and I were on the Eurostar heading towards Paris for a cremation at nine thirty the following morning.

I looked down at the body in the open coffin and tried to imagine him smiling. His forehead had broken out in a sweat and so had I as a feeling of being strangely voyeuristic crept over me. His mouth was curled with a peculiar twist and his shirt looked like it really didn't fit him but there was no doubt I was looking down at my friend and work colleague Jean Louis in a hospital morgue in Paris, on that grey and peculiarly mild and humid day. To use a hackneyed phrase, it was a day of 'roller coaster' emotions for both Peter and myself. We laughed with Mathieu about incidents from the past, we cried with Jean Louis' wife, Marie, and expressed our deepest sympathy as best we could. We laughed with Michel Merlino, who had been one of the French prop boys and part of Jean Louis' team, we sympathised with Jean Louis' daughter, Melinda, who stood up and made a little speech at the service. We still have no idea to this day what she said. Peter and I have never been very fluent with the language, but to a very large congregation she managed, despite the tears running down her cheeks, to raise a few laughs and we both admired her courage and bravery and felt so deeply for her tortured pain. Above all, the most moving sight was both his parents, neither of them in the best of health, saying goodbye to their son, an action that in the bigger scheme of things seems so unnatural and so cruel that should there be a God, I pray to him that I may never have to witness anything like that again. But being a witness can be as nothing compared to the grief that they must have suffered and I am sure are surely suffering still. After the service, and back at the flat and after what we considered a respectful amount of time had passed, Mathieu, Peter and I tried to leave the red wine engulfed wake but Marie asked us to stay for a while longer as she loved the noise of the talking. The silence when everyone had gone must have been deafening.

As we sped under the English Channel on the train journey back home to dear old Blighty, Peter looked me straight in the eye and said, 'I, er, I've never seen a dead body before.'

'Me neither,' I replied. 'And I'm not too sure I want to see one again.' Peter nodded his head in agreement.

Jean Louis Xavier was just fifty-years-old.

Finally, despite not being allowed to drive, I probably had the best eighteen months drinking of my life. However, I was glad to get my licence back eventually and return to a very controlled drinking regime, in the knowledge that if ever I was caught again I would probably be taken out and shot. It had been a salutary lesson and one of which I have no intention of ever, ever repeating!

Chapter Eleven

Hooray for Holyhead

'The way I see it,' said the Welsh police sergeant puffing on his pipe. 'To avoid a repeat of the catastrophe of this morning, which I won't dwell on because it is over and done with, and thus avoid a reoccurrence of the same thing this afternoon, we are going to need some sort of physical barrier. Yes, that's it, some sort of physical barrier.' His broad Welsh accent drew out the word physical to an inordinate length and as he blew out the blue pipe smoke into the already fog filled room, the assembled company all nodded in serious agreement. We were all sat in Holyhead police station being given a bollocking in the mildest possible way. I was in Holyhead, playing second fiddle to Dave Currie, for a *Surprise, Surprise!* insert and the morning's events had been truly amazing. The story had begun with a chap writing into the programme lamenting the fact that no one had ever mentioned Holyhead and he wanted to change that and put the town firmly on the map. To the tune of 'Hooray For Hollywood' he had written 'Hooray for Holyhead'. So, the team had been despatched for two days to the Isle of Anglesey, along with Miss Cilla Black, to record this ditty for posterity and to give Holyhead a jolly good bit of free publicity. A helicopter had been ordered and I had transported the biggest aerial in the world in a big wooden box to help me communicate from land with the camera team on board. The Winnebago was parked up and the hotel had been booked. Everything was looking exceedingly good until we came to do the opening shot on the first morning. This was to be a parade up the high street, with Cilla

187

singing and a crowd following. From memory, I think we had three cameras covering the event, one of which was positioned on a tower at the end of the high street. A couple of police had been allocated to us just to deal with any small traffic snarl ups that might occur. A small crowd had gathered but got bigger and bigger and bigger as the kick-off time approached. It began to dawn on all of us that not only had most of the inhabitants of Holyhead turned out, but the majority of North Wales as well! They were all waiting to sing happily along with Miss Black.

Someone gave the magic cry of 'action' and we were off, but such was the throng that it very quickly became obvious this was a mass of people totally out of control. Cilla was in grave peril of being trampled to death and the manager of Woolworths, seeing the danger unfold before his very eyes, kindly offered her sanctuary within the confines of his store until order could be restored. Unfortunately, as she was escorted into the shop, a large proportion of the crowd thought this was a good opportunity to do a little light shopping and consequently they followed her in. With Cilla, safe within an inner office, the crowd were pushed back out of the premises and the doors tightly shut. I breathed a sigh of relief until my eyes fell upon the emptiest rack of 'pick 'n' mix' I had ever seen and returning my gaze to the crowd, I could not resist a chuckle at the smiling, chewing sea of faces standing outside in the main road.

We had been planning to film that afternoon on the outskirts of the town but the sergeant was worried about that morning's loss of control of the crowd and really didn't want it happening again. 'Now, I've telephoned Bangor but they only have six barriers, which is just not enough.' The smoke again issued forth from his pipe and I can remember musing that even in a crisis the manufacturers of Holborn ready rubbed would be pleased at the small jump in sales figures. 'Also, I just haven't got the staff available at such short notice to police such an event.' Someone suggested incident tape but he really didn't think that would hold them. We decided that Cilla's safety was our main concern and then I think the weather intervened and it was deemed too wet to shoot anyway. So, the afternoon's activities were cancelled. We decided to recommence filming at the lighthouse the following morning. It was felt that we would be far enough away from the general masses to be able to get on in relative peace. We realised we were going to have to make a bit more of the said location than we originally anticipated. Also, we had the helicopter, which would add terrific pictures of the singing crowd and the spectacular scenery of the coastline.

I have always found that a lot of patience is required when waiting for a thick fog to clear. The directions Dave had written said something like, 'As you round the bend you will see the lighthouse clearly on the top of the ridge in the distance.' Not a chance. You were hard pushed to see the bend, let alone the distant feature. I had remained down below, to supervise a separate item of Cilla being launched off on a lifeboat, while Dave manfully had gone up to the lighthouse to try and park various vehicles up and get ready for our small tame crowd to arrive. We were one whole afternoon's filming down and there was no way the helicopter was going to fly in conditions like this. Just at that moment you really do want to be able to hold an accountant warmly by the throat and say, 'See, this is why it is not an exact science! This is why it is not a sausage factory and can never be budgeted as such. We don't do this deliberately. This is life on the road.'

189

The lifeboat men were a happy bunch, with a wicked sense of humour. Cilla was launched into the sea on board their vessel, kitted out in their bright yellow waterproof clothing. The plug for the Royal National Lifeboat Institute was well worth our time and trouble, for they do a marvellous job in quite often terrifying conditions. Thankfully, by the time we had finished the lifeboat routine the fog was beginning to clear and although my helicopter to land communications never did work, we did get the piece safely in the can.

Because in those days the police were the ones who controlled the parking meters and yellow lines, naturally it was the police you dealt with to get dispensations and meters bagged for your vehicles. There were no charges or paying scales in those days. Each request was looked at on its merit and then, depending on how well you knew the nice policeman, various things happened. One copper would meet you in a pub for a drink. You would pass him a bottle of whisky and he would slip it into his long coat pocket, where it 'fitted a treat' and the deal was done. Another would simply ask for a donation to a police fund of some kind. Finally, there were always one or two who simply wanted a few pictures of the Queen handed to them in a plain brown envelope. It was simple, uncomplicated and involved absolutely no paperwork. I loved it. Of course, it would be completely frowned upon now, but it just seemed so simple in those days. No one was hurt, the job got done and everybody benefited. But there was a slight downside to this in that the 'you scratch my back, I'll scratch yours' syndrome from time to time also crept into the equation. There were two lovable coppers, who operated out of Vine Street police station, and they got me a couple of times, because of my love of magic, to do them a few favours.

One was the annual children's Christmas party, which I did enjoy doing and my two youngsters were even invited along. But the one that they got me to do, that was one of the worse nights of my life, was their annual 'bit of a do' for adults. It was decided I would be the cabaret, just what they needed to make it a more entertaining evening than usual. I was due to go on at about seven thirty but they left it later and later so that I would get a 'good' audience. I began to get twitchy. Finally, they capitulated and let me go on. So, suddenly at half past nine the disco was halted, the lights turned on, which illuminated the assembled company, most of whom have been drinking since roughly six o'clock! Not just on the stage, but also in the whole of the room, the harsh neon's slowly flickered into life. Couples locked in each other's arms in the gloom, sprung apart and look quizzical, like rabbits caught in the headlights of a car. And almost to the sound of my own footsteps I walked onto the stage. The tricks I start doing are my best, but the feeling of hate was overwhelming, I know they just wanted me dead and gone. My scintillating patter was slightly covered in cobwebs but gags such as, 'Why do policemen have bigger balls than firemen?' allowed the whole room to join in with the punchline. The answer was, of course, 'Because they sell more tickets.' But I noticed this was not said in a jocular nice to see you sort of manner. No, it was said through gritted teeth, below piercing eyes that were saying bugger off and turn the lights back off as you go sunbeam. I had planned to do about thirty minutes with laughs. In the end, I did thirteen without and considered myself very lucky to be alive as I walked back off the stage, once more to the sound of my own footsteps. At the bar, at the back of the hall, my police friends were very complimentary and were trying hard to stop me slashing my wrists. 'No, Malcolm, they were laughing out here,' they said. 'There are funny acoustics on that stage, honest.'

'Bloody shame they didn't get any laughs either then.' I said, before ordering another large one!

I was being driven home, very kindly, by Jeremy Canny, a location production manager, who had originally introduced me to the two reprobates that were trying so hard to convince me I had done a really good job. I have never found so much solace and comfort in an after-show drink, before or since.

Cannon Row police station was another place of intrigue, or A8 as it was known within the Metropolitan Police Force. They had a Christmas bash every year but a more sedate affair than Vine Street, that various dignitaries and council members and little old me would be invited too. After the formal event, drinking wine and lager, the inner circle would make for the Superintendent's office and quaff the hard stuff. I would perform minor close-up miracles, which as they were all as drunk as me, if I could still perform under those conditions, looked truly impossible. I would depart saying complete gobbledegook, but I was convinced I was saying thank you for a splendid evening.

If I had not attended those wonderful affairs I would never have met the Chief Inspector who went back to riding a motorbike for the traffic police, which was his first love and from where he had originated. He helped me enormously when again for *Surprise, Surprise* we had an old coach and pair travelling along from Horse Guards Parade to the studios on the South Bank and, bless him, he sent me two of his very finest outriders to help speed them through and hold the traffic for us. Admittedly, it did cause absolute chaos, but with the police not only on our side, but present, we just couldn't go wrong.

During the making of *Scoop*, we did some filming in Fleet Street. We had vintage cars, ancient taxis to create old London. To get the wide shot of just our vehicles, we had hired two police constables to hold the traffic for a few minutes while we filmed merrily away. I had gone to check that all was well in The Crusting Pipe, which was the pub we were due to film in that afternoon, and as I rounded the corner back into Fleet Street, I was met by the stomach churning sight of one of the police officers having an almighty row with a bus inspector. We had chosen a Sunday to perform this character change on the street but even so the flow of public transport must go on and unfortunately, I admit, we had from time to time hindered it a little. I did one of those comic Chaplin walks and simply turned one hundred and eighty degrees and headed back in the direction from which I had come. Well, I mused, there seemed little point in getting a third party involved in such a heated discussion. Afterwards, we had a nice pint or two in the interior of the pub and the policeman decided that, overall, bus inspectors were of a much lower race of mankind, having no sense or ability and that a certain individual should consider himself very lucky he had not been arrested and thrown in a cell after swearing at the policeman. Those were the days!

The two lovable coppers from Vine Street Police Station were truly a mischievous pair. Peter Hall, a location production manager, was for the first time to meet a police officer called John Wall, who was to become a firm mate. He was responsible for the parking outside Her Majesty's Theatre when Peter first took on the task of setting up *Live from Her Majesty's* every Sunday evening. The two rogues had said to Peter that

John Wall's nickname was 'corner of the yard' and everybody called him that. They were all due to meet in a pub, but Peter met John before the other two bandits had arrived and as they shook hands Peter said, 'Hello, Peter Hall. Pleased to meet you.'

John replied, 'Yes, John Wall.'

'Ah,' said Peter. 'Corner of the Yard, eh?'

'Pardon?'

'Sorry, but I was lead to believe that everyone calls you corner of the yard, don't they?'

'No.'

'Oh.'

'Nobody calls me that,' he said, looking a bit offended.

'Ah,' said Peter, blushing.

'Shall we start again?' John suggested.

'Yes, yes, I think we better had.'

At this point the two chums arrived and John Wall needed only to take one look at them to know that both he and Peter had been set up. It broke the ice beautifully and John was top of our list for invitations to studio audience shows and indeed seats to see *Live from Her Majesty's*. Towards the end of our association with him, John, very kindly, invited three of us I think, to a private look around the Black Museum, housed within the confines of Scotland Yard. This was a great honour and a fascinating tour to boot of some of the most grisly, historic and intriguing cases that have come before our criminal courts. Yet again, it was one of the wonderful perks of doing what was mostly a wonderful job.

Our local policeman at Waterloo, who operated out of Kennington Police Station, was a chap by the name of John Street. He did many charity fundraising stunts and always dragged us, or indeed LWT, into them to

194

spice them up and add a bit of showbiz. He was also well-respected within his beat area because there is a wine bar still in existence, I believe, along Lower Marsh near the Old Vic, which is called 'Streets', and was named after him. If you gaze to your right as you come into Waterloo on the train you will see the red writing in huge letters proudly proclaiming the name. John, again, was one of the good guys and we even used the exterior of Kennington Police Station in one of the early episodes of *Dempsey and Makep*eace. Money went into their charity box and I am sure signed photographs were purloined to be sold at charity raffles.

There was one Inspector at East Dulwich Police Station who was also terribly helpful and whenever we met the meeting would be concluded by a drink of Scotch from his desk draw. A pleasantry I am sure that has long gone but he also gave me a wonderful tour of the establishment and a memorable trip around the stables and a look at those beautiful police horses that I believe are still housed there. Life was very straightforward in those days, in that you telephoned the police told them when, where and what time you would be filming, they wrote it down and that was that. Then slowly people apparently could no longer write and it became, 'Can you send me a fax?' which obviously saved them time in not writing it down but now involved more work for you. Then it became, 'Can you email me?' and finally, 'You will have to fill the form in.'

At the time of writing, Westminster Council wanted ten days' notice for filming. No commercial, and certainly not *London's Burning* or *Dempsey and Makepeace* (if they were still being made), could have operated on that time scale. We only had a two-week turn around and commercials normally are given the green light and then need to be made three days later. It forces you down the road of 'cheating' and that is bad for both sides. On a series called *The Hidden City*, which has never seen the light of day here, I wanted four meters bagged for three days outside a disused hotel to park four transit vans. It was a very small crew and set up and all the filming was to be inside. I filled in Westminster City Council's form but due to the fact for a whole day I couldn't get hold of the person I wanted to speak to in the special events office, the form went in a day short of the proper notice time and they turned me down. The hotel was booked, the crew was booked, we had done the technical recce and I was faced with mayhem. So, we fed the meters and swapped the vans round every four hours and it was probably cheaper than paying the standard rate. I had no paper work to do and I think technically I wasn't even breaking the law. But this is the stupid level of behaviour that kind of mad bureaucracy leads you to!

The superintendent from Leman Street Police Station, who helped me on *Dutch Girls*, never wanted anything in writing and gratefully received gifts of beautiful cheeses from my trips to Holland before we got to Rampart Street to film. That was the way it was then and I am still convinced to this day that it was a much more pleasant and easier way to do business. It got so that, especially with the Vine Street boys, we would just meet socially and not for business purposes. These tended to be the most dangerous liaisons, in that, 'Let's meet for a pie and a pint, at lunchtime,' would mean it was best to clear the thought of any work from your mind for the afternoon. You see, those were still the days when pubs closed at the bewitching hour of half past two, but if you knew a policeman whose main haunt was Soho, it stood to reason that he would know a club or two where a little libation could be taken during those dry hours of the afternoon. Underground speakeasies held no fear for these guys. They knew everyone and no admittance fee was ever asked for. I figured out that if you knew where the baddies hung out, then why not trouble them with your presence and let them know you were keeping a watchful eye on them, even if it did get slightly blurred towards the end of the day. How I never ran into Jeffrey Bernard during this period I shall never know. There was one watering hole that springs to mind that was situated, most bizarrely, on the top of an office block in the Haymarket. How? Why? I have no idea but there it was large as life, seemingly patronised mostly by off duty policemen and women. It was in this fine establishment late one night, while performing some wonderful magic trick, that my wallet slipped unnoticed out of my back pocket onto the floor, but was, of course, returned to me the following day in another pub. If you are going to do something quite that stupid, best that you do it surrounded by amused and honest police officers.

Exchanging ties became a bit of fad at one time. A *World of Sport* would be exchanged for a Vine Street, which had a lovely bunch of grapes on it or a rare 'M' Division tie, which was about to be made defunct as an area. I think I left this one in France on one of the *Wish Me Luck* trips, an oversight, which greatly annoyed me. Also in my collection is a River Police tie, which has a water boatman insect on the cloth with one red and one green eye, for port and starboard. I was privileged to be invited twice for a trip on the Thames, in the commissioner's barge, both times (I believe) instigated by my superintendent colleague from Cannon Row. On these occasions, I can honestly say that I always remembered the trip downstream very clearly to the

Thames Barrier where we turned around and came back. However, unfortunately, due to alcohol having been taken, the trip back upstream has always been a complete mystery to me! They were happy days and as a result the River Police were always willing to cooperate whenever my filming took me anywhere along that very under used stretch of water.

Brian Kelly and dear Peter McKay, another location production manager, were also a bit prone to this habit. The night they both wore their 'drug squad' ties, in tandem as it were, in a very posh hotel nearly got them both into very big trouble. I think the story goes that the real drug squad were operating an undercover operation and our two heroes, blissfully unaware of this, were filming in the premises where ties had to be worn. So, they strolled in with all ties blazing, as it were. Before lots of lights were punched out and heads banged, fearing that people's cover had been blown, the ties were removed at speed. It had been a nasty and potentially hazardous moment on all sides and, not surprisingly, I don't think that the ties with the magnificent syringe motif ever saw the light of day again.

There was a document issued by the police, which they would feel obliged to hand to you almost every time you met one to talk about filming, simply called form 833 – 'Filming in Streets'. When this form was first printed, I have no idea at all, but it was probably written by one of Sir John Peel's little helpers. The first line immediately ruled out the possibility of anyone making a police series because the wording was as follows:

(1) Nothing in the nature of a staged crime or street disturbance will be permitted.

The likes of *The Sweeney*, *Dempsey and Makepeace* and *The Bill* were already on dangerous ground and as for the *Bond* films, ah, well, they had money, didn't they? However, point four sort of gave them a get out clause because it said:

> (4) The Commissioner of Police has no power to authorise the use of streets for the purpose of filming and does not issue permits purporting to do so...

In which case, you may well ask, who did authorise it? And if they didn't, and no one else did, how come they could stop you? It was a confusing document but there were only five points on one piece of A4 writing paper and by the time you were on your second pint with whichever police officer you happened to be talking to, it all seemed a bit academic anyway. The Codes of Practice people in the industry work to now are, shall we say, somewhat lengthier, but again I am not too sure if you broke them who would enforce the law because they are not law in the first place? The answer is that I am uncertain because the days of having pints with police officers faded some time ago. It is not even clear if even the austere body of Film London would have an answer!

Back in my sound department days, we quite often would spend a heart-warming Sunday morning covering and transmitting a live church service. Everyone in the congregation would be very excited at the event being staged in their premises and the vicar would always be pleased at the phenomenal turnout the presence of the cameras would cause. On one wonderful occasion (and this is the difference between professionals and amateurs), the radio microphone wearing vicar, after distributing the red wine for the 'blood of Christ' disappeared behind the curtains with the props. His nerves having obviously momentarily got the better of him, he proceeded with some gusto and loud slurping noises to finish the remnants of the bottle! Unfortunately, the microphone was still faded up and the whole 'out of vision' tableau was blasted over the huge loudspeakers we had rigged up for the public-address system. Cue collapse of congregation and many a stout party and re-emergence of slightly contented but bemused vicar at all the happy smiling faces now looking at him.

LWT made a strange science fiction drama-cum comedy series called *Don Quick*, which starred Ian Hendry and Ronald Lacey. Early on, it had been the undoing of Bryan Bagge, giving him a nervous breakdown, because of the scale of a whole jungle set and delivery dates not being met. One episode featured a futuristic planet where all the women were topless and a young lady called Madeline Smith made her first voluptuous appearance onto the small screen. They don't write them like that anymore and they certainly don't show them!

In another episode, a giant dog was supposed to pee against our heroes' spacecraft. Trying to get the animal to perform against the model took up most of a morning's work. It was quite a neat gag because sat in the driving seats of the lunar module unaware of what had caused volumes of water to cascade onto the windscreen, our double act, simply turned on the wipers. I still have a vision of our special effects man David Gurdon, perched on a ladder, with a fishing rod like device attached by thread to a model spacecraft lifting the miniature off the ground in synch with blasts of smoke emitting from the engines. Eat your heart out George Lucas, these guys were pioneers!

Chapter Twelve

London's Burning

Feet! I forgot to mention my feet when I mentioned *Telethon '90*, presented by Frank Bough and Judith Chalmers in the May of that year. I stood on my feet for forty-eight hours and it got to the point where I didn't dare sit down because I knew it was quite likely I wouldn't get up again. When my wife picked me up at the railway station at Farnborough she could not believe the terrible way I was walking and it took my feet, and myself, a few days to recover from that little episode. Both the presenters had Winnebago's parked within the huge complex of the Arena so that they could relax and put their feet up when we were off the air for a few minutes. At one of the early production meetings someone, very unkindly I thought, when asked how would Frank find the trailer, had replied, 'We'll just leave a little trail of white powder from the set to the vehicle. He'll find it.' This was not long after the revelations of his excursions into the darker side of society had emerged. Michael Aspel was presenting what was seen nationally and from time to time there would be an opt out to the various regions around the country, much like the national and local news is seen today. It was a truly huge undertaking, with five-hundred telephonists taking pledges from the public, let alone all our staff. Seven cameras were covering the action and a lady called Patricia Mordecai directed the show, having on many occasions directed *World of Sport*.

Having just achieved a year without smoking a cigar, I was musing on cigar smokers I had known and Fred Dinage sprang to mind. Although in those days he was best known for presenting the children's programme, *How,* Fred was also the poor man who took over from Dickie Davies on *World of Sport* on the odd occasion Dickie went on holiday, or was linking a big special from an outside broadcast somewhere. I was present the very first time Fred did this. Although he looked as cool as a cucumber on the screen, something told me that on the inside he was probably a bag of nerves. It was no mean feat to front five hours of live television once a week and at the first available longish break Fred asked the floor manager if he could take his earpiece out for five minutes and have a smoke. The floor manager agreed and Fred came over and joined our humble sound table, lit up a Hamlet cigar and breathed out a heavy sigh of relief.

'How Dickie does that week after week, I really don't know, I take my hat off to him,' he said.

'Years of practice and self-denial, I guess,' I replied. Fred chuckled and our paths crossed quite a few times after that, because he did become the regular stand-in and a most pleasant and charming chap he is, with a superb sense of humour.

By now, I had slipped very gently into a schedule of doing the game show, *You Bet!* with the hilarious but deep thinking Matthew Kelly, during the summer months at Shepperton Studios, and the drama, *London's Burning,* during the winter in Bermondsey. One day, a very pleasant man from a crane company wandered into my office at Shepperton. These cranes are known in the trade as aerial platforms or cherry pickers and are the sort of thing your local council mends street lights with or are used for tree maintenance, anything really that needs a stable little area and not just a pair of step ladders. They are often used on outside broadcasts, especially at horse racing, to get that high wide shot of

203

the animals thundering along the course. Specialist ones are used for filming but they also get used to put lamps on usually for night shoots to represent the moon. Whatever company he was from, he explained that they had slipped a little in the media field lately and as the south-east representative he had decided to try and pick up a few extra customers by punting for business round the film studios. I asked him if business had picked up at all. 'Yes, it's not bad really. Last week we did four weddings and a funeral.' He thanked me for my time and interest, placed a catalogue on my desk and left. Simon Wallace, who I was sharing the responsibility of the *You Bet!* series with, wandered in and enquired as to who the gentleman caller had been.

'He's from that crane company but said last week they did four weddings and a funeral. I can see maybe having one at a wedding for a wide shot of the group, but what the hell would you want a cherry picker at a funeral for?' I gazed at Simon with a puzzled look.

'Search me,' came his reply, 'That is really very weird. Very weird indeed.'

Had we taken the trouble to wander around the back lot a of Shepperton a little more, we might well have noticed the various car parking spaces reserved for people who were working on a production called *Four Weddings and a Funeral.* It was not until about three months later when the film was released in the cinema that a huge penny the size of the Dome dropped loudly and for many miles inside my head.

Russell Swift is one of those manic stunt drivers that Britain seems so good at producing. He was the man who parked the cars sideways in the advert for, I suppose some brand of car, but as with all those memorable adverts, sometimes the advert is more remembered than the product it is promoting. We had designed a *You Bet!* stunt at Bruntingthorpe Airfield in Leicestershire that relied on a driver getting through a maze of cars in a certain amount of time. The cars were laid out just like a complicated maze and shifting the cars around and causing new dead ends to appear could alter the pattern of it. I think the challenge was he had to make it from one side to the other. We then altered the pattern and he had to go back again. Matthew Kelly would be in the passenger seat, being very frightened, as Russell attempted his speed trial, while the producer, Lynda Beadle, and I were also being very frightened hoping that Russell wouldn't hit any of the parked cars thus causing a massive insurance claim! Fortunately, he didn't and completed the task with a display of sheer skill and bravado. He often appeared at car or bike race meetings and other such track events and would give a display of precision driving before the race. I gave him a pair of joke glasses that look as though you have bad eyesight because of the thickness of the pretend lenses. Simon Wallace and I had tried to fool Sue McMahon, the director, and Lynda when they were first introduced to him that he had terribly bad eyesight, but they tumbled our little gag immediately and just carried on talking to him as normal, which just rubbed salt in our wounds. Some you win and some you lose!

I saw a very touching sight one-day in an idle moment while gazing out of my office window at Shepperton Studios, during the making of *You Bet*! The Muppets were making *A Muppet Christmas Carol* at the studio at the time and along the road below me walked a young lady carrying Kermit the Frog. What made it so touching was the way she was carrying him. Not like any old puppet, but cradled in her arms like a baby. No rough ride in an old suitcase for him. I quite expected the credits to say, 'Assistant to Mr Kermit the Frog'!

The other wonderful moment I witnessed was, as I walked down one of the corridors by the stage that housed the Dickensian street, someone opening a big storage cupboard. Inside were loads of Muppets all hanging up. From Animal to Ralph and Miss Piggy to Fozzie Bear. I guess if you work with them every day, it's no big deal. But having often wondered what the cupboard contained, it was a truly smile-making sight to see so many faces staring back at you!

Alf Joint was also a stunt man, but not just a car stunt man. Sword fighting, action fights, horse riding stunts, motor bikes, you name it and Alf had done it all at some point in his long and illustrious career. He became the main stunt arranger on *London's Burning*. He knew every trick in the book, every camera angle that a director should use and how to arrange murder and mayhem at the drop of a hat with economy and safety. There was nothing better I liked than to sit and chat to him about his past experiences. I told him that one day he should write an autobiography because he had so much to tell. One thing I must jot down before I forget is that when he walked into a bar he would order not a large Brandy, not a Scotch on the rocks, not even a Vodka Martini, shaken not stirred, but a simple humble Dubonnet and lemonade. It never ceased to crack me up, that such a purveyor of all things dangerous and dastardly had as his favourite drink a Dubonnet and lemonade. He had starred in the very early Milk Tray adverts where the man, all dressed in black, jumps off cliffs and swims under boats to secretly deliver his gift of chocolates. Strangely enough, one of the directors to work on *London's Burning* was Gerry Poulson, who had been the director of one of those adverts made in Malta. Alf had to jump off a cliff into the sea and badly injured his back in the attempt. He was in *Where Eagles*

Dare made in 1969, doubling a lot of the time for Richard Burton. Many of the shots of the back of Burton's head are in fact of Alf and this was probably where he met the legendary Hollywood stuntman, Yakima Canutt. He invented almost every horse trick in the book. He had been a stunt man way back working on the likes of *Stagecoach*, *Ben Hur*, *El Cid* and *Gone with The Wind*, doubling Clarke Gable riding through the Atlanta fire. These were just a fraction of his film credits and Alf spoke about *Yakima* as other people speak of God! I feel very privileged to have known Alf, because he was the fount of all knowledge about stunts and had some wacky tales of showbiz that would make your hair curl. Just a short while after writing these lines, I learned that Alf had died at the age of 78, taking with him to the grave all those stories and tales he could have told but never did.

Jacob Street Studios was the initial home for *London's Burning*, when I clambered on board to help make series four. The studios are no longer in existence and are now a complex of luxury flats that must have rocketed in value since the introduction of the Jubilee Line to deepest Southwark. A man called Steve Giudici ran the complex and, contrary to what you might think, had a broad Scottish accent and not the Italian one people frequently expected. The studios nestled quietly in the back streets of Bermondsey, almost in the shade of Tower Bridge and conveniently behind Dockhead Fire Station, which was used for all the exteriors and appliance bay sequences in the series. Well, that was until the storyline called for them to move stations. Jacob Street was the home of was the home of Blue Watch for over ten years. There was a bar and a canteen run by a mad Irish man called Gerry and his even madder wife Bridget. A frequent visitor to the canteen was the actor Paul Eddington, who lived in one of the expensive warehouse conversions somewhere along Mill Street, which ran by the side of the studios. As the years rolled by, he became very ill-looking and very stooped and it came as no surprise to eventually learn of his death. Yet again, I feel obliged to ask, if there is such a thing as a God, why take away such a talent at what these days is the relatively young age of sixty-eight years old? Perhaps God is one of those fat cats who does not recognise even the existence of Equity the actors' union. Now that would perhaps begin to make some small secular sense of his strange and peculiar ways!

Jacob Street Studios benefited from having what became known as 'The Burn Stage'. This, in effect, was a large brick built interior space, with good ventilation, where sets could be built and then, in a very controlled way, set fire to. The whole programme was a huge team effort. The sets were designed by Colin Monk and his team, constructed and built by John Carman and his team and set fire to and destroyed by Tom Harris and his team. Meanwhile, a team of actors acted in them, while a team of stunt men performed in them and a film crew, who after four years of learning and working together had also become a team, filmed the whole thing. And last, but not least, there were a team of fire fighters led by Brian Clark, who carefully watched over the proceedings, put out the flames and made sure everyone was safe. Brian, who was known as Nobby, like an awful lot of other Brian Clark's, had one of the most difficult jobs on the team. By profession, he was a uniformed fire fighter in the press office of the London Fire Brigade and was given the job of being the advisor on *London's Burning* by Deputy Chief Officer, Gerry Clarkson. It is a fine line to tread between drama and real life and as the directors kept saying, 'Nobby, we're not making a bloody documentary, love, we're making a fictional drama.' But Nobby strove manfully to keep it as close to the truth as he possibly could, otherwise there was a danger, if he wasn't careful, of the fire brigade being portrayed in a bad light and their credibility flying out of the window. He had to constantly find the middle ground between reality and drama. A classic example is that before entering a house or factory full of smoke a fire crew always but always put on breathing apparatus (BA). This is the way they are trained, in order that their lives are not put at a higher risk than they already are. Any director worth his salt could not possibly wait to watch the slow process of them putting on their BA as they always felt the pace slowed down too much. Nearly all to a man wanted the fire fighters to grab a hose and rush in to the inferno almost before the appliance (fire engine) had come to a halt. Paul Knight wanted the programme to have a documentary feel, but it was, when all said and done, a drama. Even so, Nobby always won that battle. It was a battle he fought time and time again as new directors joined and had to be taught the ways of the fire service.

The crew always greeted new directors with glee. Practical jokes were the main stay of the *Burning* team and one of the favourites they would play on a new boy was at 'watch change'. This was when a bell was rung in the morning and then again in the evening in the Fire Station signifying a new 'watch' coming on duty. A dreadful pun on the word but the first time the bell sounded in the appliance bay in front of a rookie director everyone would yell out, 'Watch change' and start taking off their wrist watches and exchanging them. Little things, maybe, but it always broke the ice

209

and caused more than a titter amongst the assembled throng.

Night shoots on *London's Burning* had their moments. We were filming one episode in Thamesmead on a huge site of waste ground. The script was one which incorporated the story of an exciting saga of boy racers and policemen on motorbikes getting stuck in quicksand like mud. Everything was going well and a cherry picker was just rising into position with a lamp, when there was a huge crash and the lamp fell to the ground from a good thirty feet or so up in the air. Minutes before the cherry picker had contained an electrician but he had got out after setting the lamp at the right angle and the lamp had ascended on its own. My assistant at the time, a lady who rejoiced in the name of Amber Valentine, had last seen the cherry picker containing both the lamp and the said electrician 'Jamie' and hearing the dreadful crash and fearing the worst, had rushed immediately off into the gloom to find the paramedics. She found them all right, sat in their mini ambulance with the door open galloping along shouting, 'Jamie' at the top of her voice she failed to see the door, which she ran into at full pelt and bounced back onto the floor. Having established the only damage had been to the lamp, luckily nobody being in close-proximity underneath it, they treated Amber for a bad bit of bruising and concussion. I sent her home early.

With the crew departed after the end of filming and with only myself, the mobile toilets, their operator, Mo, and one generator and its driver, Ken Sheppard, left behind, I prepared to depart. I could see Mo having a bit of bother on the loose sand, so foolishly I hovered just to make sure he got out all right. He didn't. He got horribly stuck and Ken, having stood smoking a Benson and Hedges watching this performance, stepped into the breach and come to the rescue. He put a stout chain around the generators rear end and the front of Mo's wagon and then he was off. His plan was to gather a lot of speed, go in a big circle and thus keep going until he was back on the harder track. As Mo hanging on for dear life passed me, flying along in the wake of the generator, he leaned out of the window and yelled, 'Where is he taking me, Malcolm?' I yelled back, 'Home Mo, he's taking you home.' Ken drove in a huge arc and ploughed the generator at amazing speed into the same soft welcoming sand.

The sun seemed to come up very slowly that morning! Ken and I shared a cigarette as we both looked at the back wheels of the generator well dug into the sand and grinned at Mo fast asleep in his marooned cab. There were some huge earth moving machines just a couple of minutes down the track from where we had been filming and I drove down there in my trusty Volvo estate a couple of times after sun up hoping for signs of life, but none was forthcoming. Finally, at about eight o'clock the workers arrived, listened to my plea for help and came along with a gigantic yellow machine and pulled, what I had always considered to be the enormous generator, out of the mire like some child's dinky toy. They rescued Mo too. It was a beautiful drive back. There is something pleasing about going completely against the rush hour traffic, knowing you were heading for a warm bath and a very snug bed.

That night shoot on *London's Burning* in Thamesmead took me back to Hemel Hempstead, to the time when I was a lad living in the now infamous area, thanks to the petrol depot explosion, called Leverstock Green. It must have been 1967 and rumours of a film being made not far away had circulated. One night,

211

being driven in the car by my father, the rumour was confirmed, when we saw in the distance bright lights burning brightly on cherry pickers high in the night sky. The film was *The Dirty Dozen* and it fired my imagination of late nights, exciting sequences and boyhood adventures beyond my wildest dreams. The reality of freezing your nuts off all evening and then looking in despair at a generator and a mobile toilet stuck in the mud was not what I expected!

Sometimes on *London's Burning* there would come an occasion when you really did think, 'where the hell am I going to find that location?' A script landed on my desk that had a whole episode set in the fog. The theme being hammered home over a few episodes was that the materials used in your car are incredibly dangerous and no manufacturer would consider using them in your living room mainly because the law would not allow them to. So why do we tolerate these dangerous substances in the car that we would never allow into our homes? In the story, an unsuspecting commercial traveller is involved in a crash in the fog on a motorway but is doomed by the electronics of a central locking system failing him and the amazingly inflammable and highly toxic nature of the interior of the vehicle. I think it was one of Nobby's pet hobbyhorses and Station Officer Nick Georgiadis in the series, played by Andrew Kazamia, gives a dramatic talk at a dinner about the subject. What stopped me dead in my tracks was after the initial crash I turned the page and read:

Scene Twenty-Two. Exterior Motorway. Night.

The road now looks like the road to Basra (a reference to the first Gulf War). There are some fifteen lorries and twenty-two cars on fire.

And that is where my little brain kicked in and whispered very gently in my head, 'Where?' I must have had more than the usual one week's notice about this one because it was indeed, as I suspected, absolutely hell on earth to find. I needed a motorway I could crash cars on and set light to, which preferably had to be in a bit of a dip so the special effects 'fog' wouldn't get blown away. The sequence was most of the last part of the episode so I would need it for some three nights. I finally stumbled upon the A3 Petersfield by-pass before it was fully open. Tarmac Construction had built one section of it between two roundabouts and was waiting for the second section to be completed before opening the entire stretch. After a lot of meetings, and reassurance from us that after the event no one would ever know we had been there, they agreed that they would help as much as they could. A donation would be given to charity, which is often the way with big companies, because to them the figure that I usually offer as a location fee amounts in their eyes simply as so much chicken feed.

We descended on the location for three nights of intense filming. The preparation took about three days before and the tidy up some three days after. It was a huge unit that invaded the by-pass, with well over two hundred people to park, feed and water. For once in my life, I did have ample parking space because I used the whole of the rest of the dual carriageway that we were not using for filming to park all the vehicles on. Of course, even that didn't suit many people because if you arrived late you had to park your car right at the end of a very, very long line. We had two mobile kitchens, three dining buses and two mobile toilets. In fact, everything that we normally had one of there was on this occasion at least another one added – if not two!

While one unit shot the main body of the action, another unit went off further up the motorway and under the guidance of Alf, shot various sequences of cars crashing into one another. This would be knitted together in the edit and give the effect of a multi car pile-up. All of which, as I said earlier, was supposed to take place in the fog. For a fortnight, we carried with us huge industrial machines wherever we went that exhaled disgusting, thick blue, noxious fog that filled the streets and caused people to slow down in cars and shut windows in houses. I had to write resident letters before and after apologising for the dreadful pong but hoped that when they watched the episode transmitted they would understand that we were trying to send a message of great importance to the seemingly uncaring car manufacturers.

Filming at night is a curious business because, obviously, everyone wants to sleep in the day and this can confuse hotels enormously. We were all billeted at a local hotel just outside Portsmouth, which wasn't too far away, and the hotel adapted to our strange ways brilliantly. They opened the bar at seven thirty in the morning when we came in from work, so that we could have a couple of jars to unwind. The expression on the other guests' faces as they appeared for their breakfasts and were greeted by the sight of grown men and women quaffing ale at such an extraordinarily early hour had to be seen to be believed. They made sure our rooms were not 'cleaned' during the day and generally did everything they could to make our stay as pleasant as possible given the bizarre circumstances of our residence.

All the cars that we set fire to and the lorries had to be 'plated', which meant a steel sheet being put underneath the vehicle to catch any burning material so

214

that the heat would not cause any damage to the road surface. This sheet was then covered with sand as an extra precaution. When we cleared up and took everything away to my huge relief the road surface was totally unaffected by what had looked like a massive blaze on camera. But what did cause some damage, and we had not thought of it, was the residue oil from two special effects flame bars called 'Dante's' (derived from *Dante's Inferno* I presume.) These long poles give an effect of huge fireballs, but as soon as someone yells 'Cut' they just turn them off and wait for the next cry of 'Turnover' to start them up again. The residue oil that had not been burnt had simply seeped into the road surface and a lovely bill of something like twenty five thousand pounds had to be paid for remedial repair work. Overall, Tarmac Construction took it quite well and philosophically – for which I was relieved! It was at this event that my assistant, Casper Mill, and I decided that the most dangerous job in the world was being a Dante lighter.

At a viewing of the episode before transmission, attended by a privileged six or seven people, one of the best comments I have ever heard came from a very senior member of the drama department: 'By golly, weren't you lucky with the weather?' Now a few people thought that this comment was a joke but then realised it was absolutely serious. We had gone through hell and back for two weeks to create that image and had obviously fooled this particular member of the audience completely. Job well done, I suppose you could say, but it did worry us that a person in such 'high office' apparently had not a clue about the process of achieving this result that had just been witnessed on the silver screen. You do wonder sometimes if those who rule our lives and destinies should not have more of a better understanding of what goes on beneath them. Mind you, it was the same person who managed to put petrol into the diesel engine of a hire car while visiting the location in France of *Wish Me Luck*, so probably enough said.

As I strolled into Jacob Street Studios one morning there seemed to be more appliances around than normal. I knew they were filming on 'The Burn Stage' for a couple of days, while I was preparing the next episode, and we always had fire cover when we did so, but somehow things didn't look quite right. And indeed, they were not. During the night, the glowing embers that Nobby to this very day swears blind had been doused the night before after a day's filming, somehow had managed to rekindle and very successfully, much to everyone's complete embarrassment, had burnt 'The Burn Stage' down. The problem was compounded by the fact that smoke frequently emanated from that part of the studios and people had learned not to take any notice of it. So, the fire fighters in Dockhead, gazing from their back yard, just assumed we had started filming early that morning. Even the call of, 'The 'Burn Stage' is on fire!' was probably answered by, 'Go away boys and pull the other one. We haven't had breakfast yet.' Paul Knight had to appear on television and explain the occurrence and for many weeks afterwards trying to persuade people that their property would be safe in our hands became very difficult. Retorts from the good burghers of Bermondsey like, 'Piss off, aren't you the tits that burnt down your own studios? What makes you fink I should let you film in my ware'ouse, you're 'avin' a right laugh, ain't you?' were pretty common. Anyway, from that day on a security man was paid another eight-hour shift to stay at any location or at the studios after we had spent a day filming fire to make sure that while everybody's backs were turned it did not flare up again.

Nobby, overall, was a happy soul but underneath was a very complicated character. He unwittingly involved me in a mental struggle that would not allow my brain to switch off. We were happily doing a technical recce before breaking for two weeks and we had reached the best part of the day – lunch! To drive around in a minibus, which was always disappointingly hard and cramped for ten hours, looking at all the places you are going to film at is not a pleasant pastime. Lunch on this occasion was also to be one of the locations, a Chinese restaurant. They were kind enough to have said we could film a simulated fire there and I felt it the least I could do was to also book eighteen of my closest friends in for a meal and combine business with pleasure. We had often used the place for lunch but never for a location. Just as the director had almost finished his little chat on what would happen where and when, and our mouths were beginning to salivate at the smells coming from the kitchen, I became aware that voices were being raised out of my eye line. It transpired that Nobby was remonstrating with the owner that his only emergency exit in the building was partially blocked by boxes and that if a fire broke out, a bit like the storyline, we would all be in danger of not being able to get out. The manager thought we had come in peace, and so did I, but to suddenly find himself attacked by the weight of the brigade unsettled him somewhat to say the least. He at first thought Nobby was from the council and couldn't believe that he was with us. I seem to remember a huge row between myself and Nobby outside the premises with him saying, 'Would you like to see twenty of your friends killed because of a load of boxes blocking their only way out of the building?' I think I probably replied that I didn't give a damn and how dare he jeopardise one of my locations. He then stormed off, missing the meal, and getting a taxi back to the studios.

Later that evening, Nobby appeared in the bar and we had another row about the day's events. For those supposed restful two weeks at home I did not know if I had a location or not; I could not get the problem out of my head and so for me the break was ruined. I telephoned the restaurant every day except Christmas Day and Boxing Day but the problem remained and the man I had spoken to said he could not now give the go ahead until he had relayed the whole story to his business partner and sought his advice. This meeting took forever to happen, until finally some three days after we returned from leave, I called again and he said it was all right and the whole matter had been forgotten and we could film there.

Nobby had been at the King's Cross fire, whereas the worst scene I have ever witnessed was my puppy being run over by a double decker bus, when I was about eight-years-old. And therein probably lies the difference in our outlooks on life. Nobby knows the worst that can happen, because he has seen it. I tend to think, like most of us I suspect, 'Yes but not to me mate.' We might just be wrong in that thought process.

There was another major incident that caused Nobby to flare up. The result was that he came dressed in his full fire brigade uniform the next day. I think it was Ray Holt who couldn't resist asking him why he was all dressed up. Nobby looked Ray in the eyes and said very seriously and very slowly, 'To remind people of where I come from.' I looked at Nobby quizzically as I passed by on the stairs and said, 'What Essex?' It broke the ice and the following day he was back in casuals.

Nobby seemed to be employed almost all the year round. He worked on storylines when we were not filming and would often approach prospective locations on our behalf. This used to upset Kevin Holden, with whom I shared almost six years of that series as the other location manager, because he hated someone approaching a possible source on our behalf. I must say it never bothered me and how else was the script department supposed to get ahead if they didn't know that what they had written was a possible option? One example was the Thames Barrier, which Nobby had approached, and a whole episode was written around it. At least in those days what was on the page was researched more often than not. A great guy called Gerry Burnan was my main contact at the Barrier. Now if you have not ever before experienced the invasion of a film unit it can be pretty intrusive. He withstood the impact terribly well and did comment at one point, 'For such a large unit, you are very tidy in your habits.' And that is all a location manager ever wants to know. I bought him a pencil sketch of the barrier as a thank you present after the shoot that I found in an art shop in Blackheath. He responded by giving myself and my family a private tour of the barrier. We viewed both above and below where we had filmed, and my wife found the whole thing absolutely fascinating. Alas, it bored my two girls a little bit because they were not quite old enough to appreciate the finer side of flood prevention in London. If I remember rightly, at that time, the barrier had only been raised something like sixteen times 'in anger', as Gerry put it. I am sure it is a lot more than that now because of our dear friend global warming. Also, security was really tight because of the fear of the IRA attacking the place. Anyway, I suppose the expense of those measures is now justified with the word 'terrorist' so frequently on the lips of every politician in the capital.

The other river 'shout' involved the Woolwich Ferry. The storyline was of a massive explosion on board and consequential fire, caused by two idiots taking a van full of explosive type contents across the river. This involved the brigade fire ship, The Phoenix, and the Harbour Masters launch from The Port of London Authority, which was loaned to us for one day free of charge because of the good publicity we were generating. The two days were very successful, except, I found out later, we nearly caused a projectionist from the local cinema to have a heart attack. He had stepped out from his room to have a cigarette on the fire escape and gaze down at the river, just at the vital moment when a huge bang erupted from the ferry, followed by a massive ball of flame and a man hurtled through the air into the water. Timing, it's all to do with timing!

Chapter Thirteen

London's Still Burning

The cast of *London's Burning* were a truly great bunch to work with and I think enjoyed their time together as much as we did. Richard Walsh, who played 'Sicknote', had a very dry sense of humour and liked red wine nearly as much as I did. Seated in the bar, we would often launch into impromptu clips from old *Hancock* episodes and I was delighted to find someone else who could quote them verbatim, after so many years thinking I was the only idiot who knew them off by heart. The late Jimmy Hazeldine, who played 'Bayleaf', got his chance to direct some of the episodes and was along with Richard, a very good mimic of most of the crew. Jimmy did an extremely funny little piece to camera for the end of series party one year, where a whole load of outtakes and clips were shown, describing how he got the job of director and how for the next series he would probably go on to write, direct and produce. Sam Beckinsale, who played Kate Stevens, was an absolute poppet and I was only wondering the other day as to where she is now. Ross Boatman, who played Kevin Medhurst, finally left the series to go and play poker as a serious professional. Having seen him back on the box recently, I wondered if he was doing it for a break or whether he had finally cashed his last lot of chips in? Knowing Ross, I suspect he still has a few in his back pocket. Sean Blowers, Glen Murphy and Stuart MacKenzie, who played 'Recall', were quite a handful for any director to call to order but with the fun went consummate professionalism of the highest quality. I personally think the acting, the special effects, the make-up, the

221

stunts, the construction, the design, the photography, the sound and even dare I say the locations, all made up a series that I was very proud to be associated with. It should have won a BAFTA many times over. It really did deserve it.

Colin Monk, the designer, had a brain as sharp as a tack. Over the years when finding locations, I would sometimes turn sites down because I knew it would be too much work for the art department – eventually you learn what they can do in the time allotted and probably most importantly what they could afford. We were looking at a house for one episode and I thought that maybe, just maybe Colin could work his magic on it and turn it into the property as described in the script. I wasn't dead sure but I had a pretty good feeling I was on safe ground. Colin slowly paced around the exterior and looked for about ten minutes and then finally turned to me, by now smoking my second cigar since arriving, and said, 'The trouble with you, Treeny, is you know what I can do. Keep looking but if you can't find anything better we will go with this one.' And I couldn't, so we did.

Anita Bronson wrote many of the early scripts and went on to co-produce *The Knock* with Paul Knight. Episode five of series four, which was one of the many that Anita penned, was about a coach crash containing a party of young children. We filmed the sequence at the test track at Chertsey and John Reardon, the director, decided that my two daughters, Laura and Hannah, would be very suitable as two of the victims. They had two very cold days filming but I think they enjoyed all the attention and wandering around in fake blood-soaked clothing for the period. The coach was rigged with a huge kick down pipe that would launch it off down an embankment and stuntman Gabe Cronnelly

222

drove the vehicle, (obviously devoid of children) and pulled the lever that operated the pipe. There was a big debate afterwards between Tom Harris from the special effects department and Gabe as to whether or not he had pulled the lever at the right moment. There was a big sign on the road that said, 'Pull the lever NOW Gabe.' The coach kicked and launched down the embankment but the rear of it crashed into the test track's 'new' shed. It also took out a telegraph pole that was the feed of a phone to the test track's control tower. Strangely, the main man in control was also a Brian Clarke and therefore called 'Nobby'. This led to a bit of confusion until we called one 'Nobby Burning' and the other 'Nobby Track' for the duration. Anyway, at this point 'Nobby Track' called me on the walkie talkie and asked me to phone the main building to let them know what had happened, 'As obviously, if you look at the wire, you will see why I can't.' Amazingly, the test track people were all very philosophical about the whole incident and just considered it 'bad luck' and 'one of those things', which was very understanding of them.

Late on the first day we were doing travelling shots of the coach from inside, the coach lurching from one side of the road to the other to simulate the driver being distracted by the kids and having momentarily lost control. The track had a one-way system in operation and no other traffic on it, so it was a very safe environment until one of the dining buses was released for the afternoon. How he failed to see all the arrows pointing one way I don't know, but he was simply retracing his route to where he had come in that morning. I realised this as I saw him pull away, the wrong way. I tried to contact the coach on the walkie talkie but got no reply and realised they must be filming and the normal thing to do was to turn your radio off, in order that other people talking to one another didn't muck up the sound on the 'take'. I was sat in my car and took off at speed because there was a short cut across the track on a minor road system and I figured that I might be able to head him off at the pass, as they used to say in the old movies. The road had been used for the exit for Batman's cave in the film of *Batman* and I drove down that stretch of road as fast as he and Robin probably had when leaving the Bat cave to dash off and fight crime! Just in time I entered onto the track pulled the bus over to one side and our hero coach drove past us, my nightmare vision of a real accident involving a head-on collision thankfully avoided. 'Nobby Track' complimented me on my swift action and I think most of the rest of the crew were blissfully unaware that anything untoward had happened. The bus swiftly did a three-point turn and went off in the right direction. And in case you are confused as to how the coach drove and went down the embankment, we had two identical coaches. The company logo on the side was labelled 'Brasset's Coaches', as a small homage to Jenny Brassett, the production coordinator. And I can still remember Colin Monk being really miffed that the sign writers had left one of the 't's out of the name 'Brassett'.

Thinking at the end of that little bout of filming it was all over, it wasn't. About two days later word came down that they wanted to do more rescue shots of kids being got out of the coach. Could I find somewhere with a similar grassy embankment as at Chertsey, but they didn't want to go all the way back there, where we could just lie the coach down and do some pick-ups for a day? They gave me two days to find it. Luckily, Southwark Council allowed us to use one of their parks and within forty-eight hours the thing was set up and sorted.

The Council were not so easy when we had an episode where a horse got stuck in a pond and the brigade had to come to its rescue. We picked Burgess Park as our location not far from the Old Kent Road. Everything seemed to be going well in that, yes, we were given permission to film there; yes, we could dig a hole to make our pond and fill it, as this was November, with warm water as we didn't want the animal getting cold. It also had to be constructed with a firm footing underneath for the animal and the actors. And yes, we could put two cardboard cut-outs of houseboats in the distance to make it look like it was near a canal. But no, we couldn't use a horse as there was a bylaw not allowing performing animals in the park. 'I can assure you it won't be performing,' I pleaded. But this didn't sway them. I would have to meet the committee and put my case and see if I could convince them to allow me to film the horse in their park.

I must admit to being rather nervous in front of the assembled group in Southwark Town Hall and I started off rather badly. 'Well, the story is that a group of gypsies has....'

'Travellers, you must call them travellers!' said the chairperson, a bit aggressively.

'Sorry, sorry, er a group of travellers are situated by a pond. They notice that one of their horses has broken free from its tethered position and wandered off and is starting to sink in sort of quicksand.'

'Quicksand, we don't get quicksand in Southwark!'

'No, well, er, soft mud really.' I paused. 'So, one of, the gypsies, er, sorry, er , sorry traveller's dashes in to pull it out and he gets into difficulties as well.' I went on to explain that there were to be two identical horses,

225

so that they could be swapped at regular intervals to prevent them getting tired or cold. They would have a heated tent to rest in and the water would also be heated. In fact, with the additional factor of a vet standing by, they would be better looked after than us humans! Two identical coaches had been bad enough to track down, but two identical horses? I remember at the time thinking how I was sometimes very pleased that I had not grown up to be a prop buyer like Will Hinton because he was often given seemingly insurmountable problems to solve. Thankfully, after what I thought was a pretty poor attempt on my part at explaining my position, the committee did give the go ahead.

We poured gallons and gallons of water into the pond and it passed through some sort of heating device and as predicted the day turned out to be bitterly cold. A man casually wandered up to me as we filmed and explained that he was from the council. Oh, here we go I thought they've changed their minds. 'Oh, no, no I'm from the library.' He explained that the library on the corner of the road had called him during the morning because they had noticed the boilers getting rather heated. It seemed the pressure had dropped because of our tapping the water off first and if it continued like that, and the boilers couldn't be cooled, then they were quite likely to explode and demolish the library!

'And, of course, the explosion and resulting fire might well disrupt your filming somewhat.'

A master of understatement! As I have said before, every day was different, you just never knew what or indeed who would be round the corner. Nobby, as often was the case, came to the rescue. He went off with the man and then came back and we decreased our supply to allow the libraries to build back up again and cool off the offending boilers. Again, the thought of the headline

226

'Location Manager destroys local library' gave me a few sleepless nights.

One of the places that you should really try and avoid with a film camera is Soho in the heart of London. Unfortunately, one of the storylines in *London's Burning* developed around that area and I was dispatched with a small second unit to film the scenes. I'd done a lot of groundwork for the shoot and warned the strip joints, bars, clubs and shops that I was coming and all seemed to be going relatively well. We had contained ourselves to a small area of sleazy, dark passages and anyway we had to keep it small because we didn't have the usual lighting kit for large areas to be illuminated. I had offered one of the 'joints' one hundred pounds for a few minutes outside their premises and went in and paid someone only to find myself summoned back into the same establishment some minutes later and asked once more for the money, but this time by a different gentleman and two rather heavy looking sidekicks. My assistant, Christopher Lee, was right by my side. He was a young enthusiastic Welshman with a broad grin, a great sense of humour and parents who had obviously been brought up on a heavy dosage of Hammer horror films. The chap became a bit threatening but I stood my ground and protested that I wasn't a bottomless pit of bungs and that I had already handed the money over. Just at that point where I was thinking 'run or stay and get a good smacking?' the girl behind the entrance counter piped up and said, 'He's tellin' the troof, Johnny. He gave it ta Ben abaat fifteen minutes ago.' I could have proposed to her there and then but did wonder why she had kept her beautiful Essex mouth so tightly shut for quite so long before coming verbally to my assistance. He looked long and hard at her, chewing in that over dramatic way many actors did in old 'B-movies'. He then turned and looked long and hard at me. 'Sounds like you ought to be having a word in Ben's shell like, doesn't it?' I said to him, I thought very bravely, considering I wasn't too sure whether I was about to vomit through sheer terror or not. Without another word, he turned on his heels nodded to his henchmen and disappeared inside the establishment. I whispered a smooth thank you to the girl and Chris and I left too.

Outside I gasped and breathed in the fresh air by the lungful.

'Bloody 'ell, Malc, you were amazing,' said Chris, reaching for his cigarettes with both hands shaking. 'I really thought they were going to turn you over. Bloody 'ell you stood your ground.' He was now beginning to laugh and in his broad Welsh accent he continued, 'and the look on his face when you said, "Ben's shell-like" well it had to be seen to be believed, Malc. Bloody 'ell, bloody 'ell, I've never seen anything like that Malc, never.' I inhaled deeply and thankfully on one of his cigarettes, turned a corner to head back to the crew and walked straight into a rather aggrieved gentleman. 'They tell me you are the one in charge here?' he said.

'Well, yes I am.'

'How much longer are you gonna be in the alley?'

'Well, we shouldn't be too long. Why?'

'My business, you are ruining my business.'

'How?"

'This is the entrance to my club,' he said pointing at a non-descript door, that for some reason I had not noticed on my previous visits. Admittedly, the visits had taken place in daylight so the door may well have been closed and sealed. After all, only a madman with a film crew would venture along these alleys at night. 'You are pointing the cameras straight down the street

228

and at my entrance,' he began to shout. 'No punter is a going to come in my place with a camera in his face, is he?'

His accent sounded Italian to me and it was only the following day, when talking to the bookshop owner on the corner, while waiting to meet the stocky little man again, that I would discover that I had had the pleasure of addressing Maltese Joe.

'Well, I really don't think they will be very long,' I started and thankfully at that point the filming lights went out and a voice yelled, 'Moving on, Scene Twenty-Three everyone, thank you.'

'Ah, well, there we are. All right, sir?'

'No, I am a not happy. I'm not happy at all. My trade has been badly disrupted. Very badly indeed.'

'Well, we are out of your hair now, sir. Thank you. Bye bye.' I suppose still flushed with success at the last encounter, this time Chris and I left at speed and went round the corner out of Maltese Joe's sight.

The lights were set up again, Chris began chatting up a girl in one of the doorways when blow me down out of the interior comes, 'No I'm nota happy. Look this is a very bad, look this is a very, very bad. Now you spoila my trade here.' I felt my shoulders droop and heard myself say quietly, 'Oh no, it can't be,' but it was. There again, large as life, was our 'friend' Maltese Joe.

'Looka, come, come with me I show you.' So off I went back round the corner into the door, down the stairs into a huge Tardis-like interior and bar area. Scantily clad girls were dancing away at the far end. 'It's empty, bloody empty. Usually this a place is packed with customers. Now look.' He led me past the girls back up another set of stairs and we came out into a street full of lights and a film crew.

'Oh! Bollocks you've got two entrances to the same place.'

'Yes. Yes.'

'Well then, while we are filming outside this one, why don't you tell the young lady to tell them to go round to the other entrance.'

'My friend, it does not worka like that.'

'No?'

'No. You have frightened them off. I have lost money. Lots of money.'

'Ah! At last we get to the point.'

'Yes, we get to the pointa. Money, you owe me money my friend.'

On the grounds of, some you win some you lose, I found that all the fight had gone out of me. We finally settled on a ridiculous amount of cash, which I didn't have on me at the time, so we agreed to meet outside the bookshop on the corner at ten o'clock the next day. He became quite chatty and very pleasant for the rest of the evening, knowing, I guess, that I wouldn't dream of not turning up the next day for fear of ending up in the Thames. In the less threatening daylight, I handed the envelope of cash and a signed photograph of the cast over to him. Well, it was his wife's favourite programme! She was madly in love with Station Officer Nick Georgiadis, played by Andrew Kazamia, as many women at that time were. We shook hands and off he went thanking me gratefully for the picture. I had taken it along in the hope I might have got some of the money back for being so thoughtful. Stupid boy.

They filmed a two-part episode of a huge fire in a gas container yard. Many appliances, many background artistes and many fire-fighters were drafted in for the major occasion. This included a one Billy Buddle, fire-fighter of some girth, who insisted on riding a bike totally naked pass the camera at one point, reducing the entire assembled company to tears. It was something fire-fighters did for a reason best known to themselves because another example happened not far away from Tower Bridge. Passing across the vast structure in a minibus off on a recce, Nobby, our brigade advisor, waved at a passing appliance from a nearby fire station. They all knew Nobby but strangely instead of waving back they lowered the windows, dropped their trousers and mooned at the happy group of passengers contained within the minibus. Just to prove it is not necessarily contained to the brigade, a certain first assistant on *Dempsey and Makepeace* paraded through a local pub completely naked, as a birthday gift for the landlord. Maybe it really is just a bloke 'thing' and I think I'll move swiftly on.

The Westminster Industrial Estate, which is positioned nowhere near Westminster and is in fact in a sort of no man's land between Greenwich and Woolwich, gave Ray Holt a huge giggle. Again, filming *London's Burning* and staging what was supposed to be a hotel fire, Ray was in-charge of a small aerial platform that you could drive and control from the bucket while elevated. We had occupied the site for the weekend by kind permission of the owner who was a huge film fan. The site was virtually deserted at weekends, as luck would have it, because most of the businesses seemed to do just five-day weeks. During a dull moment, Ray had taken himself off with the machine to test drive it after a bit of on-site maintenance. He had gone round the back of the estate into a smaller area that was by the river and completely deserted. That is except for one car, slightly steamed up and occupied by a man and a woman, which Ray came around a corner and discovered. He had a splendid view

231

from his elated position of the man's bare buttocks pressing against the windscreen. It is uncertain as to who was the more shocked, but Ray could hardly be accused of voyeurism as the machine could be heard approaching from some distance away. Unfortunately, it also had a very slow top speed so Ray could not rush past but had to trundle past very slowly. The man his, shall we say, rhythm now badly interrupted, turned around and put his hands in the air in a gesture of submission and defeat and just grinned.

It was funny how you dipped into people's lives and then dipped out again, almost like being in your own series where something different happened almost every day. One of the episodes called for 'Sicknote' to find an unexploded grenade in his allotment. I wandered around a few and finally found one I liked the look of in Peckham. I got to know the allotment holders quite well. However, it was an unusual one as you could not build sheds on the site. So, to overcome this strange council by-law, the good burghers of Peckham had tunnelled down into the soil and constructed their own little underground bunkers. We needed a shed that could be destroyed when the grenade went off. We selected, with help from the allotment committee, a plot that was owned by a lady who really could no longer maintain it on a regular basis. We built our own shed, blew it up and then took the remnants away. We paid her handsomely, restored the plot and planted a few things for her as well as giving a donation to the allotment society.

I think it was Simon Sharkey, who started off on the series as 'clapper/loader' and who went on to write quite a few of the scripts, who mused with me that probably there was a series to be had out of those allotments. You see the real intrigue was that not only was it a cross section of society that owned each plot, but many of them were happy tipplers. You would see them arrive sometimes as early as ten o'clock and realise they were carrying beer cans. They would then disappear into the bowels of the earth and re-emerge much later, slightly the worse for drink, and wend their way home. Little groups sometimes assembled and laughter would emanate from below ground. In between, a bit of weeding and planting would occasionally take place but what better excuse for a few pints than 'I'm off to the allotment darling!' and then coming back later with a bunch of carrots in your hand? I wanted to stay and watch and observe because I was sure there was endless material to be had out of those small patches of ground, each with its own story to tell.

One of my *London's Burning* colleagues, Charlie McFadden, died at the age of sixty-six on 3 September 2005, at roughly five minutes past seven in the morning, two days before my wife and I went on holiday. This meant we missed his funeral. I would dearly have liked to have paid my last respects to dear Charlie, who by profession was a boom operator. I drove him to distraction because I kept telling him it was not a boom but a fishpole he was wielding about and when I was in sound in the studios we gave that simple task usually to the trainee. A boom was something you stood on and skilfully swept around between four cameras, not just hovered over one camera as he did, which frankly was a piece of piss. I was joking, of course, because there was an art and a skill in his job, which like all jobs, if not done properly, can be the ruination of any project. He had worked on *Carry On Spying*, *Goldfinger*, *Carry On Cleo*, *The Intelligence Men*, *Carry on Matron*, *Yanks* and many others. The main thing about Charlie was that he did like to tell a joke, often at the most inappropriate moment, and he also loved a good gossip. Most of all he liked a wind up or a practical joke, both of which he was a past master at and would often trap an unsuspecting and innocent victim, who he would play along in some wild fantasy to the bitter end. He could keep the straightest of faces, imparting the most serious of stories, which would be complete cobblers, while inside he must have been cracking up. I am truly amazed that he never played poker. His other quirk was that he would give up drinking that dark drink called Guinness ever year for the whole period of lent. I still miss him to this day. I particularly miss seeing him sat chuckling over a pint. Perhaps there is a small snug bar on a fluffy white cloud somewhere labelled 'boom operators only' and he is inside now telling many of his old blarney tales. I do hope so, I really do. And when my turn comes, I hope, as an ex-boom operator, I will be allowed in to once again listen to his mighty chuckle and watch the twinkle in his eye.

The last major outside broadcast LWT ever did with their big scanner, 'Unit 1', was from Kempton Race course and it fell to me to be the production manager on the day. A whole history of that side of the business finished with a whimper not with a bang. The riggers either took redundancy or were placed elsewhere within the company. I felt sad that we didn't mark the occasion properly. One happy event did occur. Dave Currie, who was back at the mother ship, called me during the day requesting that the camera boys get a lens he needed for the following day back to the South Bank when we had finished. The home of the outside broadcast vehicles was still near Wembley at a place called Wycombe Road. Dave agreed that the simplest method of doing this was to get a taxi to run it back from Kempton. 'Just get the cabbie to ask for me at reception and I'll come down and give him the money.' I knew that a diamond geezer called Tony Street, who was one of the riggers, had on that day travelled to work in his taxi. He had seen the writing on the wall and very sensibly had added another string to his bow. So now, having done the knowledge, he was as well as a 'freelance' rigger also a cabbie.

'Do you know a bloke called Dave Currie?' I enquired.

'I've heard the name but I don't think we have ever met. Why?'

'I think I might have a nice little earner for you at the end of the day.' I didn't want Dave to think I had planned the whole thing, although knowing Dave I don't think he would have been bothered at all, so why I didn't tell him I have no idea. It was an extra bonus for Tony too, because it was on his way home anyway. We loaded the lens into his cab, he set the clock running and off he went. Dave got the lens and LWT not only paid Tony for his days' work, but also for his travel home. Was that so bad? I don't think so. I knew the goods were in safe hands and that they would get there to the right man and on time. So, a little bonus at the end of the day to a nice guy was not the end of the world. At least I felt that my last job as production manager at the last race meeting LWT was to cover had a happy ending.

In contrast, as the last truck pulled away, I felt very sad standing in the car park, very sad indeed. Worse still, such is the isolated nature of that job, I had no one to share that moment with. You are either on an unbelievable low or a magnificent high. Indeed, there seems to be no middle ground and I suppose that is the appeal of the job and indeed the industry, the whole thing is like a giant roller coaster. Every day is different, every person is unique, every journey is a mystery tour and you are not tied to a desk doing the same thing day after day, which, despite my frequent outbursts about money, is alone worth its weight in gold.

Chapter Fourteen

Beadle's About

Many articles have been written about Jeremy Beadle and many stories told. I worked on the series *Beadle's About* for three years and my opinion of him never wavered; from the outset he was a charming man, who did a lot of work for charity that went unsung but that was the way he liked it. What did waver, over the course of the years, was my opinion of the series, which in the end led to my leaving the secure staff job at LWT and becoming freelance.

Jeremy was so good with the 'punters', which was what we called the poor unfortunates paraded in front of the cameras once we hit the studio-recording period. Afterwards, in the green room, he would talk, listen and pose for pictures with this person and that person until they were sated and bid him a fond farewell. He would always hold a 'halfway through the series party' at his house for the cast and crew at which his generosity was amazing, his library fascinating and his goodwill and bonhomie boundless. Why he got so much bad press never failed to intrigue me and still intrigues me now because somewhere along the line he must have upset someone very badly, but where, how and why I could never imagine. With Jeremy, what you saw was what you got: a very clever, a very well-read and a very intelligent person with a brilliant memory. Our paths crossed again after a gap of some thirteen years, when I did the *Banged up with Beadle* sketch for a show starring the double act, *Ant and Dec*. Without hesitation, deviation or repetition he walked straight up to me and said, 'Malcolm Treen as I live and breathe. How are you?' Call me old-fashioned, but if someone remembers my name after all that time, they get my vote as an all-round good egg. No, he was fine. The show, however, was a different matter.

The producer, a mad inventive by the name of Robert Rendell, kept the ideas and stunts flowing until they began to reach a fever pitch of, I thought, rather alarmingly dangerous proportions. I always liked the thinking stunts where, for example, we would narrow a doorframe after someone had delivered a large package and watch him or her desperately struggle to get the damn thing out of the door they had come through but to no avail. They were harmless and innocent and hurt no one. The office, where a team of removers emptied the contents into their van and as fast as they emptied it, we emptied their van and stocked the place up again. Funny, gentle humour that had almost an air of Laurel and Hardy about it. But then Robert discovered special effects and I presume discovered that blowing a car up wasn't as expensive as he thought it might be.

Duxford Airfield was where I first began to wonder why I was doing what I was doing and seriously had to question if I was enjoying it. The plot was quite simple in that a lady had been tricked into visiting the airfield for the day and while she was happily wondering around enjoying the sights and sounds we would swap her car for a 'ringer' (identical make, model and registration) await her return, pretend to her that some big gun firing tests had gone horribly wrong and then blow her car up. Ha ha! What became clear almost immediately after the 'supposed' impact and explosion was that she was deeply upset. She was a district nurse and her whole life was in that car and that car was her whole life. We stopped filming for about fifteen minutes and stayed hidden. Once her running mascara wasn't too obvious and black we started filming again and all ended happily with the reveal of the stunt and Jeremy's entrance. What distressed me was that for a few admittedly brief moments her life lay before her in absolute tatters. She could easily have had a heart attack and I wasn't sure this was really showbiz as I had envisaged it. We did the same stunt again the following series and blew four cars up this time. Why? I couldn't see that the more cars that were blown up the funnier things should be. Still, I wasn't the producer and it's just my opinion.

I was, however, rather proud of my deception of the neighbours that are very close to Duxford Airfield. To prevent anyone panicking or calling the emergency services, I had to come up with a bright idea to placate them once the bangs went off and the pools of smoke rose into the air, without disclosing that we were filming for *Beadle's About* in the process. I distributed a resident's letter saying we were doing some filming for a World War Two drama called *Fire On the Runway*. As far as I know, my own little bit of deception worked and very cleverly, I thought. When we went back a second time, I simply said we were doing further inserts for the same series and once again not to be worried because it was all under control. Robert asked the special effects guy what would happen if for some reason the car didn't explode, could he guarantee that it would? He looked at Robert and replied, 'Sure, if all else fails I'll poke it with a stick!' At many production meetings afterwards, that phrase became a running gag: if someone was slightly doubtful about something they would say, 'Or we could poke it with a stick!'

As the third year of *You Bet!* at Shepperton Studios ended, I enquired about *London's Burning* for another season. I had been situated in the Light Entertainment

239

Department, when the production managers and location managers' departments were disbanded when 'total costing', don't ask, swept through the company and I was hired out to the drama department to do *Burning*. I talked to the accountant on *London's Burning*, once again the ubiquitous Mike Littlejohn, who explained that this season they weren't too sure if they would use in-house staff at all. There was a strong possibility that freelancers would service the whole programme. He had a particularly annoying habit of knowing your personnel number. In fact, he knew everybody's; again, don't ask! This meant that when he first met you or spoke to you, he addressed you with your personnel number first, as in, 'Ah, 12106 Treen, there you are'. I was told that I was one hundred pounds a week more to employ than a freelance location manager would be because I was hired out by the Light Entertainment Department at a higher rate so that they covered my overheads, and therefore he would get back to me when he had calculated things a little more closely.

It went on like that for several weeks and as the end of *You Bet!* drew closer I wandered back to the mother ship on the South Bank to see what was cooking. The head of production for Light Entertainment summoned me into her office and I explained that it looked like I might well not be doing *London's Burning* this season. Her face dropped and she said, 'Oh, that's a shame.' Obviously meaning her hurt and not mine. I raised my eyebrows. 'Well, you see,' she continued, 'It's just that I have already contracted people to fill the jobs you would have been doing this winter.'

'Ah,' was all I could muster.

'Yes. It's a shame, I just assumed you would be doing it again.'

'Yes, so had I,' I concurred. 'So, what does this mean?'

'Well, it means, er, you could help out on one or two things until next March.' I had been my own boss now for quite some time and 'helping out' just wasn't an option. I wanted to be in charge as I had been of my own projects. 'And then come March,' she mused, looking carefully at a chart on the office wall, 'Ah yes, of course, you could do *Beadle's About* again.' Oh, no, not for the fourth year, I thought. I really did need to move on as I was convinced someone was going to die. She must have seen my face drop this time because as it did, I swear to this day I saw a light bulb flash on the top of her head, 'Or have you considered seeing personnel at all?'

'Personnel?'

'Yes, personnel, you know you could take redundancy.' I felt like I was being stabbed repeatedly in the chest. I looked her hard in the eyes and tried to understand her motives or even her mind set. I had worked very hard for London Weekend for twenty-four years, twenty-four bloody years and I had known no other life. I was as dedicated a company man as you could ever wish to find. So, that was the choice was it after twenty-four years, redundancy or *Beadle's About* for the fourth time? This was really going to be a difficult decision to make and I considered that I might need well over fifteen seconds to draw it to a successful conclusion. I wasn't going to leap because I needed to know first and foremost if *Burning* would have me as a freelancer because redundancy sounded like a horrible thing and I had to make sure when I walked out I would have at least nine months' work in front of me. Luckily, as it turned out, they did want me and so I chose to go and see personnel.

241

I'm still not sure after all these years that I made the right decision. I'm still not too convinced that I didn't walk out of the front door through sheer anger, caused by the fact that I could be so little thought of that anyone would consider simply getting rid of me. I think the only consolation freelancing ended up bringing me was that I got to work for the BBC from time to time. And whenever I did, I always felt like I was getting a little bit of the licence fee back that I have paid to them over the years. People who have always been freelance seem to be able to put up with it, but I still feel lost without that security that a staff position offers. No more paid leave, pension, National Insurance, permanent desk and no more company car and parking space in London. Also, I unfortunately have never been very good at selling myself. You spend a lot of your time phoning people and networking, persuading them that you are the one they need but you can't keep calling people when you hit a run of unemployment because all they ever hear is you saying, 'Give us a job,' which in the end can put people off. No, to be freelance in my book is to be brave and I'm afraid after being cocooned for so many years, freelancing was not one of the greatest joys of my life.

When I started on *London's Burning* in the October, Chris Hall, who was the production manager said, 'Welcome on board. Regarding your salary, as you are now freelance, we had better pay you one hundred pounds a week more than last year.' Yet again, don't ask. I didn't. But my head ached for some time afterwards and I needed a lie down in a dark room.

The company car was not always a joy. I was once the proud possessor of a Montego. I wanted it in a golden colour but they couldn't get one and I got a shitty brown instead. Never mind, it was free, it was brand new and it was mine. If I had bought that car, I think I would have killed myself after eighteen months. To me, it really didn't matter what the car was. If it got me from A to B, I was happy. But this one didn't. I have never been 'into' cars as some men like Jeremy Clarkson are. I understand little of the workings, save where to put the oil, water and petrol, which is about where my knowledge of the internal combustion engine terminates. The Montego was from another planet. Everything that could go wrong did go wrong with that machine and it was the antithesis of a reliable car. It was a prime example of a Friday afternoon botched job. It leaked at the front in the drivers well, it leaked in the boot, it would overheat and no matter how many times it went back to the garage, it never got better. As I said, it didn't worry me: I wasn't the one continually paying for the machine to be patched up and really that is all it ever was, patched up. It developed strange intermittent faults all on its own. The windscreen wipers would suddenly come on in broad, dry, daylight for no apparent reason, always an embarrassment and I felt I had to spray water onto the screen to look casually as though I was simply cleaning the window! It knew, oh yes, by God it knew all right, that you had gone red in the face and looked a complete twit as they sprung into life at the most inopportune moment. I remember taking off on a trip to Southampton to have the red ignition warning light came on when I got there, only to find, when I had turned round and headed for the local garage, they couldn't find anything wrong with it and the light annoyingly went out. Oh, yes, it knew. It has only just occurred to me while writing this, that it may well have been haunted or perhaps it just didn't like leaving home. Towards the end of its short, but amusing life, I was on first name terms with the local

RAC man as more and more he was called out to find me stationary with the bonnet up in this lay-by or that. The poor brown Montego finally expired in a lay-by near Guildford some eighteen months after I had taken possession of it in the underground car park at LWT. If I had bought that car and paid hard earned cash for it, by golly I would be beside myself. I last saw it looking very sorry for itself on some gravel at the back of a workshop where I went to collect my personal belongings from it, having heard that whatever ailed it had been diagnosed as terminal. It looked like a practical joker, who has realised he has gone too far but knows it is too late to rectify the situation and sits quietly awaiting his fate.

A few weeks later, I was invited to join Dave Currie in the restaurant at LWT, just to make up the numbers really, where he was wining and dining a couple of chaps from a motor show room who had been particularly helpful to him, I think, on one of *Hale and Pace's* series. Inevitably, the talk was of motors, which Dave was very good at. Being heavily into motorbikes and go karts, he more than compensated for my severe lack of any knowledge in that area. They finally asked me about cars and I said I had just said goodbye to a Montego, where upon they held their hands up and said, 'I bet the boot leaked?' And then proceeded to list, spot on the nose, every single fault I had had with that vehicle. They didn't get the windscreen wiper one, which they admitted must have been an added super bonus that the half-past four Friday man must have thought of just as the clock clicked onto four twenty-nine!

Chris Fox, one of the directors on *Beadle's About*, was the man responsible for my first flight in a helicopter. Many people had said to me over the years,

'I expect you have flown in a helicopter hundreds of times, doing your job?' I always answered in the negative and followed this by the statement, 'and you will never catch me in one of them either, I would be scared stiff. Planes yes, helicopters I don't think so.'

I was 'resting', as they say in the trade, when the phone call came. Would I step into Dave Currie's shoes for a day and look after a *Beadle's About* stunt? The whole thing was all set up and all I had to do was babysit it. Sometimes these events happened at very short notice and although blocks of dates for filming were allocated, it often turned out that within those blocks, dates would change depending on the intended victim's availability. On this occasion, the couple were arriving back from holiday to discover that plans to build a new airfield just near their quiet and peaceful house, were nearly complete. Dave had pre-arranged to be somewhere on the Saturday when it was so suddenly necessary to grab this couple, so a deputy was needed. He was hopping mad as he had been waiting for this scam to come up. Chris Fox had suggested, 'Try Treen.' Most people always assumed I was working on *London's Burning* constantly but this was not always the case. Anyway, on this occasion I was available and off I went straight into the jaws of hell because the words 'you will be in it' and 'helicopter' were never used in the same sentence until I arrived on site, which I seem to recall was somewhere close to Cheadle. It was a pretty spot featuring some very large houses and farms.

The helicopter was on standby to fly over the property, after our actors had softened the couple up and to add insult to injury, not only did they want me in it, but I was to carry out a two-way conversation along the lines of, 'Yes, receiving you loud and clear. No trouble at all with communications. This really does seem like the ideal spot for the east to west runway to be located.'

We sat in a field with me in the front seat and Jeremy in the rear as we were to drop him near the house as the plot came to its conclusion. Anyway, we sat there for a long time and the pilot could obviously tell I was nervous either by my constant rambling or the beads of sweat breaking out on my forehead. Of course, I had told no one that I had never been in one of the dreadful contraptions before and was now wishing for my wife's sake that I really had got a much bigger insurance policy. I had bluffed it out and eventually decided that if your number's up, your number's up. I began wondering how badly Dave would feel upon receiving the news of my spectacular demise, falling so terminally out of the sky into in a field of cows. As a small drip formed on the end of my nose, the pilot leaned over to me and looking me straight in the eye said, 'I have every intention of being at home for my dinner at the end of the day and if I didn't think that, believe me I wouldn't be sat here.'

From what I can remember, I enjoyed the experience, mainly because we flew close to the ground anyway. The stunt did not enjoy the same easy ride as the couple guessed what was going on almost straight away. And before you could say this is a hell of a long way and a lot of trouble to go to for it all to fall apart, it did. Hasty conversations were had and in order not to waste an awful lot of money and come back with a blank tape, the tables were turned and the same scam was played on their cleaner – and she fell for it hook, line and sinker.

I must say the stunts did not often fail and we were very rarely spotted or sussed during the event. The whole team had become masters of disguise, hiding in vans, GPO look-alike tents and sheds. One of the other directors for a spell was a chap called Simon Cochrane. He was the son of the head of cameras I mentioned way back in the first chapter who had interviewed me for my job at LWT. We were plotting a wedding stunt and musing where the cameras could be positioned in the churchyard to best effect when, as usual, up came 'shed' from Simon and then up came 'another shed.' This led Ian Cross, who was the programme associate, who also came up with ideas and often wrote most of the scripted pieces, to exclaim, 'Two sheds?' And the name stuck and was even put into print on some of the call sheets as 'director…Simon 'two sheds' Cochrane'. Steve Joel, who was the stage manager, did shorten this eventually to 'Mr Sheds'. Rae George, one of the many designers on the project, and I know I keep saying this of the people I have worked with, but a lovely man would then be given the task of somehow erecting two sheds, without drawing too much attention to himself and his crew and then ageing them to look as though they had been in situ for many years. I still have a fake 'Telecom' pass that I was given to help me persuade anyone who thought I was putting out "no" parking cones, for no apparent reason, that I should really be there.

While in charge of one of the series, I had gone on holiday and left it in the capable hands of Kevin Holden, who was later to share many series of *London's Burning* with me. Upon my return, a handover period ensued and a trip to a location for a particularly difficult scam was arranged. I arrived at a lay-by on the busy A3 and we all poured out of our various vehicles and Robert Rendell explained the plot. It seemed awfully daunting to me, as basically it would involve putting a camera on the central reservation hidden by some construction that Rae George had already planned and worse, we would have to stop the traffic, which Robert was insistent on. My stomach began to churn, as I couldn't see how we could accomplish this, but said all I could do was ask the local police and see if they would play ball. People crossed the busy intersection in a display of measuring and taking copious notes and when the whole team seemed happy, Robert declared lunch and we retired to a nearby hostelry. He kept pushing me about how I would cope, someone began to explain something and I was aware someone else was taking Polaroid pictures of me. It turned out the whole thing was a practical joke on me! They had wound me up to believe they had picked the A3. 'You didn't think we were that mad, did you?' said Robert and before I could answer, Kevin said, 'We will need to stop the traffic but we have chosen a small lane just down the road and I have already spoken to the police about it'. The whole team had gone to the bother of finding a fake spot and then spent all morning on expanding on this elaborate hoax. I'm not too sure what this meant but I like to think that they were quite fond of me. I kept those Polaroid's for a long time and the look of relief on my face, in the last one of a series of six, was astounding!

The story of the A3 took me back to the A30 – strange how what I laughingly call a brain works sometimes! Many years ago, when I was still in the sound department, a small expeditionary force was formed to go off and see if the cameras we then had were indeed small enough to wheel out into the countryside and produce a drama. I believe it was done under the guise of a training exercise. Basically, I was to be the sound collector with my fishpole and radio mics, a young man called Dave Taylor was to be the sound mixer, a vision mixer called Mike Gibbon, a hopeful director, was to be allowed to direct and real actors were to be employed to record a play called *Picnic on a Battlefield*. It was set during the Spanish Civil War, written by Fernando Arrabal and was a very off the wall piece, with people debating the meaning of life while having a picnic with a raging war going on behind them. Gordon Melhuish was a young designer who threw himself into the project and had acquired one pretend dead horse that he kept moving about so that it looked like many.

Mike had relatives or connections in the army, which is why we ended up on army land down the A30 near Camberley, where we shot the whole piece in a week, surrounded by soldiers desperate to blow things up for us at the drop of a hat. I had my picture taken with the rifle microphone in my hand, standing on top of the horse posing like a big game hunter and put the caption 'shot on location' under it. I have a strange feeling this was before the M3 was invented, which is a strange feeling, as I type this, I wish I hadn't had. The weather was perfect and was a little too hot but we would slake our thirsts safely in the Forester's Arms lounge bar at the end of the day. It was a quaint pub with an indoor skittle alley, which nestled along the A30 opposite a garden centre. Francis Crossley, who was head of the production assistants, had volunteered to be the PA for the shoot. She had a reputation of being fierce and taking no prisoners, but I found her to be charming with a wicked sense of humour. Mary Pyke, I believe, was the stage manager, but I may be doing her an injustice because she did go on to become a PA. I always wonder what became of the tape of that production. It is probably lying on a top shelf deep in the bowels of

ITV's programme archive somewhere. There was talk of it being transmitted but as it was purely a training exercise it never did get to see the light of day. It seems a lifetime ago now in my head and a lifetime ago in reality.

It was on this production I first met Graham Armitage, an actor of some standing, who had been in many television productions such as *Doctor Who*, *Mr Rose* and many others and finally appeared in certainly two if not three Ken Russell films, most notably, *The Boyfriend*. We became friends and I found his outrageous campness was very amusing. He was a good friend of Mike's and often along with others we would be invited back to Mike's place in Fulham and long into the night we would discuss and debate on important topics of the day. Never having had a University education, I always felt I had missed out on late night talks and discussions and I felt these evenings at Mike's somehow made up for it.

It was a shame that on one of these occasions, not long after I had got married, I failed to telephone Mary and tell her I was safe at Mike's. When I realised it was so late, I decided not to call for fear of waking her. I thought I was being considerate. Wrong! As the first rays of the sun were heralding a new dawn and I opened the front door, I was mortified to see her sitting on the stairs in a terrible parlous state, shaking, crying and clutching a Paddington teddy bear, which had been a wedding gift from the people we had bought the maisonette from. Having phoned the police and hospitals and with no joy of my whereabouts, I could see from her demeanour that she had given up all hope of ever seeing me alive again. From then on, an unwritten rule was applied, that I would always phone her and explain my position and estimated time of return home, no matter how late the hour.

Graham featured in our lives for some time. He came to see our new house down in Ash in Surrey and spent the weekend with us. He fell in love with South Africa and had reported on a trip he had made there for some filming or other and amusingly described the flight with a fellow thespian in the seat next to him on the plane. As Graham looked in awe out of the window at the stunning scenery and changing landscapes passing by below he would say, 'Look, oh just look at that,' to his comrade, who would momentarily gaze out of the window say, 'Very nice,' and then go back to his book. Graham just couldn't understand how anyone could let such a spectacle go by and carry on reading. Who knows how other people's brains work, but one day he just upped and went, as they say, without so much as goodbye or farewell. No forwarding address, no communication whatsoever and we have never heard from him again. We did know he had fled to South Africa. He cropped up in a television mini-series called *Shaka Zulu*, which was made in Africa, but that was in 1987. I often wondered where he was and why he just disappeared off the face of the earth? Well, certainly off the face of England. I gave him a display of my early faltering magic skills on one visit not long before he vanished and have often wondered if just one more card trick had tipped the balance and could have been the cause of him finally fleeing the country! Mike later told me that Graham had passed away in Johannesburg on 6 March 1999. And so, another little area in my subconscious is extinguished as another soul disappears off the planet and his body is laid to rest.

Thinking about that age gone by, I can remember the first cash dispensers appearing on the outside walls of

251

banks. As someone said the other day, all they seem to have done is transferred the queue from inside the bank to outside on the pavement. The maximum you could obtain was ten pounds and it was dispensed in a little plastic holder that you could give back to the bank and they would recycle them. One late night in Wembley, I pulled up to obtain my ten pounds and when I duly counted out the contents, I discovered to my joy and delight that it contained not ten but eleven crisp one-pound notes. I felt like I had at the very least won the pools. How innocent we were, how simple the times.

Chapter Fifteen

The Knock

The ITV strike way back in 1979 went on for thirteen weeks, or so I thought, until I recently saw a documentary with Michael Grade announcing that it went on for only eleven. He said that he had gone down on the studio floor personally to ask people to work overtime but they pulled the plugs on him at ten o'clock at night. Did he never think that they might just have wanted to go home? I never saw him once on the floor of LWT asking me to work on into overtime, perhaps I wasn't around on the occasions that he did. He then moaned about the fact that some VTR (Video Tape Recording) engineers were being paid more than he was because of overtime payments! Now I may be old and stupid but how do those two statements match up? Either you want people to work the overtime and you pay them, but if they do not want to work more hours than is good for them, surely it is their right to refuse? If they do carry on, and you pay them the overtime payment, I can't quite see how you can then criticise them for earning a lot more money. The overtime payments were there to stop people being taken advantage of by companies and being made to work stupidly long hours. Nowadays it comes under the banner of health and safety.

Anyway, at the time of the strike I was unfortunately the ACTT union representative for the sound section. This meant while everyone else who had seemed to realise faster than I did, that the dispute was going to go on for some time and rushed off to find alternative work on building sites, or at film studios and anywhere else that would employ them, I couldn't. Firstly, I had a meeting every week to explain and update me on what was going on, which then every Monday I would relay back to the fifty-two people in the section. How? They each had a specific phone-in time starting at ten o'clock with a ten-minute interval between each and I would then tell them, within this ten-minute gap, all the latest news – if there was any. The last call time being at ten minutes past seven in the evening! As we weren't posh enough to have a phone in the lounge, kitchen and bedroom like we do now, all my Mondays were spent crouched in the hallway with a checklist in my hand. As more and more people got jobs, they tended to phone later in the evening. Once again, this was well before the advent of the mobile phone. The only job I could get was of a part-time variety and I became an occasional barman in a pub on the outskirts of Aldershot called The White Lion.

This long and protracted strike is I am sure what led the Prime Minister, one Margaret Thatcher, down the path of gunning for my industry. Maybe she was an avid *Coronation Street* fan and got really miffed that it wasn't on for so many weeks. But whatever the cause, she was determined to break up the power of the big five ITV stations. These were ATV, Granada Television, LWT, Thames Television and Yorkshire Television, who had happily between them for many years, carved up the schedule of what the viewers would watch, when and at what time. In 1990, the Network Centre was set up and then came the great auction in 1991 by the Peacock Committee, which everybody thought was to be resolved by the person who bid the most money getting the franchise. LWT bid seven million pounds for their franchise and won it, having beaten another consortium that had bid thirty-two million, so the highest bidder theory went out of the window. It was in the middle of this complete shambles that Thames lost their franchise having never done anybody any harm. A classic case, if ever there was one, of a government interfering in things about which they know nothing about. The real irony was that TV-am also lost their contract in the fracas, even though Bruce Gyngell, the head of the company, had almost single-handedly been responsible for the demise of the ACTT trade union. Thatcher must have been delighted that he crucified the union for her and it seemed a very strange way of thanking him to then take away his business. Such is the barmy world of politics and showbiz and people who think they know better, when in fact know no better than anyone else. I was delighted we had won the contract back but, as I mentioned earlier, my celebrations were very short lived because by late 1992 I found myself outside the front door having been made redundant.

Thatcher fragmented the entire industry and subsequently ITV set about selling off the family silver. It closed regional production houses and offices in places including Newcastle, Bristol, Nottingham, Southampton and Norwich. The BBC has also made changes to its property and production portfolio. The phrase 'Accountants know the price of everything, but the value of nothing' will haunt me forever. I do feel they have made a very big, big mistake that will lead unerringly to the death of British television, as we have known it.

I sometimes muse on the thought that Thatcher probably never even realised just how many lives, careers and jobs she affected in her determined effort to rid the planet of both the unions and the fat cats. There was a lot that was wrong with the union and I'm sure to the management it did become a severe case in the end of the tail wagging the dog. However, when I originally wrote this chapter, my wages had not risen for thirteen years and I felt somehow, just somehow, the pendulum had swung mightily back the other way and some cat has been getting very fat off my back. When Granada took over LWT, Christopher Bland made fourteen million pounds from his shareholding. I somehow think the fat cats did better than Thatcher could ever have imagined even in her wildest dreams and compared to them the rest of us faired quite badly, except for a superb pension, which if the unions had not fought tooth and nail for, would not be there in the form it is today.

Technicians are no longer trained and actors are these days infrequently employed to act and scriptwriters have become a very rare breed indeed. Reality television and make-over shows are what we are now spoon fed for what seems to me twenty-four hours a day. It's cheap television and no one is required to be creative, artistic or even semi-literate. People just sit around and watch it happen. If the late Jack Rosenthall had not written the first feature length version of *London's Burning*, I wouldn't have had work for eight seasons on that show because, obviously, the show would not have existed. Strange thought that. It applies to drama because without the written word none of us in the business would be employed in the business, if that makes sense? Well, certainly not in the drama business anyway. If you take it back even further, Jack and his wife Maureen Lipman had a Swiss au pair called Ruth who eventually married a fire-fighter, Les Murphy. If Ruth hadn't married Les, Jack would never have heard the stories from Les that were to become the seed for the programme. So, thank you to them all for many months of work and a reasonably steady income.

I slipped at some point into a sequence, not unlike before, of working on *London's Burning* during the winter and then *The Knock* during the summer. *The Knock* was an ITV drama about HM Customs and Excise, which became HM Revenue and Customs following a merger with the Inland Revenue in 2005. As seems so frequently the story these days, it was often chaos to work on. On one occasion, I had a head start on the director of two weeks, got well ahead finding locations but then he joined and didn't like the scripts at all. So then I had to wait while everything was rewritten and two new scripts were issued. I began to get well behind. I was doing all right until two days after the technical recce. Then a company that owned a recycling plant in Southwark wrote to me to say they had changed their minds and didn't want to go ahead with the filming. The dreaded domino effect sprang into place. There was a gym sequence and a park scene scheduled on the same day, so they got blown out of the water because they were certainly not near any other recycling plant, which was a crucial part of the script. Oh, by the way, this was the week before Christmas and we were supposed to close-down for two weeks and start filming on 5 January as soon as we came back. Now, if you have ever had the misfortune to have that two-week period of Christmas and New Year as a set-up period or finding time, you'll know what I was about to go through. You can't get a hold of anybody, nobody wants to talk to you, they are often on leave or they are just very simply pissed!

Then the director buggered off on holiday, the whole place shut down and I was left on my own to find an alternative site for all three locations to film on the Wednesday of that first week back. It is here I will mention Pip Short. God bless him, the first assistant, who said, 'I'll stay at work with you and come out looking.' There are not many first assistants who would do that. So apart from Christmas Day, Boxing Day, and New Year's Day, I worked those two weeks and good old Pip came with me most of the time. We found a friendly refuse-recycling place just off the A40 and, cold calling, talked to the site manager. He talked to his bosses but couldn't give the okay until after Christmas when his bosses were back from leave and could examine my paperwork. Not surprisingly, I sweated for a few days on the outcome. The David Lloyd Centre came up as the replacement gym, but I was still having trouble with a residents' association about parking round a block of flats on that fated Monday we were back!

Monday arrived and I was still struggling to get sense into the stupid twit I had been telephoning and faxing for a fortnight regarding the flats. Then I received a phone call from the guy who owned a warehouse I wanted to film at on the Saturday. He was now back from America but he had gone into liquidation. I was told he might have the keys or he might not. If he had, we could film there, if he hadn't, it would be out of the question. He asked me to call him about Wednesday for an update on the situation. The director then informed me that he wanted a high shot of the said warehouse. I was asked if I could get permission from the building on the corner overlooking the place. Between frantic phone calls to the flats, it was the third location that I still had to sort out that day. I went to Brick Lane and found that the building he wanted to shoot from was a Mosque. My Urdu was, and still is, crap and their English wasn't the best in the world, but I sort of worked out that I had been invited to return the following day at half past four to see someone in authority. I was then informed they could no-longer talk as it was Ramadan. They disappeared to the inner bowels of the emporium and I left the building.

The recycling plant gave me permission and I had to find a park near it and a unit base. I failed with the residents and for the first time in my career I had lost a location on the day we were supposed to shoot there. I had to go and see the director and say, 'sorry but you can't go there.' The unit overran at both the first two locations and we would never have made it to the flats anyway, even if we could have shot there. I felt a little bit better because of that – but not a lot! In the end, they built the damn thing in the studio, with two flats and a telephone. Don't ask me how long I looked for that location but that is the nature of the game sometimes.

When Tuesday dawned, I wondered whether to confess about the warehouse or keep quiet and just hope it will be all right! I wondered whether to find another one. The problem was I had no time as I was destined to motor down the A40 to find a park location and a base for the next day. I decided to phone the movement order into the office, which I had dictated in a very foul mood into a machine. The route to the recycling plant played back as, 'Take the next left into Carlton Mews. Past Quick Save, past McDonalds, past caring.'

A chap called Mike Liddell, the local film officer, was very helpful and found me a park and a unit base in the one place. The David Lloyd Centre came back to me and agreed to go ahead. I make a quick visit just to make sure all looked good and told them filming was confirmed for the following day. I also apologised about the short notice. The director would just have to shoot there sight unseen. I then ventured back down the A40 into town and was just in time to see the place on the first floor of the mosque for the shot. I thanked them and told them I would be back on Saturday, Allah permitting!

On the Wednesday, I left the unit to their filming as I had to be at Gatwick just to tidy up loose ends for the following week's filming. I telephoned the warehouse guy who said, 'Ring me on Friday morning I still don't know.'

The following day, Thursday, I travelled around and found a jewellery shop for the Saturday (how did I get into this mess?) to go with the warehouse and an Indian restaurant, which I have already got. The very nice man at the jewellers said he would talk it over with his wife that evening and phone me. I didn't hear back. So, on the Friday I called the jewellery shop. 'Oh sorry, I went out for a meal with my wife and I forgot all about it. I'll call you back.' By now, sweat was slowly breaking out on my forehead. I telephoned the warehouse. My contact told me he had the keys and thought it would be fine. The jeweller finally called me back and told me his wife had agreed to the filming. I then quickly telephoned the police and council, and then rushed off to do a route for the next day's movement order.

I made it to the end of the week – a bit ragged but intact. I began to relax. I worked out that we would finish filming at the Indian restaurant at about seven that evening. I thought, even if we overrun there will be no problem because they are closed all day on a Saturday. The man who owned it was cooking the food for the scene and he told me that he should be there some time around one o'clock. The jewellery shop filming went well and I relaxed a bit more. I then telephoned Michael, the restaurant owner. He was delayed due to still being at a wedding, but he assured me he would be there soon. Two o'clock came and went and there was still no sign of him. I no-longer felt relaxed any more! Three o'clock came and went and there was still no Michael. The prop master, Ray Holt, came to see me.

'When can I get into the restaurant?' he asked.

I gave him a weak smile, 'Soon I hope.' Out of Ray's earshot I squeaked into the phone, 'Michael, where the hell are you?'

'Sorry, I will be back soon,' he said. 'Look, the keys for my place, if you're desperate, are at the nearby newsagents. Help yourself, tell them I sent you. Oh, by the way, he shuts at three thirty.'

I looked at my watch and with horror realised it was already twenty past three. Luckily, it was a Saturday and the traffic was light. The prop master and I grabbed the keys just in time. We went to the restaurant and opened the doors and gasped. The crew was due there at about four. The scene was due to feature a meal for two in an up-market Indian restaurant with a few other diners in the background. With just twenty minutes to go, we gazed at the vista of the place still trashed from the night before. The tables hadn't been cleared, dirty glasses surrounded us and there was stale food everywhere.

'Oh shit! I'll start washing up in the kitchen, you start clearing the tables,' said Ray, his eyes having widened to about four times their normal size. We managed to place an Indian takeaway further up the road on standby and told him we would be back if we were really in trouble. Suddenly Michael arrived at about half past four, full of apologies. No problem, we were told, the food was already prepared and just needed heating up. The unit overran at the warehouse, thank goodness. The director walked into the restaurant at about five thirty, just as Ray and I were breathing heavy sighs of relief.

'All right, boys?' he asked.

'Oh, yes, fine thanks. Just fine.'

The director viewed the restaurant and said, 'Oh yes, this place looks bloody marvellous. Bloody marvellous.'

In a very quiet voice as the door closed I said, 'Yes, good job you didn't see it two hours ago!'

I crept round to the back of the premises and lit a cigar and said to myself out loud, 'Why? Why, oh, why do I do this bloody job?'

'Search me, Treeny,' came Ray's voice from over my shoulder. 'But you love it, don't you? You just love it?!'

Chapter Sixteen

I'd Do Anything

I ended up feeling a complete twit in Glasgow while working on the Ian Wright show, *I'd do Anything*. The basis of the show was that Ian would surprise someone in their own home or workplace and they then had to do a challenge in order that a relative could have their dream come true. They wanted a national feel to the show, so we had travelled the length and breadth of the country. The researchers had come up with two possible 'hits' as we called them in Glasgow. Now, I had been to Edinburgh before, but never Glasgow. I flew up the day before we filmed to secretly look at the two addresses where the victims were ensconced. This was so we could decide where to hide Ian, the mini bus with the crew and two cameras in it, so that we could easily just pop out, ring the doorbell and take the incumbent by surprise. The experience I had gained on *Beadle's About* had stood me in good stead for hiding crews.

I took an early flight, collected a bright red hire car at Glasgow airport, checked into the hotel and left my overnight case and videotape stock in my room. I then purchased a detailed map and headed off in the direction of the two premises. The recces didn't take me long so by about lunchtime, being satisfied of the whereabouts of both places, all that was left was to collect some lamps from a local hire company, which didn't close until six.

My hands-free lead for my mobile phone had been playing up and with some spare time now available to me to purchase a replacement I headed for the city centre and the shops. I drove around a little circular route having located the main shopping area and after about two circuits, I alighted upon a parking meter. I trotted off to the shops and had a bit of difficulty locating the right outlet, but eventually did find one. Flushed with success, I then went on to buy a Scottish rugby shirt for my French colleague, Mathieu Howlett, who I was going to be seeing in a couple of weeks or so. I headed back to the car with a good twenty minutes or so left on the meter. I rounded the corner of the street I had left it in, walked up and down along the line of cars on the meters and back again and, gob smacked, had to accept the inevitable. It had gone. Perhaps I was confused, so I went to the next street up and wandered along there. Nothing. Glasgow is quite simple to find your way round, as it has a grid system rather like New York. I spread my search area wider and slowly broke out into a sweat, probably from tension as much as fast walking exercise. After about an hour cursing that wherever it was the meter was way over by now anyway, I capitulated and admitted defeat. I stopped a passing council tow truck and the driver confirmed that if it had been over the time they just ticket them, they don't tow them away. I returned to the street that I had parked in and phoned the police to report my vehicle missing and my position. They told me to stay where I was and someone would come along and see me.

I telephoned the production office. Perhaps, inevitably, all hell broke loose with calls being made on my behalf to transport departments and hire car companies. Did I have the stock? Yes, safe in my hotel room. Thank heavens for that. I suppose I stood on the street corner not daring to move, because I didn't want to shift locations and miss the police, for almost an hour. Finally, a white police van turned up with two of Glasgow's finest officers on board. Having quizzed me about the incident one of them, speaking in a broad Scottish accent and speaking very slowly, said, 'Why don't we start at the beginning, Mr Treen. If I drive you to where you started your circular tour from, looking for a parking space, could you direct me from there to where you finally parked the car?'

'Well yes, of course,' I said. 'I'm a location manager, that's one of the skills of the job.'

So, off we went with the conversation going something like this:

'So, you started here in the underpass?'

'Yes.'

'And at the next set of lights?'

'I went straight across.'

'Right, well, let's do that. It must be quite a skilled job that directing sixty or so people to the right spot every morning?'

'Well, yes, you do learn to hone your navigational skills somewhat. Do you get much car theft in the town centre?'

'None, really. Do we Jock? Er, now at this next set of lights?'

'Again, straight across but at the next set I turned right into the street where the cars are parked on the right but at an angle, if you understand me.'

'Indeed, I do, Mr Treen. Yes, well remembered they are parked at an angle.'

I looked smugly at the cars and thought well at least they now realise that they are not dealing with a half-wit.

'And I don't suppose anyone would want to steal a hire car, would they?'

'No, I don't see why. Did you have anything of value on display in the vehicle?'

265

'No, the car was empty apart from the map on the passenger seat. Now at these lights where the scaffolding is, I turned right into the street where you picked me up and parked on the right.'

As the van turned right I had a terrible feeling in the pit of my stomach. The driver slowed.

'Is that your wee red car over there, Mr Treen?' I simply nodded unable momentarily to speak. 'You see this is not the street we picked you up in.' Looking at my face so full of disbelief, he had just the slightest hint of irony in his voice as he added, 'An easy mistake to make, would you not say Jock? I hadn't thought about it before but they do look very similar.'

'Aye, indeed they do,' replied Jock. 'An easy mistake to make, especially as you had left your map in the vehicle.'

This half-wit finally came out with, 'What a complete and utter pillock.'

'Aye, well,' retorted Jock, 'Your words Mr Treen, not mine. Och, will yer look at that, you are even luckier than you thought young man, it hasn't even got a parking ticket on it.'

I apologised profusely for wasting their time but they told me it was a relatively quiet day on the crime front. With a cheery wave, they were gone but I felt that behind the smile they were saying, 'Sassenach wanker,' and quite rightly because now I had to bite the bullet and phone the office again and confess all. The car had been discovered exactly where I had left it.

For a moment, I did toy with the idea of pretending the poor car had been found abandoned, after joy riders had made off with it, but I came clean and got such shtick back from everyone I wished I hadn't. Jo Newy, the lovable PA who worked on the programme called me.

'Have you completely lost your marbles, Treeny?' she asked. 'What the hell's going on? Have you been in the pub all day? I'll bet the police were really impressed with your navigational skills?'

'No, not really. And I haven't touched a drop all day. I think they just thought I was a complete tosser.'

'Well, Christ, can you blame them? You sure you'll be able to find your way back to the hotel? I'll make sure the crew come up tomorrow with a big map for you.'

'Thanks Jo. Shit.' It suddenly dawned on me I still had the wretched lights to collect.

'Pardon?'

Sorry, not you. I've got to go. Bye.'

It was now five o'clock. I had done a quick drive past the light shop, situated on the outskirts of the city, earlier in the day, so I knew where it was but now thanks to the afternoon's activities could I be sure? The problem was, not only was I in the middle of Glasgow, a city I was not as familiar with as I thought I was, I was also there right in the middle of the rush hour traffic. On top of that, I was now very unconfident about finding my way out in the right direction, believing that my usually excellent sense of direction had been eradicated from my brain by powers beyond my control. For the second time that day the sweat began to trickle down the back of my neck as I sat in the slow-moving traffic. I made it in the nick of time, collected the lights and retired very hurt to the hotel bar to lick my wounds and to try and undent my dented pride. You see be warned: if you dine out for years on the story of a top ITV executive foolishly putting petrol in his diesel car in France, you may find that after a few years, retribution finally catches up with you and bites you firmly and publicly on the arse!

You may recall me mentioning earlier in the book that I worked on *The Last Detective* with Peter Davison. While working on the series, I found myself looking for locations in Bledlow, a village in the civil parish of Bledlow-cum-Saunderton in Buckinghamshire. The strange thing about the area is that if you ever film there you will find that Lord Carrington owns most of the land in the vicinity. He was Foreign Secretary in the days of Margaret Thatcher. We needed to put a caravan in a field, which was supposed to be someone's permanent residence, so the art department needed about four days before we shot on the thing to put it into position and dress it. There is, or was, a pub in the village called The Lions of Bledlow, which we were using for one of our locations, and the landlord tipped me off that Lord Carrington would be the right man to speak to.

'I'm sure he won't be in the phone book,' he said. 'But let's have a look just in case.'

Sure enough, he was, which staggered both of us.

'Still, it won't be himself that answers the phone, he must have a flunky to do that surely?'

Armed with his phone number, I decided I would call him after I had been to call at the two houses at the top of a bridleway. I was in danger of cutting them off for a few hours while we filmed down below and thought it wise to sound out the ground and see how they felt about it all before I told the director he could run riot. Having visited both with favourable results, I proceeded back down the bridleway at a slow pace, as it was unmade and only room for one car over most of its length. On the radio was a programme on how one or two television programmes had affected world events a bit radically. They were talking about *Death of a Princess*, that was an ATV programme, which had been a sort of undercover documentary about the death of a princess in Saudi Arabia who had been beheaded. It had caused one hell of a stink at the time. And who was Foreign Secretary of the day? Yes, you guessed it Lord Carrington and suddenly there he was on my radio five minutes before I was going to telephone him. There was a clip of his voice saying, 'We have therefore found it necessary to close the British Embassy and we are advising everyone to leave the country.' I hadn't quite realised, or more likely failed to remember, that it had been that serious at the time. So now I am parked up back down in the village and dialling his number. Oh, my God, I suddenly think, I bet that incident probably scarred him for life against television companies. The chances of my getting any help here are probably zero, closely followed by verbal abuse. The telephone was answered not by a flunky, as Mark at the pub had presumed, but by the man himself, whose voice I immediately recognised having been listening to it only moments before. I launched into my prepared speech, which was supposed to go along the lines of 'Hello, my name's Malcolm Treen, I'm a location manager working on a television series called *The Last Detective* starring Peter Davison and I was....' Well, I got as far as, 'Hello, my name's Malcolm Treen, I'm a location manager...'

'Oh! Now then, is that fun?' interjected the good Lord. Now, this floored me completely. It was so good-humoured. Even after all these years I was a little nervous at cold calling on the phone a Peer of the Realm, but not only did it break the ice, but broke both my concentration and flow at the same time. I laughed like a complete twit for about twenty seconds. Finally, I pulled myself together and continued with the rest of my dialogue explaining the plot and my intentions.

'Hang on a minute, I'd better give you my estate manager's number, he'll be able to deal with all this.'

I gathered that the answer was yes and there was now a long interval where the number was searched for but failed to be found.

'Look, where are you now?' he asked.

'I'm actually just outside the Lions of Bledlow.'

'Well, you'd better come up to the manor house.' I drove to the manor house and there in the yard was Lord Carrington waiting to greet me. I stepped out and explained that, by extraordinary coincidence, I had just heard him talking on the radio. His reply I probably cannot print because it may well be libellous, but suffice to say that, thank goodness, he seemed to bear no malice against the long-gone ATV, or the industry in general. I gave him my business card and he said Mark, the estate manager, would telephone me. If you are ever in Bledlow, just call everyone Mark and you can't go too far wrong! Mark did call me and two days later I returned to explain on site, where, when and what we wanted to do.

After seeing Mark, I was slowly making my way back down the same bridleway, where I had first heard Lord Carrington on the radio and blow me down there he was on his way up walking his two dogs. I had to stop the car to let them pass safely. I wound down the window, 'Ah! Hello again,' he bellowed. 'Did you sort everything out with Mark?'

'Yes, I did sir and many thanks.'

'Not at all. Been doing this job, long have you?'

'Yes, over twenty years now.'

'Are you rich?' Again, the direct line of questioning took me aback.

'Actually no. I seem to be on the same wages I was on over ten years ago.' I then did think about explaining that if Mrs Thatcher hadn't destroyed the industry and indirectly making most of us redundant and forcing us to become freelance, things might be slightly different. However, I decided that this was probably not the place or the time for such an in-depth conversation.

'That's not very good, is it? That's not very good at all.'

'No.' I had to agree.

'Good luck with the filming. I'll probably come down and see you all and make a ruddy nuisance of myself.'

'Please do, I'm sure they would all like to meet you!'

'Ah, well, must get on.' He glanced over at the dogs. 'Come on you two, this man has got work to do.'

He never did come and do what he threatened. In fact, I didn't see him again but I'm sure the crew would have liked to have met him. It isn't often in this life that you get a chance to meet a piece of living history but then once again that's why being a location manager, sometimes, just sometimes, could be very rewarding.

Chapter Seventeen

Banged Up with Beadle

I awoke one morning in a rather curmudgeonly mood, a habit that seems to have become more frequent the older I get. This is a shame because I always thought the older I got, the happier I would become. Now, I firmly believe your happiness peaks quite early on and then suddenly you are on a decline that happens so quickly, that you fail to properly appreciate the high of joy and laughter has now so swiftly passed you by. The sight of an obituary had not helped my mood. It was for Christopher Blake who had died aged just fifty-five. It seems only minutes ago I was bravely swinging a boom over his head on the series, *Love for Lydia*. I am honestly beginning to worry that people may soon ask me to stop penning their name for fear of ending up six feet under! What is it about the wretched age of fifty-five?

The cause of my mood could also be fairly and squarely laid at the door of Zenith Productions after a brief encounter, which has left a rather bad taste in my mouth. I was telephoned by my agency about a job as location manager on a two-part drama series and given the number of a young lady to ring. She then made an appointment for me to see Adrian Bate, the head of drama and film at Zenith. We had a pleasant meeting where he said the job was mine, they were seeing no one else, I had been highly recommended. Would I please do an initial one week look round at St. Albans and the east coast, which were the two areas they thought they might like to film in. I was given a one-week contract but with the promise that as soon as the production finally got the green light, which was only a matter of days away, we would negotiate properly for the shoot. I looked at St. Albans and examined the place for a likely production base. I travelled to the east coast exploring a huge chunk of it, but finally had to stay overnight in Great Yarmouth, a not unpleasant experience, as I am one of those strange souls who does so love those seaside towns out of season. The following morning, it was a Saturday, I strolled along the front at about nine thirty and saw no one. It was as if a cloak of invisibility had been draped over every living person. I took a few pictures and then journeyed further north and explored some more.

On the Monday, I returned to London with my pictures and met the line producer, who was now on board. He kept my pictures in exchange for a rough first attempt at a schedule on his part and bade me study it at home and let him know what I thought about it the next time we met. 'I'll be in touch. You'll be the first to know.' I went to St. Albans again the following morning, although by now I was out of contract, and looked at another possible production base. It turned out to be no good but I emailed this to the line producer, who thanked me and then I heard nothing. I heard nothing for a long time. After a week, I decided to just lightly reintroduce myself into the picture again, so I emailed him with a gentle enquiry, asking how I could obtain my petrol money and how were things going? Three days later I received by email a reply telling me that the production was on, just, but that the producer, who had now appeared, had brought his own man with him, so my services were no longer required. He would get in touch with me regarding my expenses. He never did and in the end, I telephoned the accountant, who sent me a form and finally sorted it out. To say I was angry is an understatement; I was furious – absolutely furious. I wanted to shove the whole of the television industry up the backsides of several people and demand an apology or at the very least some manners. There may well have been nasty sides to many of the people that I have encountered, but none of them has been rude and certainly none of them have not been man enough to face me, face to face, to tell me bad news. I know people have allegedly been informed of a divorce by fax but to be dismissed from employment by email, the mind boggles. Such, I suppose, is the march of progress and the recession of good manners and a strong backbone. I was put off for several days from writing this jolly look back through rose tinted glasses of a television age gone by.

Patsy Lightfoot a mad, crazy, wild, loveable lady who was Paul Knights PA, the producer of *London's Burning* as far as series ten, had a slogan behind her desk, which read:

The television business is a cruel and shallow money trench, a long plastic hallway where thieves and pimps run free and weak men die like dogs.

I copied this slogan and went on to place it behind many of the desks I have since occupied as a freelancer. People had come in, read it and laughed. I had considered it just a joke until now. She obviously had encountered the nastier side of the industry long before I even thought that it might just exist.

What does amuse me these days is the profit that ITV makes. But it makes me want to scream, 'does any of this go back into the programmes?' I well remember being addressed at a meeting of all the staff by some chairman or other when things were quite bad at LWT and being told that we would only make a half yearly surplus of some three and a half million. Wages would have to be frozen. If we all pulled together, we could get through this crisis; after all it was our company as much as the managements. At that point, there were cut backs and the one that I remember most vividly is that they stopped giving us pencils with rubbers on the end. Why? I can only assume that, of course, if it comes with the rubber it is more expensive, but more importantly, perhaps they thought it would encourage us to write things down correctly the first time, knowing full well we couldn't rub out any mistakes!

The longer I live, the more I am becoming obsessed by my own mortality. I have not yet quite reached the stage where the first thing I do in the mornings is turn to the obituaries column and if I am not in it, I get up, but I feel I am steering very close to it. It has taken some time to write the words I have so far penned and slowly one by one, to my absolute horror, the people I have written about seem to be dying. While writing the latter part of this book I learned of the death of Ken Sheppard, the generator driver. This suddenly reminded me of the occasion when we were filming in St. Andrew's hospital just to the north of the Blackwall Tunnel. We had had a week of many overruns and by the Friday Ken had just about had enough. By the afternoon, a large card had appeared on the side of the generator on which Ken had written in huge letters,

THIS IS THE SEVEN O'CLOCK GENERATOR THAT WILL BE LEAVING AT SEVEN O'CLOCK.

This was his way of making a simple but effective one-man protest. Any question of overtime was not to be considered that day. The other thing about Ken was that wherever he went his faithful cream Labrador 'Sam' would go too. They were almost inseparable and quite often Sam could be seen at the end of the day sitting up in the driver's seat in the cab. Ken would climb aboard with a curt, 'Come on Doris, move over, it's my turn to drive.' The crew were once billeted in an hotel that bore the sign 'No Dogs' at the entrance. Ken, with the backing of the sparks crew, made out he was blind and so Sam was allowed in.

Ken's funeral was a sad and quiet affair but I was deeply moved by the news that Sam, who had died some years previously and whose ashes had resided on the sideboard in Ken's house, was finally laid to rest alongside his master in the coffin.

Banged Up with Beadle was an insert into *Ant and Dec's Saturday Night Takeaway* series and I was originally brought in to find the place where Jeremy Beadle was to be 'banged up'. The production manager of the show had started a few balls rolling, but was too busy with the main show to give time up scouting for a suitable location. When I arrived, no one had a clear idea where they wanted him located. So, I went off and looked at various locations including coalmines, caves and lighthouses. They were very far flung and viewing them was difficult and I was averaging, at best, maybe two a day, if I was lucky, but only (usually) one if I was not. This was too slow for the production manager and slight panic began to set in. I wasted a whole day trying to get to an old wartime fortification in the North Sea called 'Sealand'. The fort lies about six miles off shore and I was to travel there by dory, which is a small bouncy, and certainly not weatherproof, craft. The day was foul as we set off. I was given a suit to wear, which in the end kept all the water nicely *in*. The waves were huge! You rose and then came down with a real smack and at the bottom, it was as if two stagehands were throwing a bucket or two of water at you. Finally, we arrived at the fort. The 'swell' was just too much to safely winch the boat aboard, so we turned around and faced the dire prospect of a six-mile journey back the other way. I remember musing at the time that the fear, soaking and bruising would have cost me a lot of money at Thorpe Park.

My hosts gave me a towel and fresh clothing and we then retreated to the pub, while my soaking wet garments dried in a tumble dryer. Here, I learned that a British family created Sealand in 1966 and on 2 September 1967 they raised their own flag on the fortress. Their son, Prince Michael of Sealand, is now the man in charge. He had a bit of a problem in 1987 when Britain extended her territorial waters from three to twelve miles offshore. Nothing changed and although Sealand knows that Britain exists, they are not too sure that any favours the other way round have ever been shown.

I bemoaned my failure to the production manager and said what I really needed was a helicopter and behold it came to pass that a company called Arena Television was given the job of servicing the outside broadcast. Now, what does Arena have, being based at Redhill Aerodrome? Why a helicopter, of course; in fact they have two. So because we were now all tight for time, their boss Richard teamed up with me and we flew in the chopper from possible location to location, so that not only would I see if it was suitable but more importantly, he could look at it from the technical side and decide if the place was practicable.

We visited the lighthouse by the cliffs of Dover, we visited Sealand, for it did possess a helicopter pad, and finally we ended up at a fort to the south of Portsmouth. This indeed did become our location. Time was very tight and the Arena guys worked very hard throwing all the gear together. We needed to set up a complete control room at the location and the living accommodation for Beadle and his weekly guest. Not an easy task and one that was totally reliant on the weather, to get the gear safely out to the fortress. I had recruited Rae George, a designer I had known for many years, and with him good old Ray Holt both from my *London's Burning* and *The Knock* days. We attacked the project with gusto. I set up a production office in an hotel in Portsmouth; I recruited various launches and boats to take the gear and then punters and the audience across the seas and Richard transported some of his equipment via the helicopter.

From memory, all the gear had arrived at the quayside on a Tuesday and through no fault of our own but simply the impossible time constraint that had been put on us, we had just four days to get it all up and running. The weather, of course, was dreadful. The boatman offered to take me out to see how impossible it would be, because again the gear had to be winched up onto the Fort. The swell was just too much and the thought of monitors, cameras, lenses, mixing desks ending up in the Davy Jones' locker was too horrendous to contemplate. We turned back in the grey squall and went back to the hotel to sit it out and wait. I remember thinking how pleased I was that I was old enough not to be fazed by this adventure. I remember thinking that I was glad I wasn't younger because I would have perhaps lost control through lack of experience and panicked. I remember thinking none of it was our fault, it was purely down to nature and we would simply do the very best we could under the very difficult circumstances. Then they fired me. But I have jumped ahead a little.

We successfully started getting the gear over the following day and slowly we caught up with our schedule of rigging. The biggest problem Arena had was getting their satellite dish high enough so that the signal didn't get lost for two or three seconds, as the Isle of Wight ferry passed by. By Friday, I felt happy enough with the progress to return to London and put together a movement order and schedule and draw some stock (video tape) out of stores. I was in the office very early, when in walked John Gregory, who was then deputy head of production and had got me the gig in the first place.

'Sorry, but they want to take you off the programme.'

'Pardon?'

'They want to take you off the programme.' He was referring to the producer.

'Why?'

'For not communicating enough.'

'Me, not communicating?'

'I know, I know.'

'I've kept you informed every step of the way.'

'I know, I know.'

'Look, I'm not saying you are fired. I would like you to do the studio end of the show for ITV2. I was going to do it, but I don't want to do it every week. What do you think?'

'Well, fine, you're the boss.'

'Who will take over in Portsmouth?'

'Roger Allsop, he's, er, er, already on his way down there.'

The realisation that all this had been going on behind my back made me feel sick. Roger was a good man and we had been in the sound department together for many years, so I was not going to personally be angry with him.

'I had better get the stock down to him and show him the ropes.'

'You'll do that?' asked John almost incredulously.

'Well of course. I need to show him what's what. Introduce him to the hotel people, the boat people, and the owner of the Fort. You can't just throw someone into something like that without some sort of handover.'

'That's really good of you.'

'Yeah, well no one is bigger than the show, eh?'

I drove back down to Portsmouth and just wondered still, why? I can ramble on until the cows come home, so 'not communicating' was just bullshit. Unless John had not been passing my comments on to the producer, but Rae George had been keeping him in the picture too because at one time it looked like not only the technical side might not make the deadline, but the 'dressing' of the place had looked in jeopardy as well. From memory, I think they put it back a day, but we could have gone to air on the Saturday because we were ready. I can't ask John about it now because he too died a couple of years back at an appallingly young age, which is probably what has made me remember this grizzly episode in my life.

I showed Roger the Fort and all its technology and then took him to the hotel. I then showed him the production office I had set up; the room rate I had organised; the system we had engineered for who was staying when and where and the transport to and from shore to the Fort. He turned to me very slowly and said, 'I just don't know what to say. I am deeply embarrassed to be in this position but you are handing this to me on a plate. You've thought of everything.'

'That's okay Roger. Good luck,' and with that I drove away from Portsmouth thinking that was the last

I would see of it. The lady who owned the Fort just couldn't believe what had happened, none of the crew could either, but there you go, I thought, that's showbiz.

Some two weeks or so later I was again summoned into John's office, thinking now what is it this time?

'Sit down, sit down,' he started. 'Er, this is very difficult and, er, if you say no I can understand fully.'

I couldn't for the life of me think what was coming.

'We have a bit of a problem in week five of the run.'

'Oh, yes?'

'Yes, you see Roger has booked a week's holiday.'

'Right.'

'Well, we didn't know this when he started and but he can't get out of it.'

'Right,' I said again.

'So, I wondered, whether you would consider standing in for him for one week.' At this point I wish I could have seen the look on my own face!

'You see, we could find someone else but they would have to learn all the ropes and you know it better than anyone.'

I was speechless. This could only happen in television and it really proved the point that I still think is the case that when it all started to look as though it was all going to go horribly wrong, they needed a fall guy and I fitted the bill. But now they had the audacity to ask me to go back down to the location and run one show from there!

'Well,' I said. 'You had better ask the people who think I can't communicate first and see what their reaction is. I would hate to be sacked a second time. But if they say yes, I would, of course, cover it.'

'You would?'

'Well, I did set the whole bloody thing up. It would be nice to watch my accomplishment in action.'

How I got through that week and the eventual transmission without flattening someone I don't know. Although, if I am honest, I do. You see, as a freelancer you keep your mouth shut because you never know who may have the thought in the future that I might be worth hiring again.

Another door was closed, and another loose end was resolved and life went interminably on. Is it possible to stop yourself getting too maudlin as you get older? When this state comes upon me, I then begin to remember the bad times in this industry. *Banged Up With Beadle* was a fascinating exercise into people's personalities and how bravado is sometimes a complete front for total incompetence.

The one job that I can honestly say has never appealed to me is that of location catering. I always thought it was bad enough as a location manager, given the hours we put in, but a caterer really does work the longest. Increasingly, instead of arriving at six in the morning they will arrive at five thirty. Why? I have no idea. You would have to ask a caterer!

The other problem with being a caterer is people must like the food. Now, given the average size of a drama crew is around seventy-five people or so, you can bet your bottom dollar, someone is not going to like what you are cooking. If the unit gets tired, angry or a combination of both, the first people they always turn on are the caterers. That old expression 'an army marches on its stomach' is never so glaringly obvious than with a film crew. To cook breakfast, then prepare and serve lunch, then dish out afternoon tea and sandwiches and then if you are shooting late, serve a hot wrap break when the crew has finished for the day, all takes skill, dedication and I am sure a little pinch of madness. To produce such quality as they do from one small mobile kitchen has never ceased to amaze and astound me. They recently sent the would-be chefs on *Masterchef Goes Large* to work with a location caterer for the day and one of the contestants said it was the hardest graft he had ever done. A statement that I didn't doubt for one minute!

One of the worst parts of filming is not to have a permanent base to go back to at night. This results in having to move the entire 'circus' after you have finished filming to their new location ready for the following day. So, frequently after your five thirty start 'on site' you may well not leave for home until gone ten o'clock in the evening. This way lies insanity and an early death, but still we do it. When you are positioned in one place for a few days, life can be bliss. But when every day is a different location, life can be hell. You tend to work very closely with the caterers and their problems can very rapidly become your problems. Shooting *Wish Me Luck* in Epping Forest early one morning, I arrived at the crack of dawn and received a phone call from the caterers. A nice guy called Fred, the chef, told me that the new trainee following the kitchen in his car had ran into the back of it as they had pulled off the motorway. A shunt is a shunt you may think, but in this case, he had gone straight into the water tank and trashed it. This meant no water, which meant no tea, which meant no water to cook, which meant no food, which meant complete pandemonium for me! I rushed down to a nearby pub and asked the landlord if he could provide us with anything resembling a breakfast, even if it was only tea and toast. Also, could sixty-five of my closest friends come for lunch, Fred having assured me that even by the time a replacement kitchen got there, they could not be ready in time to do lunch. The pub happily obliged.

On the other hand, one of the most enjoyable jobs, I should think, is that of a costume designer. I have always said, 'Never knock anybody else's job until you have tried it.' I suppose the same goes for it looking enjoyable because some people can make things look so easy. When we did *You Bet!* a wonderful man called Tony Otero did a great job looking after Mathew Kelly and other bits and bobs that needed doing. He always had a smile on his face and a twinkle in his eye. I have never been, shall we say, a snappy dresser and really do not have any sort of a clothes 'thing'. Tony was determined to change this and finally took me by the scruff of the neck, while we were filming in Spain, and marched me off to the shops one night. 'You are very good looking,' he began in his smooth Mediterranean accent. You have a fine body, but you just don't show it.' He then ordered, 'Stand upright, you slouch too much.' We were walking along the harbour and he knew the area very well. 'Come, you come in here with me.' And I was dragged into a very expensive boutique. We did laugh as he ordered me about like an irate schoolteacher. 'Now try this on. No, no, that is not your colour. Try this. There look, look how wonderful it makes you look. Much better, much better.' By the time my credit card had melted, he had kitted me out and made me look about five years younger and trendy. He seemed very pleased with his work and for a while I did try to take an interest in the way I looked. Sorry, Tony, it did wear off eventually but it was a damn good try on your part!

Chapter Eighteen

Full Circle

In February 2007, I found myself walking back into London Weekend Television's former studios in Wembley, where I had started in 1968. It felt like the wheel had come full circle for me! It was now called Fountain Studios and the main entrance was on the side, not where it had been at the front. However, 'Malcolm House' an office block next door, which I had looked upon as a good omen those many years ago, had survived and the parking spaces along the side of the building were the same as I remembered them. The twin towers of Wembley Stadium were no longer visible and in my hurry to explore inside and find studios 1 and 2, I found myself facing a brick wall. The McDonalds to the left of the building had obviously eaten up slightly more than just the outside broadcast yard. Gone was the home of *World of Sport* and *Sports Arena*; gone was the home of *Who Do You Do?* and *The Kenny Everett Explosion*. Gone was the home of Harry Rabinowitz and his orchestra in Studio S; gone was the sound store and, most important of all, gone was the bar. However, I'm sure I heard the voice of the barman Rossi, coming out of the brickwork, calling, 'Fifty, fifty.'

The corridors looked narrower, the canteen smaller but Studio 5A and 5B were still just as impressive. In the days of Rediffusion, these two studios were combined and it had been the setting for *Hippodrome*, a circus show. The massive ring had been easily housed within the studio confines because there was the ability to lift the huge wall that divided the two thus making one enormous studio.

Was it really forty years ago that I had wandered along these corridors? I wanted to seek out anything I recognised and touch it like a child would hold onto a favourite toy. I wanted to relive those years. I wanted to be back in the OB garage as a young trainee, listening to Wally King tell us everything he knew about sound in outside broadcasts. In short, and quite suddenly, I wanted my youth back.

Where had the industry gone wrong that such a fine establishment should now be reduced to an eighth the size of its former glory? Well, the industry hadn't. I have, in earlier pages, laid the blame firmly at the door of Margaret Thatcher. An article appeared in *The Stage* on 2 August 2007, featuring an interview with the then sixty-nine-year-old actor, John Savident, best known to millions of viewers as Fred Elliot from the soap *Coronation Street*, a part that he played for nine years. I quote from it directly because he just nails the point firmly on the head that I have tried to portray but much tighter, unabashed and sharper than I have done. He said:

'I really do love working in the theatre. Television has changed largely due to Margaret Thatcher. What the silly cow did, and later apologised for too late, was to change the licences into franchises. Not so long ago you could take a creative idea to Southern, Anglia or Thames that did major drama series, and the like, because all those stations had creative teams. But then Maggie came along and companies had to bid for this and that and some bid so much money to keep their franchises, they had no money left for programming. That ghastly woman messed up television the way she did the film industry, and later the BBC with all the cutbacks. They got rid of things like the prestigious BBC make-up school, and the wardrobe departments suffered hugely.'

To me, that says it all. It is what we all think and what we all know. Why do politicians meddle in things they do not understand? Why must they change, alter and fiddle with everything. If it ain't broke don't fix it. When, oh when, will they ever learn? But above all, why did she muck about with the industry that I loved and in the process, completely screwed up the lives of thousands of people?

Away with the soapbox and back to Wembley! I looked at that magnificent door between the two studios as it rose majestically and very slowly into the ceiling. I had forgotten that a claxon rang out and a big red light flashed round and round just like an American fire engine, when this process took place. Safety was paramount with this event, especially the reverse of the procedure, because if you were underneath the damn thing when it came to rest on the ground, I suspect survival would not be an option. There would be very little left to give the kiss of life to. But that noise took me back in time. David Frost's theme tune played in my head and the noise of the applause from the audience bounced around in the lighting grid. I saw Vicki Carr making her entrance and heard Harry Rabinowitz and the orchestra coming from the aforementioned Studio 'S' through the foldback speakers and over the P.A. Dithers the gardener was chasing Effey the parlour maid through the set of *Hark at Barker*, as Ronnie Barker smoked a huge cigar and drank pretend Brandy. I could hear the cry of, 'I hate you, Butler!' as the end music for *On the Buses* played. I could see the set for *Gareth*, the first play I worked on, with a plethora of lights hanging down above the

287

flats. The pub, the bedroom and the corridor all sprung individually into life when the lighting console operator pushed a button and the magic of suspended belief unfolded before your very eyes. I stood there and saw myself as a callow youth, my eyes wide open and my jaw dropped low in wonderment at this adventure I was about to embark on – in discovering the secrets of making television programmes. Perhaps because this was now early February and Christmas had not long passed, I felt like I was in a scene from *A Christmas Carol* and like Scrooge was watching myself as a young lad from years gone by.

'Are you, all right?' The question shocked me back into reality. 'You look like you've seen a ghost.' It was Duncan Gaudin, the floor manager.

'I have, in a strange sort of way. Many of them.'

'Of course, I'd forgotten, you said you started here.'

'Yes, I did. A long time ago.' I realised my eyes were full of tears. 'Sorry I've just got something in my eye. Never stare up at a dusty studio wall rising, eh?' It was a limp excuse to cover my crying for no apparent reason.

'Yes. Go and see the nurse if it doesn't clear up. We are going to start rehearsals in about five minutes so can you go and see the sound department and get your radio mic fitted?'

'Sure, thanks.'

'They are in the control room, which is…'

'I think I can find it.'

'Of course, sorry. I'll see you in a minute or two.'

Kevin Paice, a gentle giant, who had been on my sound crew as a trainee was sat there now as the sound supervisor. He had gone grey, but then haven't we all?! We laughed remembering the 'old days' and had a damn good natter. I was presented with a 'covert'

288

earpiece, one for each studio. But I have raced ahead here in my haste to get my emotions onto paper, so let me back track and explain. I got the call in late October of 2006. A production manager called Nick Badham rang from Hat Trick. They were making a programme for ITV and he said, 'I've got this project and there are a few locations in it and I wondered if you would be interested?'

'Christ, Nick, you must have called a lot of people before you got down to 'T' for Treen?'

'No, I didn't cheeky bastard, you were the first person I thought of.'

I mouthed 'I wish' silently.

Nick had worked for LWT briefly as a freelance production manager and had then gone on to do such things as *The Crystal Maze*. We had sort of crossed paths occasionally over the years and I was well pleased that my name was still lurking somewhere in his subconscious. I asked what the project was, how much were they paying and when did they want me to start? The answer to these questions was, as always, 'Not sure what it will be called. Not a lot, the budget is low. As soon as possible.' At the point Nick phoned me, Hat Trick thought they were in a race with the BBC, to get very similar ideas off the ground. Both were trials set largely in a courtroom; both were to be rolled out over a period of nights and both featured celebrity juries, who would decide the fate of the accused. I was initially employed for a couple of weeks to scout round and look at any courtrooms I could think of to see if they would be suitable to place up to twenty-two hidden cameras in. This was a task I already knew the answer to!

During this quest for a courtroom, I had telephoned Richmond court, which was often used as a bolthole.

'Now, that's a funny thing,' said my friendly contact down there, 'I wondered why they had been so hush, hush about it.'

'Who?' I enquired.

'The BBC. You have described exactly what they have in mind for a drama series. They were very cagey on the recces and didn't let me know much about it.'

'And?'

'And if you were in a race, you aren't any longer.'

'Why?'

'Why? Because they started filming here yesterday for a week, celebrity jury and all. Gosh I'm sorry, Malcolm, looks like they have beaten you to it.'

I reported back that we were no longer in a race but everyone seemed philosophical. Anyway, Richmond would not have fitted the criteria that we wanted. Having found that, as suspected, the property did not exist, Nick booked the studio in Wembley in which to build his courtroom set and the jurors' room. At that point, I thought that would be that. However, although most of the action did take place in the studio, there were some inserts to be done, which were supposed to have come from CCTV cameras. There were a couple of scenes in a restaurant; one at a wedding of home video type footage and quite a few at a mansion house where the murder that results in the trial being held was committed. About four days filming had been allowed for these inserts, so I was asked to concentrate on these locations now and do the filming.

I began my search for the right sort of restaurant and property. I was asked if I knew of a director who would be likely to take the project on. A director had already been allocated for the studio but did I know of one that would be willing to take on a mostly static camera shoot? I put forward the name of Keith Washington who had got me onto the *Jonathan Creek* series so I felt a return compliment would be greatly in order. He got the job and in turn asked for Paul Bond to light the project. He was another dear colleague from *London's Burning.* He in turn employed another ex-*London's Burning* teammate, Joe Spence, as the gaffer spark. I did ask them all at one point for a 10% fee from their wages but my request was declined! It is always so good to work with people you know and people you enjoy working with. The job seems so much easier. We had developed such shorthand with each other as a team on *London's Burning*, that it took newcomers into the fold quite a while to catch up.

The filming of the inserts did indeed only last four days, but it was enough. It was enough for me to reflect that standing in the pouring rain at five thirty in the morning was really a young man's game. That breaking your non-smoking habit that you had had for almost eighteen months because all your bagged meters had cars parked on them, was not worth the stress.

On the last day, the phone rang and it was Nick to ask how things were and I told him that unfortunately the house would need a good clean because of the atrocious weather and the large number of people going in and out. This would mean spending more money as a facility fee for the house as well as the cleaning. He said that was not a problem and then said, 'The usher.'

I turned my collar up against the wind, 'Did you say the usher?'

'Yes, the usher.'

'What about him?' I asked, not understanding what on earth this was leading towards.

'Well, the jury usher in the courtroom.' I just waited for him to continue. 'We don't want to choose an actor because he will dominate the role. It needs to be someone who can work with talkback in his ear, so it needs to be someone on the production side. We really are looking for a grey haired, middle aged, amiable sort of bloke and round this office your name keeps coming up. Don't decide now, but it would be five days in the studio and probably quite a bit of fun really. Have a think and let me know, I'll talk to you tomorrow.'

The line went dead. I sat in the car to get out of the wind and rain and lit another cigar. 'Well, at least I would be in the warm,' I mused to myself. I told Mary when I got home that evening. With a slight giggle in her voice, she said, 'I should just hold the thought and be flattered they said, 'middle aged.' So, the following day I rang Nick and said 'yes.'

I was made-up, no dressed-up, in a gown put on by Billy from wardrobe, who again I had not seen for years, and back in the studios where it had all started. *The Trial of Gemma Lang*, as the show was now called, was about to begin and I met my celebrity jury: Julian Clary, Robert Kilroy-Silk, June Sarpong, Gemma Atkinson, Lee Ryan, Derek Akorah, Wendy Richard, Lisa Faulkner, Timmy Mallett, Immodesty Blaize, Brian Sewell and Nancy Dell'Olio. I was told not to tell them who I really was but try to fool them into believing I was an usher because they wanted the experience to be as real as possible. The judge was a retired judge, the Clerk of the Court, John Edwards, was also a real one but now retired and the two solicitors were both real and not retired. All the others were actors except me, who was neither one thing nor the other. Anyway, I carried off my part well, I thought. Not only did I have a radio mic, but they also fitted a 'covert ear piece'. In fact, as I said, I had two of these. There was one for the courtroom studio and one for the jury room studio as different directors controlled them separately from different control rooms. All the cameras were hidden in the style of *Big Brother* and not only did I have to look after my jury, I was one of the few people allowed contact with them, and so I brought in their lunch every day. They kept me on my toes as much as the production team did.

The highlight of the whole week came from Timmy Mallet, who in a rather mischievous vein, on the Thursday morning (thank God, he hadn't had this bright idea on Monday!) decided that we should put a pound in a sweep and pick a number, guessing how many times during the first session the judge blew his nose. It had never really dawned on me that he was a nose blower but on reflection I did concur that he was a blower of some 'gusto'. I had not noticed because I was sat down below in the courtroom with my back to him. The jury in the jury box, of course, faced him. Anyway, thirteen pounds was collected and Timmy insisted that I join in. Then numbers were chosen and in we went to the courtroom. You could see it coming and I should have been more prepared but on the first blow of the nose from M'lud, facial anarchy ensued. I looked straight at Timmy who just corpsed, as did Lisa Faulkner, who was sitting beside him. I then studied the rest of the jury: none of whom could make eye contact with anyone else and almost all to a man and a woman had his or her head bent down studying the studio floor. I bit my lip, long and hard and John, the clerk of the court, gazed round at us all trying to work out what on earth in the middle of a serious murder trial had caused such mirth. He looked puzzled for some time and nobody looked at anybody for some time too. The second blow to M'lud's nasal passage, saw us all grimacing again and the third was near destruction, at which point the jury thankfully, for legal matters in the trial, was dismissed back to the jury room for a few moments.

We entered the corridor and were told to stay there, as we would be returning to the courtroom very quickly. I asked was it two blows or three as I thought the second one had been a bit half-hearted. Lisa Faulkner said, 'Ah, see!' There had obviously been some discussion between the jury as to the answer to this question. However, three was decided upon and the winner was Immodesty Blaize. Another thirteen pounds was collected for the next round. The director yelled in my ear to tell them to stop thinking about the judge and concentrate on the trial.

It was a very nostalgic way to finish my career. Never, say never, as they say, but as the phone has not rung since October 2006, I have a feeling that maybe, just maybe, that could be it. As Barry Cryer once said when he was asked why he still hadn't retired yet, 'You don't retire in this business, the phone just stops ringing!'

As I came out of the studios on the last night, I looked at the new Wembley Stadium in the distance. I had seen many a football match in the old one and even been working and watching as Evel Knievel the mad American motorbike guy failed to jump those London buses. The show had started with a little old man climbing up an enormous ladder and then throwing himself off into six inches of water. The atmosphere was electric as the build up to Evil's jump came. The strangest thing was that as he parted company with the motorbike it went in a long curve on a journey of its own but then came back and hit him as if to say, 'No one puts me down like that and gets away with it.' At least the new stadium contains no less than two thousand six hundred and eighteen toilets, so perhaps the chances of getting urinated on from a great height are somewhat diminished these days!

I walked towards the car park and took one long look back, remembering Graham Thor-Straten and myself leaning on the foldback speaker and falling in love with Lulu. The funny thing was I could remember doing the same thing with Graham when we moved to the new studios on the South Bank. However, on that occasion the object of our affection was a young lady called Suzi Quatro. Perhaps it was something Graham and I did frequently? Maybe it was a male 'thing', who knows?

As I drove away from the building, I wondered why *On the Buses* stuck in my mind so much. Only after a bit of research did I realise why. From 1969 onwards, LWT transmitted seventy-four episodes, which explains why I can never get the theme tune out of my head. Also, the other thing that has always stayed with me was the answer I once got from one of the lovely ladies who used to man(?) the switchboard. If it was a personal call, you gave your name and the operator would get the number you wanted for you and they would then dock your wages for the cost of it. Those were the days! I was ringing home to talk to Mum and Dad, which was then in Newbury. The conversation with the operator went along the lines of, 'Could you get me a number, please?'

'I *can*, it is a question of whether I *will* or not.' Feeling suitably rebuked for such dreadful misuse of the English language I started again, 'Sorry, *would* you get me a number, please?'

'That's better.' And that small conversation has remained firmly planted in my head ever since, for better or worse. It is strange what you do or do not remember. For instance, when I was still in the sound department, working happily away in the new studios on the South Bank, I had developed a mouth ulcer. Keith Warren, who had recently been conveyed to us from the BBC, promised that he would bring in the following day an instant cure. The next day, and again with amazing clarity I know it was in Studio 2's control room, Keith produced a bottle and a cotton bud from his pocket. He had the look of a slightly manic dentist on his face as he said, 'Now open wide. Good. Ah, yes, I can see it. My, it is quite a red, angry looking one.' He raised the doused cotton bud above my mouth, 'Now this may sting, just a little.' And I presume he gently dabbed the offending area. It didn't feel like a dab to me. To me it felt like a knight with a jousting pole had galloped up on his horse doing at least fifteen miles per hour and thrust the weapon with amazing force and uncanny accuracy into the back of my mouth and pierced the ulcer. I have seen stunt men in the movies on wires that pull them back at speed against a wall, to represent being blasted by a shotgun. I performed the same acrobatics but included sinking to my knees at the end as the pain took hold. My eyes began to water and so did Keith's but his from hysterical mirth that gripped his body until it shook for many minutes. Happy days!

Time has erased many memories but kept some pin sharp. The programmes were endless. There was *The Secret Life of Edgar Briggs*; *The Train Now Standing*; *Yus, My Dear* and an interesting one called *If It Moves, File It*. The latter was a situation comedy starring John Bird and Dudley Sutton, originally shown in 1970. I was co-opted onto this to make noises into a microphone that sounded like explosions. The reason being that the technical equipment in those days operated by the grams operator could not be re-cued quick enough for the required series of fast action bangs. The producer was Humphrey Barclay, a master of his art, who spotted many comedy ideas and turned them into accessible laughter. I have tried, in vain, to source a recording of this show but feel perhaps not time in this case but a machine, aptly named a 'bulk eraser', may be responsible for its non-availability. Many old videotapes, once transmitted, were recycled in the early days because of cost. So two, half-hour episodes of *If It Moves, File it* may well have made way for a one-hour episode of *Upstairs Downstairs.*

The lights of Wembley faded into the distance, as have the lives of quite a few people since I started writing this epistle. They include Trevor Carless, the sound mixer on many programmes I worked on as a location manager. At Trevor's funeral in Berkhamstead, I talked afterwards with the producer of *London's Burning*, Paul Knight. My opening gambit was, 'You know, I'm thinking of getting my name taken off the end credits of *London's Burning.*' Paul immediately thinking something was terribly wrong, as all producers do, retorted with, 'Why, Mal, why? What's wrong?'

I explained, 'It's just that the grim reaper seems to be working his way, slowly but surely down the cast and crew list.'

He looked at me hard and long, 'I think we've got a few years left in us yet, Mal.' And we agreed to hang on for as long as we can before the 'bulk eraser' takes us both and replaces us with a new show!

Postscript

From Wembley to France, Morocco to Jersey and Ireland to Holland, along with Sir David Frost, Herbert Lom, Jane Asher, Gordon Jackson, Tommy Cooper, Ronnie Barker, Barry Cryer, Bill Patterson, Stanley Baxter, John Thaw, Googie Withers and many others, you must admit it's been one hell of a ride! Many years ago, in my youth, I saw Vincent Price and Jane Asher in a film directed by Roger Colman called *Masque of the Red Death*, and I fell immediately madly in love with Jane Asher. So imagine how overwhelmed I was when many years later and one day on location for *Wish Me Luck*, she asked to use my car phone. She could have seduced me there and then! Day dreams are just such wonderful things, aren't they? Another of his films that springs to mind, again adapted from an Edgar Allen Poe story, is *The Fall of the House of Usher*. Made some four years before *Masque of the Red Death* in 1960, it also starred Vincent Price. Again, I was very lucky and privileged enough to have worked with the actor.

The countries and the people have all been so important. One memory that has just come to mind relates to when I was working on *The Hidden City*, a funny drama never transmitted in this country. There were two producers, one of whom wasn't even twenty-one, so couldn't drink alcohol at the meetings held in the States! Also part of the team was a great designer called Robin Tarsnane. He had worked on *Inspector Morse* for many years. On the day of 9/11, Robin and I dropped a film off for developing in the Portobello Road in London. As we entered the building, I noticed the television was on with everyone just staring at the screen, in silence. We rushed back to the production office and sat watching the horror unfold along with our colleagues.

To me, the studio buildings I have worked in are a major part of my memories. I consider those buildings to be important, but some of my friends disagree. They are only bricks and mortar they cry, it's what was inside them that is important. Yes, to a certain extent, I agree. But that title *The Fall of the House of Usher* got me thinking about the buildings I have worked in, and all but lived in, during my career.

As previously mentioned, Jacob Street Studios, home of *London's Burning* for many years, was demolished ages ago and replaced by flats. Is there a blue plaque outside that pays any acknowledgement to my encumbrance within those walls for many hours. I think not. We then moved to a new base in Long Lane, which was a fascinating old brewery, still safely in the land of my media upbringing – SE1. But that too has now been demolished and turned into flats. Again, any sign of a 'Treen was here' plaque? Alas no!

I have recounted elsewhere my last encounter with Wembley Studios, by then known as Fountain Studios, and the case of the disappeared OB garage, but now even bigger plans are afoot to demolish the whole damn lot. So, what was the biggest studio in Europe at one time, will soon cease to exist and am I the only one to think that quite a few people will shed a tear over this demise? My one little reassuring feeling when I arrived in Wembley Park Drive in 1968, was the fact that nestled on the corner was an office block called 'Malcolm House', which reassured me at the time that I was exactly where I should be, and that my mother's crystal gazing was all so true. Alas and alack, I see with an indubitably sad heart, that since I was there for *The Trial of Gemma Lang*, a programme that never did get

299

transmitted, 'Malcolm House' has also met its demise and has been felled. Gulp. Wembley Studios were originally a film studio complex before it became the base for Rediffusion from 1955 until 1968. I was there during LWT's time from 1968 to 1972 before we relocated to the South Bank and established ourselves in SE1.

Finally, Kent House, LWT's one-time home, is itself now standing empty and scheduled for who knows what? Truly the end of an era. Everywhere I seem to have worked they have demolished. The same has happened to Teddington Studios, which was home to Thames Television, but that too has succumbed to the bulldozer. I really do hope that Pinewood Studios and Shepperton Studios are not too panic stricken at this news, as I have also graced their premises over the years!

The real misery of all this is that people have been made redundant. Many of them old working colleagues, who are not so old because they were young when they joined me in my middle age, have now seen their careers thrown to the wolves. After years of security being 'staff', you no doubt have gathered my feelings by now on being suddenly made 'freelance'.

Thank God that my 'vulgar final salary pension', as my chiropodist once called it, has cushioned my retirement. Just as with my career, I have been extremely lucky. With hindsight, I wouldn't change one minute, except only to make much more of it at the time had I really realised that, compared to many other working folk, what a ball I was having. I was talking to someone the other day and I said, 'Well, of course, when I was working,' as a preface to some profound statement I was about to make. He swiftly interrupted me and said, 'Work? Work? You didn't work, you were

300

in the media for Christ's sake!' And do you know, I couldn't deny it. Thanks to my Mum, and all those people and places I met and saw, it has been a rich pathway to tread. But removing the buildings is like taking away the rock on which all those experiences were built and were based. Happy days reduced to rubble. It is hard not to feel that someone is removing your emotional legacy.

Thank you so much for buying and reading this ramble. If you want to know how the retirement has gone, please visit:

www.malcolmandmary.wordpress.com